*Numbers, Predictions and War:
Using History to Evaluate Combat Factors
and Predict the Outcome of Battles*

Books by the author:

NUMBERS, PREDICTIONS AND WAR:

USING HISTORY TO EVALUATE COMBAT FACTORS AND PREDICT THE OUTCOME OF BATTLES

by

Colonel T. N. Dupuy

U.S. ARMY, RET.

THE BOBBS-MERRILL COMPANY, INC.
Indianapolis/New York

Copyright © 1979 T.N. Dupuy

All rights reserved, including the right of reproduction
in whole or in part in any form
Published by The Bobbs-Merrill Company, Inc.
Indianapolis   New York

Library of Congress Cataloging in Publication Data

Dupuy, Trevor Nevitt, 1916-
    Numbers, predictions, and war.

    Includes index.
    1.   Military art and science—Mathematical models.
2.   War games.   3.   Battles.   I.   Title.
U104.D85   355.4'01'84   77-5243
ISBN 0-672-52131-8

Manufactured in the United States of America

First printing

This book is dedicated to my son Arnold,
the war game buff of the family.

Contents

Preface

The purpose of this book is to describe the Quantified Judgment Method of Analysis of Historical Combat Data, the complete title of an analytical methodology that I have been primarily responsible for developing and perfecting. As is the custom these days, this long title has been condensed to a series of initials (not quite an acronym)—QJMA—by which it is commonly known to the relatively small group of professional operations research analysts and military men who are familiar with it. A major component of the methodology is a long but simple mathematical equation which is called the Quantified Judgment Model, or QJM.

This is, then, a model which I—a retired Regular Army officer and rather widely published military historian—have used for analysis of military operations. In the technical sense of the terms, however, this is not a typical operations analysis methodology, and I am not an operations research analyst.

Some people—including a handful of properly accredited operations research analysts—believe that the QJMA is a more realistic tool for analysis of combat than any standard operations research (OR) methodology, and that the QJM is a more faithful representation of real-world contemporary combat than any other standard OR model or simulation. Thus it seems useful, in describing the method and the model, to explain their background and the developmental process from which they emerged.

In writing this book I have assumed that three rather distinct, but somewhat overlapping, audiences would be interested in the QJMA, and its *raison d'être*. First there is what I call the Defense Research Community, a disparate group of people in Government, in research organizations, and in defense industry; most of these are OR analysts, but the group includes a few serious military historians, military planners, and military bureaucrats in and out of uniform, serving in the Defense Department or the armed services, or subsidiary agencies.

Second are the military professionals—including planners and civilian bureaucrats, of course—of the several services, most of whom are somewhat removed from the day-to-day use of OR techniques, but who find themselves increasingly affected by OR analysis.

The third group consists of military "buffs," who are civilians (although they may formerly have been in uniform or in civilian jobs in the military establishment) who are interested in military matters. Particularly important in this latter group are the war game enthusiasts, most of whom are as much interested in games that portray, with reasonable accuracy, military operations of the historical past, as they are in models that appear to project and predict warfare of the future.

In addition to these three main and rather sizable groups, there may be some interest in the methodology and the model—because of its historical derivation—among professional military historians who do not think of themselves as belonging to any of these three main and rather sizable groupings. A handful of other historians may also be interested in the methodology as an approach to the quantification of history.

The book is organized to lead the reader through the developmental process of the QJMA, partly in the assumption that the narrative will have some human interest appeal, but mainly because I believe that in this way the method and the model can best be understood. Thus the book begins with a chapter which attempts to demonstrate the chaotic nature of raw historical data, and how easily this can be interpreted and misinterpreted in a number of different, and often mutually contradictory ways. From then on the book devotes itself to showing how these chaotic, confusing, and contradictory facts and numbers can be tamed, brought under control, and made consistently meaningful. (The word *consistent* is extremely important to this process.)

The easiest aspects of military affairs to quantify are weapons and their effects. Weapons have well-known and easily measurable physical characteristics; they obey the standard laws of physics; they are, in short, quite predictable in their performance. (At least theoretically.) So the next chapter deals with weapons and their predictability. But, as all soldiers know from experience, and as is reasonably self-evident to anyone who gives the matter any thought (or who reads Chapter 1) when employed on the battlefield weapons tend to drift away from their consistent predictability. So Chapter 3 is devoted to consideration of the various external causes—which we call variables of combat—which disrupt and distort the consistent and predictable performance of weapons.

Chapter 4, then, tells how my colleagues and I went through the first crude processes of trying to understand combat variables, and their effects upon weapons performance—and thus on battle outcomes. From this learning process a mathematical formula, or model, began to emerge, with the weapons essentially as constant numbers, while the variables were reflected in the equation as modifying factors to which—when considered in isolation—values or ranges of values could be attributed.

For a variety of reasons—partly because of the availability of data, partly because of self-evident relevance—we concentrated these efforts initially on World War II, and mostly those operations of that war involving German, American, and British troops in 1943 and 1944. Slowly, but rather breathtakingly (or so it seemed to some of us), the numbers we had calculated for weapons and their effects, and the values that seemed to represent the variables, began to fit together in consistent relationship patterns that were, in turn, consistent with the outcomes of the World War II battles we were trying to analyze. Chapter 5 tells about that.

The following two chapters focus a bit more sharply on two of the problems discussed generally in Chapter 5. The first of these problems is that of representing, in combat formulae concerned with land-based weapons, the effects of air support provided by aircraft that appear only fleetingly over the battlefield. The second problem was to account for a troubling quantitative deviation or inconsistency in the performance of German troops, on the one hand, and British and American troops on the other. When it became evident that this deviation was quite consistent, and resulted from a standard German ground combat effectiveness superiority of about 20% over the Western Allies, we recognized that we were opening up a whole new field of behavioral factors, of which relative combat effectiveness was the most obvious and probably the most important. Chapter 7 is devoted to the effects of behavioral variables on combat outcomes, on both Western and Eastern Fronts of World War II.

Some of us began to think that if this methodology could so faithfully represent historical combat—at least of World War II—it might well be able to project hypothetical combat of the future. The next chapter shows how we adapted the model to extrapolate from history to predict some hypothetical future possibilities. But many people found it difficult to accept the possibility that a model based upon history could be reliable in projecting the future.

Then came the Arab-Israeli October War of 1973, when modern armies were really using the modern weapons and technologies with which the QJM had been coping hypothetically in Chapter 8. Now it was possible to demonstrate, from real-world examples, that the methodology was as reliable and realistic in portraying modern weapons as it had been with World War II weapons.

At this point it seemed appropriate to look back at the problems which the developers of the QJMA had encountered in trying to explain the method and the model to various people in the Defense Research Community. Chapter 10 discusses that.

During the process of development of the model we had given some attention to its capability to represent military operations before World War II. Chapter 11—with an eye primarily on military buffs and military historians, but also to demonstrate to military analysts and planners that there is continuity in combat processes—reviews some applications of the model to pre-World War II warfare.

Next there is a chapter almost entirely for the benefit of the military buffs, showing how the model can be adapted to the entertainment world of the wargamer. But the other audiences should also find Chapter 12 a useful demonstration of the flexibility of the method and model in adaptations to a variety of analyses. After all, the entertainment wargame is a kind of analytical process for the participants.

Finally there is an Epilogue, pulling together all of the strands dangling from the earlier chapters. And following that are various appendices; one commentator has suggested that the data compilations alone are worth the price of the book.

I hope, however, that is not its only value.

Acknowledgments

I am grateful to a number of people, who fall into three general categories: those who helped me develop the methodology; those who have recognized its value and encouraged me to continue my work on it, despite many frustrations; and those who have made direct contributions to this book.

My colleagues at the Historical Evaluation and Research Organization belong, to some extent, to all three categories, but I shall try to be specific.

In the development of the methodology, my original collaborator was my esteemed HERO colleague, Colonel Angus M. Fraser, USMC, Retired. As we began to try to find values for variables, other HERO colleagues and consultants joined in assisting me, primarily Colonel Ashton Crosby, USA, Retired; Brigadier General Edward Chickering, USAF, Retired; Colonel Donald Quackenbush, USA, Retired; and Colonel John A.C. Andrews, USAF, Retired. In the details of applying historical data to specific analysis, I received considerable assistance from Mrs. Grace P. Hayes, Mr. Frank Pichini, Mr. John Rabb, and Colonel Andrews. Mr. Robert McQuie, a HERO consultant, worked with me on the structure of the model. So, too, did Dr. William Fain and, in particular, Dr. Janice B. Fain.

In the Defense Research Community I received considerable encouragement in my development work from a number of people, but particularly again from Dr. Janice Fain. Among others who encouraged me were Dr. Francis Kapper, Scientific and Technical Advisor to the JCS Studies, Analysis, and Gaming Agency; Dr. J. Stockfisch of the Rand Corporation; and Lt. Col. Lannie Walker, of the Weapons Systems Evaluation Group.

In the preparation of this book I have received valuable advice and comments from my HERO colleagues Mrs. Hayes, HERO Director of Research; and Mrs. Gay M. Hammerman, Editorial Director. Dr. Janice Fain, Mr. McQuie, and Dr. Kapper were also very helpful with advice and comments.

I am extremely grateful to Mrs. Billie P. Davis, Mrs. Virginia M. Rufner, and Miss Alicia Boyd for the work they did in typing the manuscripts, and in helping me with charts and diagrams.

However, it is all my book, and nobody else's. If it is any good, many people deserve credit for helping me to make it so; but if it is bad, I alone am to blame.

Author's Note:
Formulae and Symbols

The reader of this book has been warned by its title that it has much to do with numbers. A major purpose of the book, in fact, is to show how simple formulae can make these numbers both manageable and meaningful.

Let me hasten to reassure those who feel at all uncomfortable when faced with pages of complex mathematical equations; I feel exactly the same way. So, if I can understand it, you probably can. I am not a mathematician, and all of the formulae which appear in this book are merely means for organizing numbers or quantities, and can be understood by anyone who is able to add, subtract, divide, and multiply.

SYMBOLS, ABBREVIATIONS, AND GLOSSARY

Because there are so many different and variable numbers to be considered in warfare, we have to use standard symbols to represent them in formulae. These symbols are usually letters or combinations of letters, often in the form of abbreviations. Listed below are all of the symbols which will be found in the formulae and discussions on the following pages. These, with their meaning, also provide a kind of glossary of terms.

SYMBOLS, ABBREVIATIONS AND GLOSSARY

A	Accuracy	cas	Casualties
a	Attacker identifier	CEV	Relative Combat Effectiveness Value
AAA	Antiaircraft artillery		
AAM	Air-to-air missile	CL	Ceiling factor (for aircraft)
AD	Air Defense		
AE	Aircraft mount effect	D	Depth (in kilometers)
AME	Amphibious effect	d	Defender identifier
APC	Armored personnel carrier	Di	Dispersion factor
ASE	Ammunition supply effect	E	Effectiveness or effect
ASM	Air-to-surface missile	e	Enemy identifier
AT	Antitank weapon(s)	ex	Exhaustion factor
b	Logistics (supply) factor	F	Factor

f	Friendly identifier	PF	Punishment factor
FCE	Fire control effect	PR/PR	Combat power ratio reflecting result
g	Artillery identifier		
GE	Guidance effect	PTS	Potential targets per strike
h	Weather factor		
hw	Heavy weapons identifier	Q	Distance of opposed advance (km)
i	Armored force identifier		
IC	Intensity of Combat (casualties incurred in relation to strength)	R	Result (quantification of engagement outcome)
		r	Terrain factor
J	Vehicles (number)	RA	Radius of action factor
le	Leadership factor	RF	Sustained rate of fire
M	Force mobility characteristics	RFE	Rapidity of fire effect
		RIE	Relative incapacitating effect
m	Mobility factor, QJM formula		
		RL	Reliability
MBE	Multiple barrel effect	RN	Range factor
MF	Mission Factor (numerical assessment of qualitative performance)	S	Force strength (inventory of OLIs modified by environmental factors)
MFM	Mobile fighting machine		
MCE	Multiple charge effect	s	Small arms identifier
mg	Machine gun identifier	SAM	Surface-to-air missile
MOF	Mobility factor for OLI calculation	SE	Score effectiveness (unit ability to inflict casualties)
MV	Muzzle velocity (meters/sec)	SME	Self-propelled mobility effect
N	Personnel strength, numerical	sp	Spatial effectiveness measure and identifier (ability to gain or hold ground)
n	Infantry identifier		
o	Morale factor		
OB	Order of battle		
OLI	Operational lethality index value*	SSM	Surface-to-surface missile
		sur	Surprise factor identifier
OR	Operations research	t	Training/experience factor
P	Combat power or combat potential		
		TD	Tank destroyer
P/P	Combat power ratio	TLI	Theoretical lethality index

*This can be expressed as a value for a single weapon, or be the sum of values for an inventory of weapons, and can be used as a unit of measure for the unmodified or ideal performance of weapons ("Proving Ground"), for weapons performance modified by environmental factors (Force Strength), or for weapons performance modified by environmental and operational factors (Combat Potential).

T/O&E	Tables of organization and equipment	W	Proving ground OLI; weapons effects firepower
u	Posture factor		
V	Force vulnerability characteristics	w	Weapons identifier
		y	Air support identifier
v	Vulnerability factor	z	Season factor

Numbers, Predictions and War:
Using History to Evaluate Combat Factors
and Predict the Outcome of Battles

1

Numbers
and Military History

THE SEARCH FOR QUANTITATIVE ANSWERS

Since the dawn of history men have been calculating the chances of success in future war by assessing the available statistics on past wars. We find evidence of this in the writings of Sun Tze, half a millenium before the Christian era, and in the subsequent writings of such commentators on military affairs as Vegetius and Machiavelli. Then, in the early 19th Century, Jomini and Clausewitz ushered in a new, more sophisticated, and more complex era of military analysis. And even this new era did not satisfy the fascination of the military analyst with numbers and quantification. Jomini was more concerned with patterns than with numbers, and Clausewitz's approach to analysis was generally qualitative and philosophical. However, his concern about quantities is evident in his significant conclusion, which has been paramount in military theory for more than a century, that "Defense is the stronger form of combat."

Another example of how military men tend to think in numerical terms is the famous statement—attributed to both Wellington and Marshal Blücher—that the mere presence of Napoleon on a battlefield was worth 40,000 men.

But that quotation also demonstrates one of the problems which military men have always had with numbers. The figure 40,000 is rather precise. It is hard to believe that either Wellington or Blücher would have used that number to represent the value of Napoleon if he had only a squad of ten men with him. Or that Napoleon's influence on the outcome could have been worth precisely 40,000 both at Austerlitz in 1805 (where the opposing armies were less than 100,000 strong, and when the Allies still did not understand Napoleon's methods of war) and at Leipzig in 1813 (where each opponent was more than 200,000 strong, and after the Allies had learned much from Napoleon). Furthermore, neither Wellington nor Blücher could have been very certain of what the opposing strengths were at Leipzig, where Napoleon's influence (whatever it may have been) was not enough to give him victory. Different historical sources, of comparable reliability, differ by as much as 50 percent in their estimates of the opposing strengths at that battle.

So, we are confronted with the two principal problems affecting quantitative analysis of war data. First is the question of accuracy or precision of the numbers—how reliable are they? Second, to the extent that they are reliable, how do we interpret them? What do they mean? What attributes do they measure?

THE QUESTION OF DATA RELIABILITY

There is no quick, easy, or general answer to the first problem. Each war is unique, and the accuracy of the data it generates must be assessed independently of all other wars. Within a war, of course, some general characteristics are common, but in a multi-front war (like the two world wars of the Twentieth Century, or even the more recent and smaller Middle East wars), each front has to be considered as a separate campaign, with individual characteristics. To assure accuracy there must be time-consuming, frustrating, tedious, and expensive research, with frequent comparison of differing data sources, different engagements, and different campaigns. Simple, logical, consistent, and militarily sound procedures must be used to fill gaps, or to deal with any discrepancies that emerge from this research. We will look further at such matters later in this book.

If we assume that reasonably reliable and accurate numerical data can be obtained for a war, a campaign, or a battle (frequently such an assumption is justified; sometimes it is not), then comes the question of determining what it means.

THE INTERPRETATION OF DATA

Presumably if we can collect enough reliable data from military history we should be able to determine patterns of conduct, performance, and outcomes that will provide basic insights into the nature of armed conflict, and that will indicate trends to assist military planning for the future. In fact, just such a line of reasoning led in the early Twentieth Century to the development of the generally accepted concept that there are a number of fundamental "Principles of War." However, there has never been firm agreement as to what these Principles are, or how firmly they govern performance in war.[1]

[1] In 1976, for the first time in more than 40 years, the Principles of War were omitted from the US Army's standard statement of basic doctrine, FM 100-5. The author deplores this omission which leaves a void in the structure of doctrine.

It should also be noted that there are some respected and respectable modern military operations research analysts who believe that the changes in weapons and technology of the past few decades have made all military history—even that as recent as World War II—irrelevant. At this point, therefore, the reader should know that this book totally rejects this belief and asserts that all military history is relevant to modern combat, as long as due allowances are made for the significant (but not usually over-whelming) impact of changing weapons and technology—particularly in the fields of communications, observation, and transportation.

DRAWING LESSONS FROM MILITARY HISTORY

Despite differences of opinion as to the relevance of military history, and its significance as a guide to what happens or is likely to happen in modern combat, it is very common to hear strategic concepts or theories presented with the introductory words: "Military history proves that. . . ." Surprisingly, such statements are often made by the very analysts who otherwise reject the relevance of history to future war. I certainly agree that military history proves a great deal, but I have found that it is not a reliable guide unless the analyst uses a different approach from that of most people who think or say, "Military history proves that. . . ."

For instance, in Figure 1-1 are ten propositions that are commonly presented—in such places as the Pentagon or the pages of serious books on military theory and strategy—as being derived from military combat experience. Three of these are based upon "lessons" drawn from the 1973 Middle East October War—the most recent important war at the time these words are written.

Figure 1-1.
SOME FORECASTING PROPOSITIONS FROM MILITARY HISTORY

1. As advancing technology has made weapons increasingly lethal, changes in warfare have become more radical than in the past.
2. Casualty rates have declined over the years.
3. History proves that a successful attacker should be three times as strong as the opposing defender.
4. The numerically inferior force is usually victorious.
5. The moral is to the physical as three is to one (Napoleon?).
6. God is on the side of the heavier battalions (Napoleon?).
7. Modern technology permits faster advance rates in combat.

SOME PROPOSITIONS FROM THE OCTOBER WAR

8. October War casualty rates were greater than those of previous wars.
9. In the October War more tanks were lost to AT missiles and rockets than to guns.
10. In the October War, 70% of the tank casualties were knocked out by guns (mostly tank guns); the tank is still the best AT weapon.

The first thing to be noted is that some of these propositions contradict each other and some—notably Proposition 4—appear to defy logic, thus reinforcing my earlier suggestion that a major problem of the military historian and the military analyst is deciding what the data means. In the following paragraphs we shall see that some of those propositions most generally accepted are wrong; that some most often challenged are right; and that sometimes apparently contradictory assertions can *both* be proven right. I will go further, however, and say that none of the propositions is *always* right, and none completely wrong.

A closer look at these propositions reveals two things: (1) numerical combat data is contradictory and confusing, and (2) it is very easy to draw erroneous conclusions from such data, adding more contradictions and confusion. No wonder Henry Ford said, "History is the bunk."

INCREASING WEAPONS LETHALITY AND CHANGES IN WARFARE

Figure 1-2 appears to substantiate the first of the ten propositions. It portrays the lethality, or destructive power, of weapons during history and shows how, in the aggregate, lethality has increased over the years. The graph is semilogarithmic; the weapons values of the ordinate represent destructive force in terms of the number of men a weapon can theoretically kill in one hour under certain artificial, laboratory-like circumstances; the dispersion value of the ordinate shows how troops have dispersed (taking up more square meters per man) in response to increased weapons destructiveness. The abscissa, of course, shows the passage of time over the course of history.

But, despite the evidence of this chart, the second part of the first proposition of Figure 1-1 is just plain wrong. It is wrong because the technological change that has most influenced modern ground warfare came in the decade between 1850 and 1860. No other change—not even the aircraft or the tank, not even tactical nuclear weapons (at least not yet)—has affected warfare so quickly, or so fundamentally.

Let's examine the background of that momentous change that took place more than a century ago.

At the close of the Napoleonic wars, the dominant weapons of the battlefield were the flintlock and bayonet, and the smoothbore, muzzle-loading cannon. Cannon had marked superiority in range and accuracy over the flintlock, and inflicted nearly half the casualties in combat. In battle, armies formed in line to defend, or to attack by fire, and usually formed in greater depth (the so-called column) to charge. By 1820 this linear tactical system, introduced by Gustavus Adolphus, was about 200 years old. Until the Napoleonic era, the proportion of casualties (killed and wounded) to total effective forces had declined steadily from about

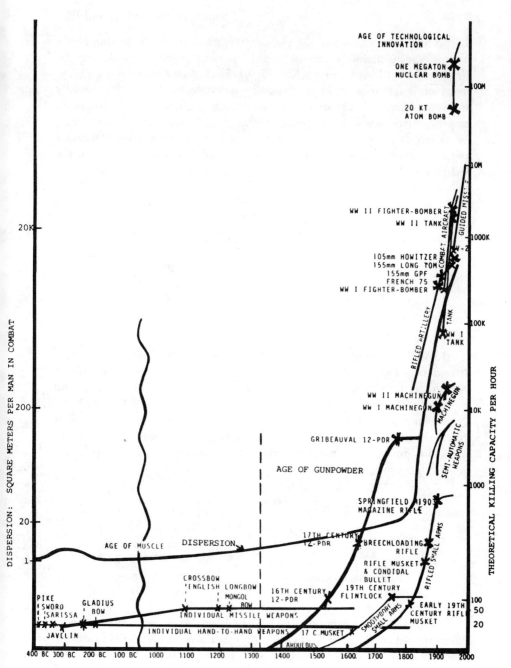

Figure 1-2.
INCREASE OF
WEAPON LETHALITY
AND DISPERSION OVER HISTORY

7

15 percent for victors and 30 percent for losers in battle in the Thirty Years' War to about 9 percent and 16 percent respectively during the French Revolutionary wars. (See Figure 1-3.) Napoleon's later employment of "column" attacks with hastily raised levies drove the casualty rates up sharply to 15 percent for winners and 20 percent for losers. In several minor wars fought under this same weaponry system after Waterloo, casualty rates fell even below those of the French Revolutionary period. This would suggest that a balance had been struck between the lethality of weapons used and the combat effectiveness of linear tactics by men so armed.

Figure 1-3.
CASUALTY TRENDS
17th TO 19th CENTURIES

			Victor	*Loser*
c.	1630	(Thirty Years War)	15%	30%
c.	1795	(French Revolution)	9%	16%
c.	1812	(Napoleonic wars)	15%	20%
c.	1848	(Mexican War)	8%	15%

Although there are no accurate statistics, authoritative sources agree that during the late Eighteenth and early Nineteenth Centuries artillery accounted for 40-50 percent of casualties, muskets 30-40 percent, and swords or bayonets 15-20 percent. (Figure 1-4, left column.) During the Napoleonic wars British musketry seems to have been better than that of the continental powers, so that in Wellington's Peninsular army small arms fire probably inflicted slightly more casualties than did artillery—but the preponderance was not great.

Figure 1-4.
NINETEENTH CENTURY CAUSES OF
BATTLEFIELD CASUALTIES

	Before 1850	*After 1860*
Artillery	40-50%	8-10%
Infantry Small Arms	30-40%	85-90%
Saber and Bayonet	15-20%	4-6%

The costliness of frontal attacks against a combined arms team of infantry and artillery, or against infantry marksmen behind field fortifications, was clearly demonstrated in such battles as Bunker Hill and New Orleans. At the same time, it was amply demonstrated that well-trained, well-led, determined troops could overcome such defensive firepower if their commanders were willing to pay the cost. Bunker Hill was also an example of this, as were the Napoleonic victories of Wagram and Borodino, and our victory over the Mexicans at Monterrey.

However, commanders preferred to employ maneuver to strike the flank of an opponent in order to achieve surprise, if possible, and in any case to reduce the volume of hostile firepower that could be brought against the attacking force. Typical examples were the British at Long Island and the Brandywine in the American Revolution, and Napoleon at Austerlitz.

Then, in the 1850s there came a revolutionary change in infantry weapons. (Figure 1-4, right column.) This was the introduction of the muzzle-loading rifle musket, designed to fire an elongated or conoidal bullet, replacing the old smoothbore musket and musket ball. The rifle musket was the standard weapon used by both North and South in the Civil War. The conoidal bullet was lethal at longer ranges than canister or spherical case shot fired from contemporary smoothbore cannon, and could reach almost as far as solid shot and shell from cannon. Furthermore, spherical shells, if they burst, broke into only two to five fragments, while direct hits with solid shot cannon were extremely rare. Finally, whatever slight theoretical advantage the artillery piece enjoyed in range was meaningless on the battlefield, where the new rifle musket could reach the next ridge just as easily and just as accurately as the cannon. In short, the relation of lethal capability between infantry weapons and artillery had been overwhelmingly reversed in less than a decade. In the Civil War, small arms (mostly rifles) caused 85-86 percent of the casualties, cannon caused 9-10 percent, and edged weapons caused about 5 percent.[2]

Both sides used linear tactics during the Civil War. On many occasions, most notably when fighting over broken ground, troops would spontaneously break into little groups and fight from one cover to another. But to attack or defend, men would still be formed in lines of two or three ranks; to weight an attack, one regimental line would follow another to make a great column, as in Napoleon's day. There was no other way to control or maneuver troops in battle. The resulting imbalance between infantry weapons of greater potential lethality, on the one hand, and tactics better suited to the weapons of a previous generation, on the other, sent casualties on both sides soaring to levels comparable to or greater than Napoleon's bloodiest battles. (Figure 1-5.) By the end of the war there was a clear, although slow, trend toward dispersal of men on the battlefield. This trend, which continued in the subsequent Franco-Prussian and Russo-Japanese wars, was the first major change in infantry deployments since Gustavus Adolphus introduced his linear system in the 1620s.

From 1866 on in western Europe breech-loading rifles were the

[2] Historical Evaluations and Research Organization (HERO), *Historical Trends Related to Weapon Lethality*, mimeographed, Washington, 1964, p. 18.

Figure 1-5.
SAMPLE CIVIL WAR CASUALTIES
(% casualties, entire battle)

	Victor	Loser
Shiloh	20.7(U)	26.5(C)
Antietam (draw)	28.9(C)-17.7(U)	
Second Bull Run	19.0(C)	21.1(U)
Corinth	11.0(U)	19.2(C)
Fredericksburg	6.8(C)	11.8(U)
Chancellorsville	29.7(C)	23.0(U)
Gettysburg	27.7(U)	37.4(C)
Atlanta	17.7(U)	28.9(C)

standard weapons for infantry. About this time, also, the capabilities of field artillery were improved by the introduction of breech-loading and rifling in cannon. This improvement in performance did not alter the fact that theoretical range was unimportant when targets could not be seen beyond the next ridge line. Thus, in the Franco-Prussian War, as in the American Civil War, casualties from rifle bullets were still about ten times those from artillery. The implications of this fact were not appreciated initially in the Prussian or French services any more than they had been by either North or South in the American Civil War. Even at the end of the Franco-Prussian War, the linear tactics of Gustavus Adolphus were still in vogue, for commanders still had no other way to exercise control.

Thus, despite a truly revolutionary change in weapons effects, the resulting changes in tactics were evolutionary and could not have been otherwise.

DECLINING CASUALTY RATES IN HISTORY

You will note from the numbers in Figures 1-3, 1-4, and 1-5 that there has *not* been a steady decline in casualty rates (percentage loss per battle or per day) over the years. Rates have fluctuated widely. This is reaffirmed in Figure 1-6, which includes selected combat casualty statistics, summarizing most American experience for the past century and a half, and also including some selected foreign statistics, particularly from the Middle East wars.

And in this regard, note that the widely prevalent idea—presented in Proposition 8 of Figure 1-1—that October War casualty rates were horrendous is just not supported by the facts. Personnel casualty rates for that war actually seem to have been less than those for comparable size units in World War II. Tank losses were indeed very heavy, but in assessing them other factors must be considered. In some World War II

Figure 1-6.
SELECTED COMBAT CASUALTY STATISTICS
(Approximate Data)

	% Combat Theater Troops/Year	Representative Casualties % Per Day	
US Forces			
Mexican War	14.5		
		Antietam:	U–17.7
Civil War	23.2		C–28.9
		Gettysburg:	U– 9.8
			C–12.5
Spanish-American War	1.0		
Philippine Insurrection	1.2		
World War I (½ Year)	25.5	Per Division	2.0
World War II	21.3	Per Division	0.9
Korea	17.3	Per Division	0.8
Vietnam	20.6		
Soviet Forces			
1944 (12 Months)	82.0	Kursk (1943)	3.7
Middle East Wars			
1967 Israel (6 Days)	2.2	Overall	2.8
Egypt (3 Days)	6.2	Overall	1.6
Jordan (3 Days)	5.7	Overall	5.6
Syria (2 Days)	3.0	Overall	4.0
1973 Israel (19 Days)	3.9	Overall	1.8
Egypt (19 Days)	8.0	Overall	2.6
Syria (17 Days)	6.8	Overall	2.9

battles the *percent* losses of tanks were three to four times the percent of personnel casualties. No detailed study of tank loss rates for the October War has yet been published, but in that war the *percent* loss of tanks was approximately 5.4 times as great as the percent personnel casualty rate. (The factor was about 5.6 for the Israelis, and about 5.3 for the Arabs.) However, since there was a higher tank-to-manpower ratio in the October War, and since—as indicated just above—personnel casualty rates for that war were less than those for World War II, the absolute tank loss rate has increased little, if at all; in fact, it may possibly have declined. In any event, the casualty and loss rates of the October War do *not* demonstrate any startling increase over those of World War II—or even over those of the preceding Arab-Israeli war.

THE 3-1 SUPERIORITY REQUIREMENT

Next, let's examine Proposition 3 of Figure 1-1: the requirement that an attacker should have a three-to-one superiority over the defender. It is easy to find examples of attackers who have assembled such a superi-

Numbers, Predictions and War

ority in order to achieve success. A few examples come quickly to mind; the Allied breakout from Normandy in July 1944, the Soviet offensive toward Kharkov in August 1943—indeed almost any Soviet offensive between 1943 and 1945—the Egyptian attack across the Suez Canal in October 1973, and many others.

But it isn't very difficult to assemble a list of attacks in which the attacker was successful without having any such 3-1 superiority. In fact, in most of the examples shown in Figure 1-7 the successful attacker was actually outnumbered by the defender. In most or all of these cases, there were special considerations which permitted the attacker to undertake an offensive despite the equal or greater numerical strength of the defender: superior combat effectiveness; overwhelming air power superiority; higher morale; and so forth.

Figure 1-7 shows why the 3-1 force ratio requirement for the attacker cannot be of useful value without some knowledge of the behavioral and other combat variable factors involved.

FORCE SUPERIORITY AND BATTLE OUTCOMES

By working from an unrepresentative sample of battles, and by careless assembling of data on force strengths, it is not hard to "prove" that there is no relationship between force ratios and battle outcomes. Pentagon military officers and civilian officials in responsible positions really have been heard to state that there is no such relationship, and they really can cite studies that support their statements.

Figure 1-7 also shows how it is possible to take a collection of battle statistics and find no relationship between the size of the force and the outcome, or in fact be able to assert—as in Proposition 4 of Figure 1-1, that the numerically inferior force is usually victorious. In fact, since our history books focus on battles won by underdogs or great leaders, one can easily prove from readily available statistics such as those in Figure 1-7 that the smaller force has been successful in the majority of the best-known battles of history. These best-known battles, however, do not provide a statistically valid sample. Despite the statistical sleight of hand of Figure 1-7, thorough research has demonstrated (even if not precisely) that in 81 World War II engagements in Europe the larger force, or a barely outnumbered defending force, is successful about 65 percent of the time. When a smaller force is successful, this is because its numerical strength has been multiplied by physical or behavioral factors peculiar to that battle and the forces engaged in it.[3]

In other words, we can see how Napoleon could have said *both* of the apparently self-contradictory aphorisms attributed to him (Propositions

[3] See HERO staff paper, "Significance and Effects of Surprise in Modern War," *History, Numbers, and War*, vol. I, No. 1 (Spring, 1977), p. 4.

5 and 6[4] of Figure 1-1) and have meant both sincerely because (as Number 5 demonstrates) he was a firm believer in the mathematical interaction of forces—including moral, or behavioral forces.

Another thing Figure 1-7 does is to raise questions about the meaning of the term "force ratio." For instance, what is the force ratio to be used with the 3:1 force ratio planning factor? Is it numbers of men, or weapons? Is it firepower? Is it some other calculation of a combat power ratio? In any event, it is clear that neither numbers nor firepower tells us much unless we know the circumstances under which these numbers face each other, and the manner in which the firepower is applied.

TECHNOLOGY AND RATES OF ADVANCE

Figure 1-8 shows the advance rates in fifteen campaigns of the past 200 years that are noted for speed and/or distance of advances. This demonstrates that, for short distances, modern motorized-mechanized armies can move more rapidly than the foot-marching, horse-drawn armies of the Nineteenth and early Twentieth Centuries. Even so, the quickest "Quick Win" of World War I—the British victory at Megiddo, achieved by horse cavalry—was as quick as the most rapid Israeli armored force success of the Six Day War, nearly half a century later.

Note also how long it took Napoleon to reach Moscow (83 days; 13.6 kilometers a day). It took the Germans 167 days to reach the outskirts of Moscow (7.5 kilometers a day)—and they never quite got to the city.

Thus speed of opposed movement of large forces over great distance appears to reflect limitations on human capability much more than it reflects the road speed of tanks or trucks.

TANK LOSSES IN THE OCTOBER WAR

Propositions 9 and 10 in the list in Figure 1-1 are completely contradictory assertions of what should be simple, easily verifiable facts from very recent military history. These conflicting assertions are rather dramatic examples of the kinds of discrepancies with which military historians and military analysts have to cope when they seek insights or "lessons" from military history.

In support of Proposition 9, General Chaim Herzog has written the following in his reliable and responsible *War of Atonement:*

Contrary to the hasty conclusions published throughout the world after the Yom Kippur War, the tank still remains a dominant factor on the field of battle. . . . The results achieved by the Sagger antitank missile bore no proportion whatsoever to the publicity accorded it. In fact, surveys published indicate that less than 25% of the Israeli tanks damaged were hit by such a missile.[5]

[4] Proposition 6 is properly attributed to Voltaire, but was quoted by Napoleon.
[5] Chaim Herzog, *The War of Atonement,* Tel Aviv, 1975.

Figure 1-7.
SELECTED BATTLE STATISTICS, 1805-1973

Battle	Date	Attacker*	Strength	Defender*	Strength	A/D‡	V/L‡
Austerlitz	1805	FRENCH	75,000	Allies	89,000	0.84	0.84
Auerstadt	1806	Prussians	50,000	FRENCH	30,000	1.67	0.60
Borodino	1812	FRENCH	130,000	Russians	120,000	1.08	1.08
Dresden	1813	FRENCH	100,000	Allies	150,000	0.67	0.67
Leipzig	1813	ALLIES	300,000	French	180,000	1.67	1.67
Ligny	1815	FRENCH	77,000	Prussians	83,000	0.93	0.93
Waterloo	1815	ALLIES	129,000	French	72,000	1.79	1.79
Buena Vista	1847	Mexicans	16,000	AMERICANS	16,000	3.20	0.31
Cerro Gordo	1847	AMERICANS	8,500	Mexicans	12,000	0.71	0.71
Shiloh	1862	Confederates	40,335	UNION	62,642	0.64	1.55
Antietam	1862	Union	80,000	CONFEDERATES	45,000	1.77	0.56
Fredericksburg	1862	Union	106,000	CONFEDERATES	77,500	1.46	0.68
Chancellorsville	1863	Union	161,000	CONFEDERATES	57,352	1.76	0.57
Gettysburg	1863	Confederates	75,000	UNION	88,289	0.85	1.18
Chattanooga	1863	UNION	56,359	Confederates	46,165	1.22	1.22
Cold Harbor	1864	Union	107,907	CONFEDERATES	63,797	1.69	0.59
Koeniggraetz	1866	PRUSSIANS	220,000	Austrians	215,000	1.02	1.02
Sedan	1870	PRUSSIANS	190,000	French	110,000	1.73	1.73
Frontiers	1914	GERMANS	1,200,000	Allies	1,390,000	0.86	0.86
Tannenberg	1914	GERMANS	187,000	Russians	160,000	1.17	1.17
Marne	1914	ALLIES	1,200,000	Germans	900,000	1.33	1.33
Masurian Lakes	1914	GERMANS	288,600	Russians	273,000	1.06	1.06
Champagne II	1914	French	500,000	GERMANS	190,000	2.63	0.38
Gorlice-Tarnow	1915	GERMANS	175,000	Russians	300,000	0.58	0.58
Arras	1917	British	276,000	GERMANS	120,000	2.24	0.45
Aisne II (Nivelle)	1917	French	1,000,000	GERMANS	480,000	2.08	0.48
Meuse-Argonne	1918	AMERICANS	600,000	Germans	380,000	1.58	1.58

Battle	Year						
Flanders	1940	GERMANS	2,500,000	Allies	3,000,000	0.83	0.85
Crete	1941	GERMANS	20,000	Anglo-Greek	41,000	0.49	0.49
Barbarossa (Kleist Group)	1941	GERMANS	132,000	Russians	150,000	0.88	0.88
Malaya	1941-1942	JAPANESE	60,000	British	130,000	0.46	0.46
El Alamein	1942	BRITISH	177,000	Axis	93,000	1.90	1.90
Stalingrad	1942	RUSSIANS	1,000,000	Germans	800,000	1.25	1.25
Kursk-Oboyan**	1943	GERMANS	62,000	Russians	90,000	0.69	1.45
Anzio, "Bowling Alley" (US 45th Inf Div)	1944	Germans	41,974	AMERICANS	20,496	2.05	0.49
Velletri (US 1st Armd Div)	1944	Americans	14,620	GERMANS	12,327	1.19	0.84
Metz (US XX Corps)	1944	Americans	60,794	GERMANS	39,580	1.54	0.65
Ardennes (US 4th Inf Div)	1944	GERMANS	10,000	Americans	8,634	1.16	1.16
Iwo Jima	1945	AMERICANS	68,000	Japanese	22,000	3.09	3.09
Sinai, Six Day War	1967	ISRAELIS	54,993	Egyptians	100,000	0.55	0.55
West Bank, Six Day War	1967	ISRAELIS	45,650	Jordanians	43,300	1.05	1.05
Golan, Six Day War	1967	ISRAELIS	40,450	Syrians	60,000	0.67	0.67

Summary:

In 42 battles: 28 attackers, 14 defenders, were successful.

13 numerically inferior attackers; 12 of these successful.

18 victors were numerically superior (43%).

24 victors were numerically inferior (57%).

°Where both sides attacked (as at Waterloo and Marne), relates to final posture; victor capitalized.
°°German XLVIII Panzer Corps sector, first seven days, before arrival of a fresh Russian army group.
†Attacker/Defender
‡Victor/Loser

15

Figure 1-8.
ADVANCE RATES IN SOME
19th AND 20th CENTURY CAMPAIGNS

Campaign	Distance (km)	Days[c]	Distance /Day (km)
Marengo[a], 1800	350	31	11
Ulm[a], 1805	475	22	22
Jena[a], 1806	140	6	23
Friedland[a], 1807	210	9	23
Danube (Aspern), 1809	405	30	14
Russia, 1812	680[b]	57[d]	12(13.6)[f]
Lutzen-Bautzen, 1813	300	20	15
Vicksburg, 1863	190	19	10
Savannah-Raleigh, 1865	1,010	121	8
Appomattox[a], 1865	100	6	17
Sadowa[a], 1866	230	18	13
Metz-Sedan[a], 1870	390	30	13
Marne, 1914	560	28	20
Caporetto, 1917	160	20	8
Gaza III, 1917	150	39	4
Somme II, 1918	110	16	7
Megiddo[a], 1918	167	3	56
Flanders[a], 1940	368	12	31
Barbarossa, 1941	700[b]	24[e]	29(7.5)[f]
Malaya[a], 1941-42	515[b]	28	18
Luzon I[a], 1941-42	216	15	14
Caucasus, 1942	775	34	23
Normandy Breakout, 1944	880	32	28
Luzon II, 1944	230	26	9
Manchuria[a], 1945	300	6	50
N. Korean Offensive, 1950	560	42	13
UN Offensive, 1951	790	42	19
Sinai 1967[a]	220	4	55
Samaria 1967[a]	80	3	27
Golan 1967[a]	35	2	18

[a]"Quick Wins"; complete victory in 30 days or less.

[b]Overall campaign distance exceeded 1,000 km.

[c]Days required to go distance shown, by which time a decision was reached; some campaigns continued for a number of days and considerable distance following decision.

[d]Days to Smolensk; Napoleon reached Moscow on 83d day.

[e]Days to Smolensk; Germans reached Moscow suburbs after 167 days.

[f]Rates for distance and time shown; number in parentheses shows rate for entire campaign.

There are indications that similar information can be found in classified US Government documents, compiled with Israeli assistance in Israel.

Yet when the author discussed this question with an Egyptian officer, in connection with a recent book,[6] the Egyptian insisted that at least 70 percent of the 300-400 Israeli tanks that were left behind the Egyptian lines had been hit by the Sagger missile or RPG-7 rocket. (See Figure 1-9.) The author has seen the published and the classified reports to which General Herzog refers, and they are quite scientific and convincing. No similar Egyptian survey is available; although this of course would be helpful, there is no doubt of the sincerity of the Egyptian officer's statement.

Figure 1-9.
CAUSES OF TANK CASUALTIES

	Israeli Assessment	Egyptian Assessment
Guns, Tanks and AT	65-70%	20-25%
Missiles and Rockets	20-25%	65-70%
Mines	5-10%	5-10%
Aircraft	2-5%	5-10%
Artillery	2-5%	2-5%

Both sides are right, in fact, despite almost diametrically opposed conclusions. The damage inspected and reported by the Israelis was done to tanks that ended up inside the Israeli lines, most of them from the Egyptian attack on October 14th and during the subsequent operations in the Chinese Farm area and on the west bank of the Suez Canal. This was damage inflicted after the Israelis had learned, from their bitter experience of the first three days, how to deal with the Egyptian antitank missiles and rockets. These tank losses were also incurred in combat in which either the Israelis were on the defensive, after the effects of the initial Arab surprise had worn off, or they were on the offensive and the Egyptians were the ones who were disrupted. Furthermore, during the period of 18-24 October the Israelis were concentrating most of their fighting on the west bank of the Suez Canal against Egyptian units that had very few Saggers and RPG-7s, since most of these had been transferred before October 6 to the units that were to operate on the east bank, and that were still there.

[6] T.N. Dupuy, *Elusive Victory, The Arab-Israeli Wars, 1947-1974,* New York, 1978.

The damage reported by the Egyptian officer was to tanks that the Egyptians had inspected behind their lines after the war. These tanks were mostly the victims of the first three days of fighting, when the Sagger and RPG-7 gained their reputations, which (despite what Herzog writes) apparently were fully deserved, under the then existing circumstances of combat.

BRAVING THE DATA JUNGLE

These few examples serve to illustrate the problems of trying to analyze trends in ground combat by making sense out of the anarchical masses of data that lie in the dark and musty records of warfare. To some extent, they illustrate why it is both vain and dangerous to seek immutable lessons from the records of the past; the facts are too contradictory, too specialized, too subject to misinterpretation, to support unequivocal conclusions. Certain generalized principles can be substantiated—usually. But the specifics of combat processes and relationships are elusive.

These examples illustrate, also, why there is so little data—relative to the potentially available volume—in analyzable form for the use of analyst and military planner. The task of digging it out is too great, and the obvious utility of the result too questionable to warrant the effort by busy and impatient analysts; it is easier to guess, to assume, or to generalize.

Subsequent chapters will describe how, despite these problems, the author of this book and his associates have gone about the process of translating the numbers of military history into a coherent, consistent, quantitative theory of combat and combat relationships. In the telling, it may appear to the reader that our efforts were systematic, orderly, logical, and efficient. It wasn't really that way. Our results came from a combination of considerable thinking, many false starts, numerous hunches, some strokes of good luck, and the application of the combat experience of several retired professional military officers to the various problems of combat analysis.

2
The Effects of Weapons

Partly by accident, the efforts to quantify warfare which are described in this book began with a consideration of weapons lethality. This was in a historical analysis of trends in weapons lethality which I did in collaboration with several colleagues of the Historical Evaluation and Research Organization—or HERO, as we modestly call ourselves—in 1963 and 1964.[7]

If the numbers of military history mean anything, it appears self-evident that there must be some kind of relationship between the quantities of weapons employed by opposing forces in combat, and the number of casualties suffered by each side. It also seems fairly obvious that some weapons are likely to cause more casualties than others, and that the effectiveness of weapons will depend upon their ability to reach their targets. So it becomes clear that the relationship of weapons to casualties is not quite the simple matter of comparing numbers to numbers. To compare weapons to casualties it is necessary to know not only the numbers of weapons, but also how many there are of each different type, and how effective or lethal each of these is.

The effectiveness, or lethality, of weapons is obviously a function of their ability to inflict damage. In our study we defined weapon lethality as "the inherent capability of a given weapon to kill personnel, or to make materiel ineffective in a given period of time, where capability includes the factors of weapon range, rate of fire, accuracy, radius of effects, and battlefield mobility." We then attempted to ascertain and quantify the inherent (or potential or theoretical) lethality of the most important weapons in history on a basis that would permit valid direct comparison of such weapons and their theoretical effectiveness.

The lethality of a weapon in actual use is affected by many variables, such as terrain, weather, morale of the users, the extent of their training, and the effectiveness of the users' leaders. There is no obvious way in which to give precise values to the effects of these variables. Furthermore, different weapons, or even identical weapons, can never be employed at different times and places under exactly identical circumstances with precisely identical results. Thus, in order to have a reliable basis for comparing the lethality potential of different weapons it was necessary to

[7] *Historical Trends Related to Weapon Lethality,* HERO, October 1964.

19

postulate a standard, theoretical, laboratory-like environment which could be common for all weapons.

Rate of fire, range, accuracy, radius of effects, and battlefield mobility are factors quantifiable for all weapons, and essential for inclusion in a quantification effort. Research indicated that other measurable characteristics which should be considered are: the number of potential targets rendered ineffective by one blow or one round fired by a weapon, the relative incapacitating effect of each such impact, the weapon's reliability, and (for a weapon which is a mobile fighting machine) its radius of action, its speed, and its ability to absorb punishment and still retain some effectiveness.

Having identified the essential factors that could be readily expressed in numbers, we were faced with the problem of what standards of measurements could be used in order to get comparable lethality values, what we called a Theoretical Lethality Index (TLI). Each factor had its peculiar characteristics, and we had to treat them all differently.

1. *Rate of Fire (RF)*. This is the number of effective strikes which a weapon, under ideal conditions, can deliver against a target in a given period of time. A time unit of one hour was selected because it is long enough to permit consideration of sustained rates of fire for missile weapons (that is, weapons that achieve their effect by hurling an object through the air, or by being themselves hurled through the air, like an arrow from a bow, a stone from a sling, or a projectile from a gun). It was assumed (under the postulated laboratory conditions) that there is no logistical problem for any weapon during the period of one hour.

2. *Number of Potential Targets per Strike (PTS)*. In order to establish a basis for comparison of the relative theoretical lethality of hand-to-hand or early missile weapons (which we can call point fire weapons) and later weapons with the capability of incapacitating more than one enemy per strike (area fire weapons), it is essential to establish a standard of target density. A realistic, universally applicable standard is men in mass formation, each individual assumed to occupy one square meter. While artificial in terms of battlefield circumstances, this standard permits consideration of the relative theoretical lethality of high-explosive shells, and of the multiple casualty possibilities of non-explosive solid projectiles, as well as the one-for-one lethality of such point weapons as the sword, pike, or bayonet.

3. *Relative Incapacitating Effect (RIE)*. Since single blows from some weapons are more likely to be lethal or incapacitating than single blows from others, a factor has been selected for each weapon on the basis of historical experience, to represent the likelihood that an individual blow if it hits a target will incapacitate the target.

4. *Effective Range (RN)*. A weapon's range clearly affects its practical lethality. History proves conclusively that a longer range gives a weapon

more opportunity to be lethal or incapacitating than does a shorter range. Moreover, all enemies within the effective range of a weapon are forced to take some kind of passive or active countermeasure to protect themselves from the direct effect of the weapon's employment within its effective range (considered as 90 percent of maximum range if no other value is available). This indirect effect (sometimes called suppression or neutralization) may be as significant as the direct. It was decided to establish as a norm for range the length of a man's arm, called Normal Range, with a value of 1, for 1 meter. On this basis the following empirically derived formula expresses the historical significance of effective range:

$$\text{Range factor} = 1 + \sqrt{.001 \times \text{Effective Range (meters)}} \tag{1}$$

Thus the value of the range factor will always be 1 or greater, and will increase proportionately as the reach of a weapon extends beyond that of a man's arm.

For greater consistency of results and increased precision for comparisons of the lethalities of tube artillery weapons (particularly for high muzzle velocity weapons such as AT and AA guns designed for maximum penetration and reduced time of projectile flight) it was found that results comparable to and compatible with those of equation (1) can be obtained by another empirical formula—based upon the weapon's caliber in millimeters and its muzzle velocity (MV) in meters per second —rather than effective range, as follows:

$$\text{Range factor} = .007 \times \text{MV} \times \sqrt{.01 \times \text{caliber}} \tag{2}$$

The constant of .007 assures a value comparable to that of the formula based on range; in any event, as suggested above, the value of this factor can never be less than 1.0.

Where accurate performance data is available, lethality should be calculated for both range and muzzle velocity. Where the MV result is higher, this should be adopted. Where the range factor is higher, the OLI value should usually be the mean of the two calculations. For mortars and missiles (rockets), however, the higher value (whether muzzle velocity or range factor) is taken.

5. *Accuracy (A).* The probability that a single blow, aimed precisely at the target, will hit it must be considered as an inherent quality of the weapon and not of the user, whose performance is affected by practice, training, excitement, and other outside influences. For weapons whose accuracy factors at mean battlefield ranges are not included in available official manuals, factors are estimated.

6. *Reliability (RL).* This factor recognizes that all mechanical weapons can and will break down. It provides for such things as misfires, duds, and jamming, whose possible occurrence reduces the potential lethality of a weapon. Hand-held, non-mechanical shock weapons (sword, spear,

etc.) are assumed to be entirely reliable. The degree of reliability has been estimated on the basis of known operational experience.

The six factors discussed above relate to stationary, towed, or carried weapons. When combined (multiplied) they yield a theoretical lethality index (TLI) value for any given weapon with any characteristics, and this index is directly comparable to the similarly derived index value of any other weapon.

The formula for the calculation of theoretical lethality indices for stationary, towed, or carried weapons thus is:

$$\text{Lethality index} = \text{rate of fire} \times \text{targets per strike} \times \text{relative effect} \times \text{range factor} \times \text{accuracy} \times \text{reliability} \qquad (3)$$

○ ○ ○

The following six factors are applied to weapons that incorporate some motive capability, and that can be considered mobile fighting machines. The mobile fighting machine, such as tank or fighter-bomber, generally carries more than one weapon and, by virtue of such protective characteristics as armor and/or speed, also can increase the security and reduce the vulnerability of the personnel manning it. The overall lethality of such a machine is calculated by adding the individual lethality indices of all weapons it carries and applying (by multiplication) a mobility factor and a radius of action factor, adding a punishment (or relative invulnerability) factor, and multiplying this result by three performance factors: rapidity of fire effect, fire control effect, and ammunition supply effect. These factors are not applied to self-propelled artillery because it is assumed that the enhancing effects are at least in part offset by increased vulnerability and decreased reliability due to mechanical considerations not affecting towed artillery; however, a bonus factor is applied to the towed weapon calculation to reflect the tactical flexibility of self-propelled artillery.

7. *Battlefield Mobility (M)*. The ability of a weapon to change its position on the battlefield necessarily affects its potential lethality. A valid representation of that effect, involving a relationship of speed, weight and power, is produced by multiplying the weapon's theoretical lethality (based upon its stationary characteristics) by 0.2 times the square root of its road speed in kilometers per hour. This factor (an empirically derived relationship translated from miles per hour) is applied only when the following factors are also applicable to fighting machines.

8. *Radius of Action (RA)*. The combat potential of a fighting vehicle is affected by its operational range, that is, the distance it can travel without refueling. For a ground vehicle, this is assumed to be the distance it can move cross-country over "average" terrain on a tankful of fuel. For

an air vehicle it is the radius of operation, allowing sufficient fuel to perform its combat mission after reaching the target area, and sufficient fuel to return to its base. Values derived from this effect that are consistent with historical experience are obtained by assuming that the factor can be represented by 0.08 times the square root of its range, or radius, in kilometers.

9. *Punishment Factor (PF)*. The vulnerability of the weapons combined in a fighting machine is diminished either by armor, by speed, or by both. The vulnerability-reducing effect of speed is assumed to be taken care of by the Battlefield Mobility factor, above. The contribution of the effect of armor in enabling a fighting machine to absorb or inhibit punishment from hostile weapons is assumed to be primarily related to the weight of the armor, and is calculated as follows:[8]

$$\text{Punishment factor} = 3000 \times \frac{\text{weight(tons)}}{4} \times \sqrt{2 \times \text{weight(tons)}} \qquad (4)$$

The punishment factor for an armored personnel carrier, an assault gun, or a tank destroyer is assumed to be half of that of a tank of identical weight (since a smaller proportion of its weight is attributable to protection). Similarly, the punishment factor for an aircraft is assumed to be half of the result obtainable from the application of equation (4) to aircraft weight. The full value is used for armored reconnaissance vehicles (ARVs) and armored cars. The value is additive.

☼ ☼ ☼

After these first three mobile fighting machine factors have been applied (total weapons TLI value multiplied by battlefield mobility factor and radius of action factor, plus the calculated punishment factor), the resulting TLI value is multiplied for armored vehicles by each of three performance factors, as listed below.

10. *Rapidity of Fire Effect (RFE)*. The speed with which the principal weapon of an armored vehicle can be fired and reloaded has a significant bearing on its survival in combat against other armored vehicle or antitank weapons. A curve has been prepared (Figure 2-1) to represent this effect, as related to the sustained hourly rate of fire of the basic weapon.

[8] This value was derived empirically, after testing various possible relationships of weapons vs. armor; it gives results which seem consistent with the observations of experienced military specialists. Note that it does not reflect slope or metallurgical characteristics of armor, and clearly is susceptible to refinement. The constant factor of 3,000 is a reflection of the effect of troop dispersion in relation to firepower, which is discussed below.

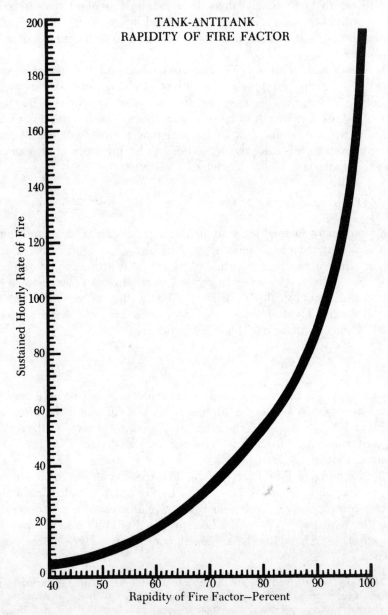

Figure 2-1
TANK-ANTITANK
RAPIDITY OF FIRE FACTOR

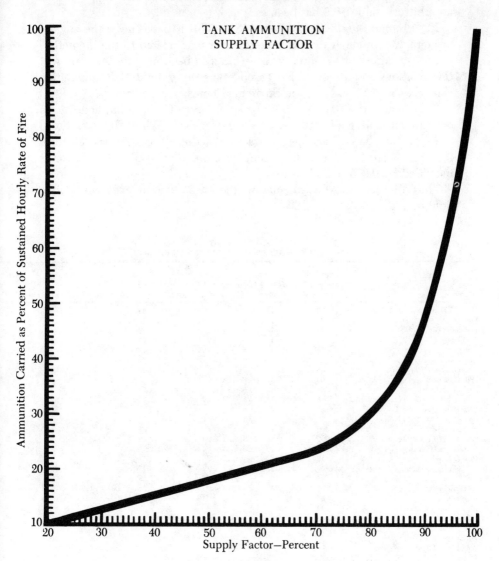

Figure 2-2
TANK AMMUNITION
SUPPLY FACTOR

11. *Fire Control Effect (FCE)*. This is a judgmental factor representing practical fire control effectiveness, not necessarily sophisticated equipment. Values derived for tanks operational in 1973 have been related to the assessed fire control effectiveness of the US M60A1 tank, to which an arbitrary value of .9 has been assigned.

12. *Ammunition Supply Effect (ASE)*. This is based upon the amount of ammunition which the machine can carry, as related to the theoretical hourly sustained rate of fire. A curve has also been prepared to represent this relationship (Figure 2-2), based upon the quantity of ammunition carried as a percentage of the theoretical hourly rate of fire.

For aircraft of all types a ceiling performance factor is applied; for an operational ceiling of 30,000 feet the factor is 1. When the operational ceiling is less than 30,000 feet, the factor is reduced by 0.02 for each 1,000 feet below 30,000; when the ceiling is more than 30,000 the factor is increased by 0.005 per 1,000 feet.

Thus the formula for calculating the theoretical indices for mobile fighting machines is:

Figure 2-3
INDEX OF RELATIVE THEORETICAL LETHALITY

Weapons	Rate of Fire Strikes/hour	Targets /Strike	Relative Effective- ness	$1+\sqrt{Range/1000}=$	Range Effect	Muzzle $.007 \times velocity \times \sqrt{Cal/100}=$			Muzzle Velocity Effect
Hand-to-Hand (Sword, pike, etc.)	60	1	.4	$1+\sqrt{.001}$	1.03				
Javelin	60	1	.4	$1+\sqrt{.02}$	1.14				
Ordinary bow	55	1	.4	$1+\sqrt{.08}$	1.28				
Longbow	55	1	.5	$1+\sqrt{.2}$	1.45				
Crossbow	50	1	.5	$1+\sqrt{.23}$	1.48				
Arquebus	40	1	.6	$1+\sqrt{.1}$	1.32				
17th C musket	45	1	.7	$1+\sqrt{.15}$	1.39				
18th C flintlock	60	1	.8	$1+\sqrt{.2}$	1.45				
Early 19th C rifle	40	1	.8	$1+\sqrt{.55}$	1.74				
Mid-19th C rifle with conoidal bullet	65	1	.8	$1+\sqrt{2.0}$	2.41				
Late 19th C breechloading rifle	120	1	.8	$1+\sqrt{1.5}$	2.22				
Springfield Model 1903 rifle (magazine)	300	1	.8	$1+\sqrt{2}$	2.41				
World War I machinegun	4000	1	.8	$1+\sqrt{1.5}$	2.22				
World War II machinegun	5000	1	.8	$1+\sqrt{1.5}$	2.22				
16th C 12-pdr cannon	10	10	1.	$1+\sqrt{.5}$	1.71				
17th C 12-pdr cannon	20	12	1.	$1+\sqrt{1.5}$	2.22				
Gribeauval 18th C 12-pdr cannon	30	18	1.	$1+\sqrt{2.5}$	2.58				
French 75mm gun	150	675	1.	$1+\sqrt{10.4}$	4.23	.007×	697	×$\sqrt{.75}$ =	4.23
155mm GPF	60	3370	1.	$1+\sqrt{18}$	5.00	.007×	573	×$\sqrt{1.55}$ =	5.00
105mm Howitzer, M-1	120	1570	1.	$1+\sqrt{9.5}$	4.08	.007×	570	×$\sqrt{1.05}$ =	4.08
155mm "Long Tom"	60	3370	1.	$1+\sqrt{30}$	6.47	.007×	742	×$\sqrt{1.55}$ =	6.47
World War I tank									
World War II medium tank									
World War I fighter-bomber									
World War II fighter-bomber (P-47)									
V-2 ballistic missile	6	75,000	1.	$1+\sqrt{200}$	15.14				
20 KT nuclear airburst	1	600,000	1.	$1+\sqrt{1000}$	101.				
One megaton nuclear airburst	1	8,500,000	1.	$1+\sqrt{1000}$	101.				

*Does not reflect multiple charge versatility.
** $\sqrt{.01} \times$ range (mi)
*** $\sqrt{.1} \times$ speed (mhp)

Lethality index=(summed total of lethality indices of all weapons) ×mobility (or speed) factor×radius of action (or endurance) factor;+the punishment factor; all of this ×rapidity of fire effect×fire control effect× ammunition supply effect×ceiling effect (5)

Formulae (3) and/or (5) can be applied to any weapon to produce a TLI value for that weapon. Figure 2-3 shows the computed TLI values for a number of weapons, in use from ancient times to the nuclear age. As evident from the table, these numbers provide an interesting comparison of historical weapons capabilities, but are not easily relatable to any of the many different kinds of battlefields on which they have been used. (In the previous chapter, Figure 1-2 showed theoretical weapons lethality trends through recorded history.)

Despite the constantly increasing lethality of weapons over the years as shown by Figures 1-2 and 2-3, we noted in the previous chapter that battlefield casualty rates have generally declined over history, even though this has not been a smooth transitional curve. This is in large part

				Mobile Fighting Machines			
Accuracy	Reliability	TLI	Total TLI	Endurance**	Mobility***	Punishment	TLI
.95	1.0	23					
.75	.95	19					
.8	.95	21					
.95	.95	36					
.95	.95	33					
.55	.6	10					
.55	.8	19					
.65	.95	43					
.8	.8	36					
.9	.9	102					
.9	.8	153					
.95	.9	495					
.65	.75	3463					
.7	.8	4973					
.5	.5	43					
.6	.7	224					
.75	.9	940					
.95	.95	386,530					
.95	.95	912,428					
.9	.95	657,215					
.95	.95	1,180,681					
			6,926	$\sqrt{.5}$	$\sqrt{1.5}$	$3000 \times 9/4 \times \sqrt{18}$	34,636
			575,000	$\sqrt{1.}$	$\sqrt{2}$	$3000 \times 24/4 \times \sqrt{48}$	935,458
			6,926	$\sqrt{2}$	$\sqrt{10}$	$3000 \times 1.4 \times \sqrt{2}$	31,909
			135,000	$\sqrt{2.6}$	$\sqrt{32}$	$3000 \times 6/4 \times \sqrt{12}$	1,245,789
.7	.7	3,338,370					
.9	.9	49,086,000					
.9	.9	695,385,000					

because formations of troops have become more dispersed as weapons have grown more lethal and as their ranges and potential effectiveness have increased. Thus, the actual battlefield effectiveness of weapons in producing casualties has been decreased by the presence of fewer targets within a given area. A more realistic representation of the actual practical, or operational, lethality of a weapon can therefore be obtained if, for any given period of history, it can be related to the normal dispersion pattern of the forces against which the weapon would be employed.

Figure 2-4 shows the areas covered by typical armies or forces of 100,000 troops in six different periods of history. From a comparison of these dispersion patterns, it becomes possible to calculate the effect of dispersion on real-world, battlefield lethality.

Figure 2-4.

HISTORICAL ARMY DISPERSION PATTERNS

	Ancient Armies	Napoleonic Wars	American Civil War	WWI	WWII	1973
Area occupied by deployed force 100,000 strong (sq km)	1.00	20.12	25.75	247.5	3100	4000
Depth (km)	.15	2.5	3.0	12	60	67
Width (km)	6.67	8.00	8.33	20.83	50	60
Dispersion factor	1.0	20.0	25.0	250	3000	4000

13. *Dispersion Factor (Di).* The second of the factors used for calculating the original TLIs for hand-to-hand and early missile weapons—Number of Potential Targets per Strike—assumes a mass formation which approximates the tightly packed deployment patterns of the ancient phalangial formations that preceded the Roman legion. As shown in Figure 2-4, a theoretical ancient army of 100,000 men when so deployed would have occupied an area of approximately 1.0 square km. A dispersion factor value of 1 is assigned to this massed formation; dispersion factors for any subsequent tactical system of deployment and dispersion are obtained by calculating the area in square kilometers which would be occupied by a tactically deployed military force 100,000 strong.

Application of the Dispersion Factor converts Theoretical Lethality Indices (TLIs) to Operational Lethality Indices (OLIs). Figure 2-5 demonstrates the application of these dispersion factors to the weapons listed in Figure 2-3. Note in particular how the battlefield lethality potentials for the same or comparable weapons have markedly declined in later

Figure 2-5

TABLE OF COMPARATIVE OPERATIONAL LETHALITY INDICES

Weapons	Historical Period	Ancient or Medieval	17th Cent	18th Cent	Nap. Wars	Civil War	W.W. I	W.W. II	1975
Dispersion Factor		1	5	10	20	25	250	3,000	4,000
	TLI Values								
Hand-to-Hand	23	23	4.6	2.3	1.1	0.9	0.09	0.007	0.006
Javelin	19	19							
Ordinary Bow	21	21							
Longbow	36	36	7.2	3.6					
Crossbow	33	33	6.6						
Arquebus	10	—	2.0						
17th C musket	19	—	3.8						
18th C flintlock	43	—	8.6	4.3	2.2	1.7			
Early 19th C rifle	36	—	—	3.6	1.8	1.4			
Mid-19th C rifle	102	—	—	—	—	4.1			
Late 19th C rifle	153	—	—	—	—	6.1	0.61	0.05	
Springfield Model 1903 rifle	495	—	—	—	—	—	1.98	0.17	0.12
WW I machinegun	3,463	—	—	—	—	—	14.0	1.15	0.87
WW II machinegun	4,973	—	—	—	—	—	—	1.66	1.24
16th C 12-pdr cannon	43	43	8.6						
17th C 12-pdr cannon	224	—	45.0	22.0					
Gribeauval 12-pdr cannon	940	—	—	94.0	47.0	38.0			
French 75 mm gun	386,530	—	—	—	—	—	1,546.	129.	97.
155 mm GPF	912,428	—	—	—	—	—	3,650.	304.	228.
105 mm Howitzer	637,215	—	—	—	—	—	—	219.	164.
155 mm "Long Tom"	1,180,681	—	—	—	—	—	—	394.	295.
WW I tank	34,636	—	—	—	—	—	139.	12.	
WW II medium tank	935,458	—	—	—	—	—	—	312.	234.
WW I fighter-bomber	31,909	—	—	—	—	—	128.	11.	
WW II fighter-bomber	1,245,789	—	—	—	—	—	—	415.	311.
V-2 ballistic missile	3,338,370	—	—	—	—	—	—	1,113.	835.
20 KT nuclear airburst	49,086,000	—	—	—	—	—	—	16,362.	12,272.
One megaton nuclear airburst	695,385,000	—	—	—	—	—	—	231,795.	173,846.

eras, as weapons have become more powerful and tactical dispersion has increased correspondingly.[9]

Logical though it may appear from this discussion, and from the relationship shown in the illustrations, the conversion of Theoretical Lethality Indices (TLIs) to Operational Lethality Indices (OLIs) was not a quick and easy matter. In fact, it was more than three years before we realized that dispersion was the key to making such a conversion. An article by Major William G. Stewart in the professional journal *Military Review*, provided the stimulus.[10] In that article Stewart demonstrated that there has been a historical, dynamic relationship involving firepower, mobility, and dispersion. He showed that an increase in weapons lethality requires an increase in dispersion, but that the response of tactical doctrine to this requirement has been at least partly dependent upon the means of mobility available.

It had by this time become apparent to me and my colleagues that the TLIs and their related OLIs really represent the "proving ground" values for weapons effects, i.e., the maximum possible lethality under ideal conditions. On the battlefield, however, the actual effects vary widely from one situation to another, depending upon the circumstances of combat. The performance of weapons on the battlefield could be represented only if we could modify the "proving ground" values by a variety of realistic combat variables, such as the effects of weather, terrain, season, mobility characteristics, and vulnerability. Our earlier research suggested that it should be possible to derive specific values for many of these variable effects to reflect the varying circumstances of combat. We recognized that there were such other things to consider as surprise, leadership, training, morale, and logistical efficiency; but at that time we assumed that these intangible variables could not be quantified.

At this point in our explorations we mused that if we could figure out how different combat circumstances and variables affected the ideal, or "proving ground," OLI values, we could then determine the actual battlefield value of each weapon under those special circumstances, and arrive at an overall value for the inventory of weapons for each of two opposing sides in a battle. If our original OLI values were reasonably

[9] It should be noted that the great increase in dispersion factors between World War I and World War II was only partially due to increasing weapon lethality; it was in part due to improved means of mobility, permitting greater dispersion, since in an emergency forces could be more rapidly concentrated. Thus, for conventional warfare, the dispersion factor increase since World War II—as demonstrated in subsequent wars—has been less dramatic, representing some increase in lethality and some increase in mobility, due primarily to the advent of the helicopter.

[10] William G. Stewart, "Interaction of Firepower, Mobility, and Dispersion," *Military Review*, March 1960, pp. 26-33.

Figure 3-1
VARIABLE EFFECTS FACTORS QUANTIFIED JUDGMENT MODEL

A. Weapons Effects
　1. Rate of fire
　2. Potential targets per strike
　3. Relative incapacitating effect
　4. Effective range (or muzzle velocity)
　5. Accuracy
　6. Reliability
　7. Battlefield mobility
　8. Radius of action
　9. Punishment (vulnerability) factor
　10-13. Armor performance factors (4)
　14. Helicopter
　15-21. Special weapons effects factors (7+)
　22. Dispersion factor
B. Terrain Factors
　23. Mobility effect
　24. Defense posture effect
　25. Infantry weapons effect
　26. Artillery weapons effect
　27. Air effectiveness effect
　28. Tank effect
C. Weather Factors
　29. Mobility effect
　30. Attack posture effect
　31. Artillery effect
　32. Air effectiveness effect
　33. Tank effect
D. Season Factors
　34. Attack posture effect
　35. Artillery effect
　36. Air effectiveness effect
E. Air Superiority Factors
　37. Mobility effect
　38. Artillery effect
　39. Air effectiveness effect
　40. Vulnerability effect
F. Posture Factors
　41. Force strength effect
　42. Vulnerability effect

G. Mobility Effects
　43. Characteristics of mobility
　44. Environmental effect
H. Vulnerability Factors
　45. Exposure consideration, general
　46. Environmental effects, general
　47. Across beach
　48. Across unfordable river
　49. Across major fordable or minor unfordable river
I. Tactical Air Effects
　50. Close air support damage and casualties
　51. Close air support morale effect°°°
　52. Interdiction logistical movement°°
　53. Interdiction delays on ground movement°°
　54. Interdiction damage and casualties
　55. Interdiction disruption effect°°°
J. Other Combat Processes
　56. Mobility effects of surprise
　57. Surpriser's vulnerability effect
　58. Surprised's vulnerability effect
　59. Other surprise effects°°
　60. Degradation effects of fatigue and casualties°°
　61. Casualty-inflicting capability factor
　62. Disruption°°
K. Intangible Factors
　63. Combat effectiveness°
　64. Leadership°°
　65. Training/experience°°
　66. Morale°°°
　67. Logistics°
　68. Time°°°
　69. Space°°°
　70. Momentum°°°
　71. Intelligence°°°
　72. Technology°°°
　73. Initiative°°

°Sometimes calculable
°°Probably calculable; not yet calculated
°°°Intangible; probably individually incalculable

fiable at a given time or place, and which are descriptors peculiar to the engagement.

It is only during the process of general analysis of a *body* of combat results, within terms of some theory or concept, or some simulation of combat, that the mathematician's variable elements become the unknowns, and different values for these are sought with respect to ranges of values among the parameters.

CLASSIFYING COMBAT VARIABLES

The military generalist, however, is not concerned with the difference between variable elements and parameters. He classifies combat variables in various other ways. We prefer to use three pairs of contrasting categories:

     a. Environmental and operational variables;
     b. Tabular and formular variables; and
     c. Tangible and intangible variables.

Environmental variables are those which affect the effectiveness of weapons; they are included in the four categories B through E in Figure 3-1. *Operational* variables, those influencing the employment of weapons and forces, include some of the factors listed in categories B through E and all of those in categories F through K in that Figure.

Tabular variables are those which lend themselves to representation in relatively simple tables of values, usually presented in matrix format. *Formular* variables are those which are more complicated, and which can be represented only by formulae, usually involving interactions of two or more tabular variables.

Tangible variables are those to which, as a result of observation, research, or some form of analytical process, specific quantitative values can be assigned which are believed to represent the practical effect of the variable in modifying the value of one weapon, or a collection of weapons. *Intangible* variables are those which are—at least for the present—impossible to quantify with confidence, either because they are essentially qualitative in nature, or because for some other reason they currently defy precise delineation or measurement.

SPECIFIC VARIABLES

First let's look at some tangible, tabular variables.

Terrain effects. Table 1 in Appendix A (p. 228) is a list of certain terrain-related factors. The relative effects of different kinds of terrain upon weapons effectiveness (infantry weapons, artillery, armor, and close air support) are environmental. The effects upon mobility and posture are operational. For instance, terrain can limit fields of fire; this is an environmental effect. Also terrain can inhibit movement of weapons and forces, an operational effect.

Weather effects. Table 2 in Appendix A (p. 229) presents values for different weather factors. These include the relative environmental effects of different kinds of weather conditions upon weapons (artillery, armor, and direct air support) and operational effects upon mobility and posture.

Season effects. Table 3 (Appendix A, p. 230) shows season factors. The environmental effects include seasonal variations affecting weapons (artillery and direct air support); the operational effect is on posture, mainly reflecting the hours of daylight and darkness in different seasons in the Temperate Zone.

Air Superiority effects. Table 4 (Appendix A, p. 230) presents air superiority factors. The presence or absence of air superiority can affect a land battle in four major ways, two environmental and two operational: (1) its presence will enhance the effectiveness of tactical air support (both close support and interdiction) and degrade the effectiveness of air forces operating against it; (2) it will slightly enhance the effectiveness of friendly artillery and degrade the effectiveness of hostile artillery; (3) it will slightly enhance the ground mobility of the force possessing it and will substantially degrade the mobility of the opposing forces; and (4) it will reduce the vulnerability of a force with air superiority while increasing that of the hostile force.

Posture. All offensive-defensive posture factors are operational in their effects. Posture effects reflect Clausewitz's well-proved dictum that "defense is the stronger form of combat." The force strength of a unit is enhanced by defensive posture; its vulnerability is decreased proportionally to its defensive readiness. Table 5 (Appendix A, p. 230) presents the apparent effects of different postures.

Mobility and *Vulnerability* are combat variables that reflect somewhat complex interactions of several other combat variables. Thus they cannot adequately be represented by tables, but require formulae.

Mobility. There are three major aspects to force mobility (as distinct from mobility of weapons, which is considered in the OLI calculation). The first is the way the *inherent characteristics* of the two forces affect their relative capability of movement. The second is the degrading effects of *environmental influences* on mobility. And the third is the *relationship between the inherent mobility characteristics and the environmental influences,* and the relationship of both to the force strengths of the opposing sides. All three aspects must be reflected in any meaningful mathematical representation of force mobility.

The first aspect requires a formula that will portray the effect upon the relative combat power of two opposing forces of their own operational characteristics relating to mobility and maneuver. In World War II these characteristics were essentially the relative size of the forces, their quantities of motor transport, and the quantities and fighting power of armored vehicles. After considerable experimentation with World War II data, the following formula was found to give satisfactory results for Mobility Force Characteristics (M), here shown for the attacking force.

$$M_a = \sqrt{[N_a + 20J_a + W_{ia}) \times m_{ya}/N_a]/[(N_d + 20J_d + W_{id}) \times m_{yd}/N_d]} \quad (6)$$

The subscript a identifies the attacker; d identifies the defender; N represents personnel strength; J is a vehicular constant which for World War II was numbers of vehicles other than tanks; W_i armored "proving ground" firepower; and m_y the effect of air superiority upon mobility (from Table 4).

The value of J is further refined as follows: all unarmored vehicles, plus $2 \times$ armored non-fighting vehicles including self-propelled armored artillery platforms, plus $10 \times$ all organic aircraft (fixed wing or helicopter) available. For the 1970s the constant modifier of J in the formula has been changed to 15 to reflect a different dispersion factor. The value of M_d is always 1.

The second aspect of mobility—the degrading effects of environmental influences—is concerned mainly with the effect upon mobility of difficult terrain (r_m) and inclement weather (h_m); these factors are shown in Tables 1 and 2. After experimentation and analysis it became evident that these terrain and weather effects on mobility should not be applied directly to either the Weapons Firepower (W) or the Force Strength (S) of either side. Firepower is not degraded directly by the effects of environmental factors on mobility. Also, to avoid distorting the relative importance of vulnerability and mobility, the degrading effects of environment on mobility should be applied to the relative mobility of the two forces as determined by their inherent characteristics.

The third aspect of mobility is the relationship of the technical characteristics of weapons and machines (M, as calculated above) to the environmental effects of mobility, and the relationship of both to the force strengths of the opposing sides. The attacker is always more directly affected by differences in mobility and by environmmental influences than is the defender. Further, the degrading effects of terrain and weather have a tendency to reduce the inherent mobility differential of both forces. From this reasoning emerges the following formula for a mobility factor affecting the attacking force:

$$m_a = M_a - (1 - r_m \times h_m)(M_a - 1) \quad (7)$$

For the defender, m always is 1.

Vulnerability. The few military models and war games that consider vulnerability (most do not) assume that the vulnerability of a force to hostile firepower should be represented by a factor which reflects either the posture or the relative size of the opposing force. HERO, however, has adopted the diametrically different concept that the vulnerability of a force to hostile firepower is dependent upon a number of factors which are only indirectly related to the relative strengths of the opposing forces. Among the considerations affecting a force's vulnerability are its personnel strength, combat deployment exposure (in terms of terrain and posture), relative firepower of the opposing forces, presence or ·absence of air superiority, and increased exposure in amphibious and river crossing situations.

As with mobility, the first step is to calculate vulnerability characteristics (V). Also as with mobility, this formula—reflecting all of these considerations—resulted from considerable experimentation with World War II data.

$$V_f = N \times c \times (\sqrt{S_e/S_f}) \times v_y \times v_r \qquad (8)$$

The value v_y is obtained from Table 5 (Appendix A, p. 230). The value v_r (for amphibious or river crossing operations) is obtained from Table 6. Exposure (c), is expressed as a relationship between posture (u_v), and terrain (r_u), as follows:

$$c = u_v/r_u \qquad (9)$$

The vulnerability characteristics—represented by a rather large cardinal number V—are converted to a vulnerability factor (v) by relating V to Force Strength (S) in the following formula:

$$v = 1 - V/S \qquad (10)$$

The minimum (numerically) vulnerability factor has been arbitrarily set at 0.60. When the calculated values of V/S is greater than 0.30, its effective value above 0.30 is calculated to be 0.1 times the difference between the calculated value and 0.30. Thus, if V/S is calculated at 0.42, the effective value is 0.312 (0.3+.012), giving a vulnerability factor (v) of 0.688.

◦ ◦ ◦

Now for the "intangibles." The results of HERO's work to date suggest that ranges of values may often be applied to some of these intangible variables on the basis of professional military experience. Some (such as logistics) may lend themselves to assessment indirectly through measurement of their effects.

Leadership, Training, and Morale. These subjective qualities are almost impossible to assess in absolute terms with complete objectivity. However, the relative capabilities of the opposing leaders in terms of skill, nerve, and determination can probably have more influence on the out-

come of a battle than any of the other qualitative variables of combat—
if there is a substantial difference in the qualities of leadership of the
opposing sides. The same is true, probably to a somewhat lesser extent,
if there are substantial differences in the state of training or of combat
experience of the two sides, and if there are great differences in their
respective states of morale. Accordingly, where solid historical information
warrants, these three variables can be given mathematical weights, either
individually, or in relationship with the other elements of combat effectiveness, on the basis of professional military judgment, but (under the
present "state of the art") this weighting process is bound to be highly
subjective. A typical approach (for morale) is shown in Table 7 (Appendix A, p. 230).

Logistics. Logistics or supply capability is basic in its importance to
combat effectiveness. Yet, as in the case of the leadership, training, and
morale factors, it is almost impossible to arrive at an objective numerical
assessment of the absolute effectiveness of a military supply system. Consequently, this factor also can be applied only when solid historical data
provides a basis for objective evaluation of the relative effectiveness of
the opposing supply capabilities. One such basis is a calculation of the
effect of air interdiction upon supply capability, which is discussed briefly
in Chapter 6.

Time and Space. Time and space are major factors in combat, both
separately and in combination. They are two of the three basic "coins"
of war (the other being military manpower).

However, at present we believe it is neither possible nor necessary to
express directly the impact of the passage of time, or the effect of timing,
as factors affecting combat outcomes, since these are reflected indirectly
in various other factors, principally mobility, and are of course inherent
in leadership. Furthermore, time is represented directly in most dynamic
models and simulations.

The concept of utilization of space is also inherent in leadership. So,
too, is space considered with respect to advance or retrograde movements
in combat, and thus as an element contributing both to force substitution
calculations and to calculation of the quantifiable outcome of an engagement. For reasons to be shown later, we are convinced that unopposed,
or only partially opposed, rates of advance of units across space over
extended periods of time are not relevant to assessments of combat
power, or vice versa.

Momentum. Momentum is an intangible comprised of both the space
and time factors. However, it does not seem to warrant expression in a
calculation of relative combat power. In circumstances in which momentum might be a factor, the difference in combat power of the opposing
forces is probably already too great to be affected significantly by a relatively modest bonus value.

Intelligence. This is an aspect of leadership, also related to training and experience. We don't know enough about its influences on combat effectiveness. It is reflected to some extent in surprise, a variable which is discussed later (see p. 63).

Technology, or relative technological development of the opposing cultures, we know plays a part in combat effectiveness. Technology is also, of course, represented in evaluating weapons characteristics to arrive at OLI values. Otherwise, we don't know much about the effect of technology on military operations, although Chapters 7 and 9 will demonstrate that it is subject to analysis.

Initiative. The side which possesses the initiative in combat operations has an unquestionable intangible advantage over the opponent. What is not clear at this time, however, is whether this variable can be represented by itself, or whether it can or should be included within leadership, or combined with momentum. It certainly is an element within the larger intangible of general combat effectiveness.

Combat Effectiveness. As a group, all or most of these intangible variables are components of another—combat effectiveness—which can be quantified rather precisely if the data base is sufficiently large. The most important elements of combat effectiveness are probably leadership, training/experience, morale, and logistics. For instance, we have found that in 1943-1944 during World War II the Germans had a ground combat effectiveness superiority over the Western Allies of 20-30 percent; at the same time they had a ground combat superiority over the Russians ranging between about 200 percent (1941) and 80 percent (1944). More recently we have been able to calculate that in 1967 and 1973 the Israelis had a combat effectiveness superiority of nearly 100 percent over the Egyptians. It must be recognized, however, that these combat effectiveness comparisons represent an oversimplified statement of a complex relationship.

SUMMATION

It is in its concept of variables, and their application, that the methodology described in this book differs most radically from other modern models, or simulations of combat. We believe that the concept of variable factors, representing environmental and operational effects upon the readily calculable firepower effects of weapons, is a reasonable, logical approach to representing the actual battlefield influence and effects of such weapons. It is not necessarily the only approach which can be reasonable and logical but at this time it is the only approach that we know of that makes *consistent* military sense.

This concept of variables, then, is the essence of the Quantified Judgment Model, and of the Quantified Judgment Method of Analysis of Historical Combat Data. For that reason, the discussion in this chapter is crucial to the presentation in the rest of the book.

4

Constructing a Model

When I was a cadet, some of the practical field work for the West Point Engineering Department was done under the supervision of a hard-bitten old (at least so we thought then) sergeant of the Engineer Corps, who knew his business, and was a superb instructor, despite a thick accent and unparsable sentences. One of his favorite class introductions was: "Now we constrooct a bridge." This chapter describes how we at HERO constroocted a model.

Seeking Basic Relationships

The theory of the effects of the variables of combat, as presented in the previous chapter, did not emerge in a continuous process of research and analysis. That some kinds of variables had degrading or multiplicative effects on numbers or on firepower was an intuitive judgment, not at all original. It is obvious from the writings of such military thinkers as Napoleon and Clausewitz—and even Sun Tze, five centuries before the Christian era—that they had sensed the same thing.

THE CONCEPT

That it might be possible to obtain systematic and consistent values for such variables of combat as weather, terrain, and posture (or offensive-defensive attitude) began to suggest itself to me and my colleagues in 1966 and 1967 as a result of research in US Army records on casualties and materiel losses in World War II and the Korean War. The thought became stronger the following year as a result of some analyses we did for the US Air Force of ground and air-ground operations in Italy in 1943 and 1944. Then in 1969 we were asked by the Air Force to do a further analysis of the combat data we had been compiling and analyzing for them, to explore the use of historical data in evaluating military effectiveness.

As military historians we had discovered that some operations researchers and planners are interested not only in obtaining data from recent conflicts, but also in obtaining the qualitative judgments of historians on

40

trends or effects of weapons and combat processes in modern warfare as revealed in that data. We had also found that at least as many OR analysts and planners are convinced that neither history nor data from past wars has any relevance to modern combat, and their abrupt dismissal of the observations of military historians has raised doubts in the minds of those who would otherwise be intuitively certain that there must be some relevance between the real world of history and the real world of today.

Recognizing that the results of the research requested by the Air Force would be subjected to review by both hesitant believers and obdurate unbelievers, we felt that it was important to buttress with quantitative facts any qualitative observations we made about the relationship of historical data to historical combat effectiveness. Accordingly, we decided to try to measure the combat potentialities of opposing forces by quantifying their total weapons firepower by use of the Operational Lethality Index (OLI) concept. To this firepower we would then apply reasonable factors, consistent with historical facts and the estimates of professional military judgment, for all identifiable and presumably quantifiable combat variables.

While this study for the Air Force was in process, we were asked by the British Defence Operational Analysis Establishment (DOAE) to analyze the relationship of tactical air support to land combat. In this new study, profiting from the lessons learned in our work for the Air Force, we applied fundamentally the same methodology, somewhat refined, but focusing entirely on 60 division-sized engagements in the American Fifth Army zone in Italy between September 1943 and June 1944. Italy was selected for this analysis because both the Fifth Army's ground and air operations were canalized to the area between the Tyrrhenian Sea and the Apennines, permitting the analyst to assume weapons interactions with greater assurance than was possible in other less strictly defined operational areas.

Based upon our previous studies, we calculated proving ground OLI values for the German, British, and American weapons used by both sides in the 60 engagements selected from the Salerno, Volturno, Anzio, and Rome Campaigns—our initial 60-Engagement Data Base. A group of retired officers who had served in the Artillery, Infantry, Armor, Army Air Forces, and Marine Corps in World War II[11] postulated values for combat variables' effects under all of the circumstances of combat encountered in Italy during those ten months, and then tried various ways of applying these variables to the weapons inventories of both sides in

[11] Those involved in this process were Brig. Gen. Edwin S. Chickering, USAF, Ret.; Col. Ashton Crosby, USA, Ret. (armor background); Col. Angus M. Fraser, USMC Ret. (infantry background); Col. Harold Quackenbush, USA, Ret. (infantry background); Col. John A.C. Andrews, USAF, Ret.; and Col. T. N. Dupuy, USA, Ret. (artillery background).

each of these engagements. Slowly there emerged from this work a fundamental concept, two basic formulae, some tables of variable effects factors,
and formulae for calculating other values for the variables of combat
that we could identify from our surveys of the detailed unit records of
the engaged American, British, and German forces.

A COMBAT POWER FORMULA

In the earlier study for the Air Force it had become evident that a
formula based upon a comparison of the opposing combat power values
—"proving ground" OLIs modified by the various applicable variables—
would be meaningful only if the resulting ratio of combat power values
could be compared with a quantification of the actual outcome. The
combat power ratio would indicate what the outcome of the engagement
theoretically should have been. This would be compared with the quantification of the battle or engagement outcome.

For the first of these formulae, using data from combat records, we
applied the variables from our tables or formulae to the weapons inventories of each side, to get a value P, representing the Power or Power
Potential of a force. If the ratio of the two Power Potentials—P_f for the
friendly force divided by P_e for the enemy force—was greater than 1.0,
we postulated that this meant that the friendly side *should* have been
successful; if the ratio gave a value less than 1.0, then the enemy side
should have been successful.

QUANTIFYING BATTLE OUTCOMES

As to the second formula—quantification of battle outcome—it was easy
enough to suggest, but there was no known method for quantifying actual
battle results. As military historians and former professional soldiers,
however, my colleagues and I assumed that a battle outcome should
reflect three things: (1) the extent to which each side accomplished its
assigned or perceived mission; (2) the ability of each side to gain or
hold ground, giving due consideration to their respective firepower inventories; and (3) the efficiency with which they did these first two things
in terms of casualties, i.e., casualty effectiveness, derived by comparing
casualties incurred to the starting strengths of the two opponents. (We
didn't realize it at the time, but these three evaluation criteria were
what operations researchers call "measures of effectiveness.") After considerable experimentation with a number of historical battles, going back
as far as Austerlitz in 1805, a scale for evaluating mission performance
was prepared, and two sub-formulae for spatial effectiveness and casualty
effectiveness were derived.

A MODEL AND PROSE

When discussing the two major formulae with an operations research analyst friend, I was somewhat surprised when he referred to them as "models." He assured me that these were indeed the kind of formulations which OR analysts called models. I felt a pride akin to that of Moliere's Bourgeois Gentleman when he realized that he had been speaking in prose for forty years.

Thus, the Quantified Judgment Method of Analysis of Historical Combat Data (QJMA) emerged from this study. In essence it was a comparison of two component models; the Quantified Judgment Model formula for ascertaining the theoretical winner of an engagement, and the outcome or Result Model formula, for quantifying the actual outcome of the engagement. There have been a number of refinements in both models since, but the fundamental theory, procedures, and tabular values had been tested successfully.

The Model Formula

Having previously developed a concept for quantifying the ideal, or proving ground, value of weapons, and another concept for calculating variable factors to modify the weapons in such a way that they conform to the circumstances of combat, we then had to bring these two concepts together. In the following paragraphs are summarized in an orderly fashion the results of a somewhat messy process of trial and error.

FORCE STRENGTH

First the proving ground values of the weapons had to be modified to reflect the effects of environmental conditions upon their theoretical effectiveness. In this process four different classes of weapons were considered: infantry weapons, artillery weapons, armor weapons, and air support weapons.[12]

To show how the variables affect the proving ground values of weapons, Figure 4-1 provides examples of the effects of environmental variables upon typical weapons of each of these classes in four different kinds of hypothetical situations: (a) attack under favorable circumstances; (b) attack under unfavorable circumstances; (c) defense under favorable circumstances; and (d) defense under unfavorable circumstances.

---

[12] In subsequent refinement of the methodology, two additional classes of weapons are considered: antitank weapons and antiaircraft weapons (see p. 112). For purposes of considering environmental effects the variable factors for infantry weapons are applied to antitank weapons, and the factors for artillery are applied to antiaircraft artillery and other air defense weapons.

Figure 4-1

APPLICATION OF ENVIRONMENTAL AND
OPERATIONAL VARIABLES TO WEAPONS LETHALITY VALUES

	Symbol	Tables or (Formulae)	60mm Mortar Attack F°	U°	Defense F	U
WEAPONS EFFECTIVENESS-STRENGTH						
Infantry						
Lethality (Proving ground) (W_s, W_{mg}, W_n)		–	126.0	126.0	126.0	126.0
Terrain	r_u	1	0.9	0.7	0.9	0.7
Result	–	–	$\overline{113.4}$	$\overline{88.2}$	$\overline{113.4}$	$\overline{88.2}$
Artillery						
Lethality (Proving ground)	W_g	–	–	–	–	–
Terrain	r_{wg}	1	–	–	–	–
Weather	h_{wg}	2	–	–	–	–
Season	Z_{wg}	3	–	–	–	–
Air Superiority	W_{yg}	4	–	–	–	–
Result	–	–	–	–	–	–
Armor						
Lethality (Proving ground)	W_l	–	–	–	–	–
Terrain	r_{wl}	1	–	–	–	–
Weather	h_{wl}	2	–	–	–	–
Result	–	–	–	–	–	–
Air Support						
Lethality (Proving ground)	W_y	–	–	–	–	–
Terrain	r_{wy}	1	–	–	–	–
Weather	h_{wy}	2	–	–	–	–
Season	Z_{wy}	3	–	–	–	–
Air Superiority	W_{yy}	4	–	–	–	–
Result	–	–	–	–	–	–
Total (Σ)	S	(11)	113.4	88.2	113.4	88.2
MOBILITY FACTOR						
Personnel (N)						
Vehicles (J)	M	(6)	(1.2)	(0.8)	(1.2)	(0.8)
Armor (W_l)						
Air Superiority (m_y)						
Weather	h_m	2	(1.0)	(0.9)	(1.0)	(0.9)
Terrain	r_m	1	(0.9)	(0.8)	(0.9)	(0.8)
Factor	m	(7)	$\overline{1.1}$	$\overline{0.9}$	$\overline{1.1}$	$\overline{0.9}$
VULNERABILITY FACTOR						
Personnel (N)						
Posture (u_y)						
Terrain (r_u)	V	(8)	(0.1)	(0.3)	(0.1)	(0.3)
Relative Strength (S_s/S_t)						
Air Superiority (v_y)						
Shoreline Vulnerability (v_r)						
Factor	v	(10)	$\overline{0.9}$	$\overline{0.7}$	$\overline{0.9}$	$\overline{0.7}$
OTHER OPERATIONAL FACTORS						
Terrain	r_u	1	1.0	1.0	1.5	1.2
Weather	h_u	2	1.0	0.8	1.0	0.8
Season	Z_u	3	1.1	1.0	1.0	1.0
Posture	u_s	5	1.0	1.0	1.5	1.5
Leadership	le	–	1.0	1.0	1.0	1.0
Training/Experience	t	–	0.9	0.9	0.9	0.9
Morale	o	7	1.0	1.0	1.0	1.0
Logistics	b	–	1.0	0.9	1.0	0.9
COMBAT POWER POTENTIAL	P	(12)	$\overline{111.1}$	$\overline{36.0}$	$\overline{227.3}$	$\overline{64.8}$

*F = Favorable circumstances; U = Unfavorable circumstances.

| 105mm Howitzer | | | | M-4 Medium Tank | | | | P47 Fighter-Bomber | | | |
| Attack | | Defense | | Attack | | Defense | | Attack | | Defense | |
F	U	F	U	F	U	F	U	F	U	F	U
–	–	–	–	–	–	–	–	–	–	–	–
–	–	–	–	–	–	–	–	–	–	–	–
–	–	–	–	–	–	–	–	–	–	–	–
239.0	239.0	239.0	239.0	–	–	–	–	–	–	–	–
1.0	0.8	1.0	0.8	–	–	–	–	–	–	–	–
1.0	0.9	1.0	0.9	–	–	–	–	–	–	–	–
1.0	0.9	1.0	0.9	–	–	–	–	–	–	–	–
1.1	0.9	1.1	0.9	–	–	–	–	–	–	–	–
262.9	139.4	262.9	139.4	–	–	–	–	–	–	–	–
–	–	–	–	288.0	288.0	288.0	288.0	–	–	–	–
–	–	–	–	0.9	0.3	0.9	0.3	–	–	–	–
–	–	–	–	1.0	0.3	1.0	0.3	–	–	–	–
–	–	–	–	259.2	25.9	259.2	25.9	–	–	–	–
–	–	–	–	–	–	–	–	121.0	121.0	121.0	121.0
–	–	–	–	–	–	–	–	1.0	0.9	1.0	0.9
–	–	–	–	–	–	–	–	1.0	0.2	1.0	0.2
–	–	–	–	–	–	–	–	1.0	0.9	1.0	0.9
–	–	–	–	–	–	–	–	1.1	0.8	1.1	0.8
–	–	–	–	–	–	–	–	133.1	15.6	133.1	15.0
262.9	139.4	262.9	139.4	259.2	25.9	259.2	25.9	133.1	15.6	133.1	15.0
(1.2)	(0.8)	(1.2)	(0.8)	(1.2)	(0.8)	(1.2)	(0.8)	(1.2)	(0.8)	(1.2)	(0.8)
(1.0)	(0.9)	(1.0)	(0.9)	(1.0)	(0.9)	(1.0)	(0.9)	(1.0)	(0.9)	(1.0)	(0.9)
(0.9)	(0.8)	(0.9)	(0.8)	(0.9)	(0.8)	(0.9)	(0.8)	(0.9)	(0.8)	(0.9)	(0.8)
1.1	0.9	1.1	0.9	1.1	0.9	1.1	0.9	1.1	0.9	1.1	0.9
(0.1)	(0.3)	(0.1)	(0.3)	(0.1)	(0.3)	(0.1)	(0.3	(0.1)	(0.3)	(0.1)	(0.3)
0.9	0.7	0.9	0.7	0.9	0.7	0.9	0.7	0.9	0.7	0.9	0.7
1.0	1.0	1.5	1.2	1.0	1.0	1.5	1.2	1.0	1.0	1.5	1.2
1.0	0.8	1.0	0.8	1.0	0.8	1.0	0.8	1.0	0.8	1.0	0.8
1.1	1.0	1.0	1.0	1.1	1.0	1.0	1.0	1.1	1.0	1.0	1.0
1.0	1.0	1.5	1.5	1.0	1.0	1.5	1.5	1.0	1.0	1.5	1.5
1.0	1.0	1.0	1.0	1.0	1.0	1.0	1.0	1.0	1.0	1.0	1.0
0.9	0.9	0.9	0.9	0.9	0.9	0.9	0.9	0.9	0.9	0.9	0.9
1.0	1.0	1.0	1.0	1.0	1.0	1.0	1.0	1.0	1.0	1.0	1.0
1.0	0.9	1.0	0.9	1.0	0.9	1.0	0.9	1.0	0.9	1.0	0.9
257.7	56.9	527.0	102.4	254.0	10.6	519.6	19.0	130.5	6.4	266.8	11.5

The sum of the values of the weapons of a force—modified to reflect environmental variables—is termed Force Strength. A formula for Force Strength (represented by the symbol S) is as follows:

$$S = (W_s + W_{mg} + W_{hw}) \times r_n + W_{gi} \times r_n + (W_g + W_{gy})(r_{wg} \times h_{wg} \times z_{wg} \times w_{wg})$$
$$+ (W_i \times r_{wi} \times h_{wi}) + (W_y \times r_{wy} \times h_{wy} \times z_{wy} \times w_{yy}) \qquad (11)$$

The symbols represent the following:

S —Force Strength (overall weapons inventory value of a combat force, as modified by environmental variables)

W —Weapons Effectiveness or firepower inventories of a force, a summation of the OLI values of all small arms (W_s), machine guns (W_{mg}), heavy weapons (W_{hw}), antitank weapons (W_{gi}), artillery (W_g), air defense weapons (W_{gy}), armor (W_i), or close air support (W_y)

r_n —Terrain factor, related to infantry weapons

r_{wg} —Terrain factor, related to artillery

h_{wg}—Weather factor, related to artillery

z_{wg} —Season factor, related to artillery

w_{yg}—Air superiority factor, related to artillery

r_{wi} —Terrain factor, related to armor

h_{wi} —Weather factor, related to armor

r_{wy} —Terrain factor, related to air support

h_{wy} —Weather factor, related to air support

z_{wy} —Season factor, related to air support

w_{yy}—Air superiority factor, related to air support

COMBAT POWER POTENTIAL

The Combat Power Potential (P) of the force in the circumstances of combat is then calculated by applying all identifiable operational variables to the Calculated Force Strength (S). The effects of the various operational variables on the value of each individual weapon can be seen by a continuation of the process shown above for four sample weapons in the four hypothetical combat situations:

Expressed as a formula, this is as follows:

$$P = S \times m \times le \times t \times o \times b \times u_s \times r_u \times h_u \times z_u \times v \qquad (12)$$

The symbols represent the following:

P —Combat Potential (Force Strength as modified by operational variables)

m—Mobility factor (as calculated in Equations (6) and (7); m for a defender is always unity)

le—Leadership factor (when data permits an assessment)°

t —Training and/or Experience factor (when data permits an assessment)°

o —Morale factor (when data permits an assessment)°

b —Logistics factor (when data permits calculation or assessment)°

° This is incorporated in a relative combat effectiveness value (CEV) or factor, when it has been calculated.

u_s—Posture factor, related to Force Strength
r_u—Terrain factor, related to Posture
h_u—Weather factor, related to Posture
z_u—Season factor, related to Posture
v —Vulnerability value (as calculated in Equations (8), (9), and (10))

All of the equations required for the overall model calculations—(6), (7), (8), (9), (10), (11), and (12)—can be related to each other diagrammatically as shown below:

$$P = S \times \text{operational variables}$$

$$S \times [M_a - (1 - r_m \times h_m)(M_a - 1)] \times le \times t \times o \times b \times u_s \times r_u \times h_u \times z_u \times v$$

$$\sqrt{\frac{(N_a + 20J_a + W_{ia}) \times m_{ya}/N_a}{(N_d + 20J_d + W_{id}) \times m_{yd}/N_d}} \qquad 1 - (N \times c \times \sqrt{S_e/S_f} \times v_y \times v_r)/S_f$$

$$u_v/r_u$$

$$(W_s + W_{mg} + W_{hw}) \times r_a + W_{gi}{}^{\circ} \times r_n + W_g + W_{gy}{}^{\circ\circ} + (W_i \times r_{wi} \times h_{wi}) + W_y$$

$$\times r_{wg} \times h_{wg} \times z_{wg} \times w_{yg} \qquad \times r_{wy} \times h_{wy} \times z_{wy} \times w_{yy}.$$

$^{\circ}$ Up to total of W_{ei}; thereafter only half value.
$^{\circ\circ}$ Up to total of W_{ey}; thereafter only half value. (13)

We can now ascertain the theoretical outcome of an engagement between two forces, by means of the ratio of the opposing combat power potentials. But before further analysis is possible it is necessary to compare this theoretical result to the actual historical outcome.

Outcome Evaluations; The Result Model

MEASUREMENT OF HISTORICAL RESULTS

As noted earlier, we decided as military historians that the outcome of a battle should be assessed on the basis of three different, almost intuitive, evaluations: (1) the accomplishment of the opposing missions as assigned or perceived; (2) the effectiveness of the contestants in relation to space—the ability of the attacker to gain ground, and the ability of the defender to hold ground; and (3) casualty effectiveness, involving a comparison of casualties suffered by a force with its own initial combat strength, as well as that of the enemy.

The concept of these three measures of effectiveness—or performance criteria—in determining outcomes of historical engagements is quite simple; its application is something else again. No one had apparently ever before attempted to develop a system for quantifying battlefield outcomes before we did so.

MISSION ACCOMPLISHMENT

Most difficult of the three measures to quantify is assessment of the degree of accomplishment of the mission. The military historian must make an essentially subjective judgment based upon the weight he gives to the largely contradictory views of the engagement as reported to and by the opposing commands. After some experimentation, however, it soon became obvious that experienced military historians could quite consistently agree on a subjective assessment value of mission accomplishment in a scale between 1 and 10. From these assessments the evaluations of Mission Factor (MF) shown in Table 8 (Appendix A, p. 230), have been derived. Unless the historian has reason to show gradations in mission accomplishment, the Normal values are usually applied.

SPATIAL EFFECTIVENESS

The measure of spatial effectiveness (E_{sp})—that is, gaining or holding ground—of a force in an engagement should recognize both the relative strengths of the two forces, and the relative depths of the areas occupied by each (D), in comparison with the average daily distance of advance—or withdrawal—(Q), as ground changes hands during the course of the engagement.[13] This was tried and adjusted and tried again on literally hundreds of battles and engagements from Austerlitz to the Bulge until the following empirical formula (shown for the friendly side) gave results that seemed to military historians to be consistent with what had occurred in these battles.[14]

$$E_{fsp} = \sqrt{[(S_e \times u_{se})/(S_f \times u_{sf})] \times (4Q + D_e)/3D_f} \qquad (14)$$

[13] In World War II the average depth per 10,000 men was 3.8 miles or 6.08 kilometers. This can also be considered as 1,644 men per kilometer in depth. Based upon apparent trends and combat performance in the Middle East, in the mid 1970s the depth per 10,000 men seemed to be about 4.7 miles or 7.5 kilometers, or 1,333 men per kilometer in depth.

[14] This equation has been derived empirically by applying all of the reasonably different combinations of the obviously operating variables to the reported results of all 60 of the engagements of the original data base, plus some 50 more engagements analyzed later, and a substantial number of earlier historical engagements. The relative strengths of the opposing forces, affected only by environmental variables and posture, is another essential element of the comparison. The square root has been used since the iterative, trial and error process suggested that it is necessary to dampen the effects of major variations, without changing their relative significance, in relating spatial effectiveness to the Mission Factor values.

Q is a plus value for one side, and a negative value for the other. Whenever $(4Q+D_e)$ has a negative value, the whole factor E_{sp} is negative. Transposition and substitution of values to obtain the spatial effectiveness of the opposite, enemy, side is obvious.

CASUALTY EFFECTIVENESS

The casualty effectiveness (E_{cas}) of a force in an engagement should reflect not only the relative efficiency of the two sides in inflicting casualties on each other (in terms of daily losses), in consideration of their respective sizes, but also the daily casualty rate of the force in relation to its own size. The following formula (shown for enemy forces) does this:

$$E_{ecas}=v_f{}^2[(\sqrt{(Cas_f \times u_{se}/S_f)/(Cas_e \times u_{sf}/S_e)} - \sqrt{100Cas_e/N_e}]\qquad(15)$$

Transposition and substitution of values to obtain the casualty effectiveness of the other, friendly, side is obvious.[15]

RESULT FORMULA

In order to permit a comparison of the actual outcome with the theoretical outcome, the three measures of effectiveness—mission accomplishment, spatial effectiveness and casualty effectiveness—are combined in a Result Formula:[16]

$$R=MF+E_{sp}+E_{cas}\qquad(16)$$

Since it is possible to obtain a negative value from this result formula, the results for the two different sides cannot be related by a simple proportion, as is the case in predicting the theoretical outcome of an engagement. A satisfactory relationship is obtained, however, by subtracting R_e from R_f:

$$\text{Result Comparison}=R_f-R_e\qquad(17)$$

A positive value represents a friendly success, a negative value an enemy success. When P_f/P_e is greater than one, predicting a theoretical friendly success, R_f-R_e is expected to be positive; when P_e/P_f is greater than one, R_f-R_e is expected to be negative.

[15] The derivation of this equation followed a pattern similar to that representing spatial effectiveness; see previous footnote.

[16] Each of these measures of effectiveness says something different about the outcome of the engagement, and ideally a force commander hopes for success in all. Since we have arrived at quantified representations of all three it is logical to add them to get a total degree of success for the whole engagement.

Consolidation of Model and Result Formulae

When we first began to compare the P_t/P_e ratios with the $R_t - R_e$ values, the results were often contradictory or confusing. We would then review the variable factors to see if slight modifications in any of these would improve the comparison. Obviously we couldn't make any major changes in any of the variable factors as originally set by professional military judgment, since this would throw away that important judgmental element which we considered fundamental to the analytical process. It was a painful, time-consuming, exhaustive, and sometimes stormy process, as airmen, artillerymen, tankers, and infantrymen argued. In any event, after some months of this process, we arrived in early 1970 at tables of factors and formulae for calculation of other factors which seemed to give the best possible fit and interrelationship for each of the 60 engagements. These tables and formulae—which are summarized in Appendix A—have proven to be applicable to all modern combat situations and have been revised only very slightly since that time.

Summarizing the Concept

The QJMA, then, is a method of comparing the relative combat effectiveness of two opposing forces in historical combat, by determining the influence of environmental and operational variables upon the force strengths of the two opponents. The heart of the QJMA is a model of historical combat called the Quantified Judgment Model (QJM). The model is applied to statistics of selected historical engagements and produces values for the Combat Power Potentials of the opposing forces under the circumstances of the engagement, and a Combat Power Ratio to ascertain which of the opposing sides—on the basis of data available in the records—should theoretically have been successful in the engagement, and by what margin.

This Combat Power Ratio is next compared to a quantification of the actual outcome of the battle. This outcome value, derived from consulting the records, represents (as we have seen) the comparative performance of the opposing forces in terms of (1) their accomplishment of their respective missions, (2) their ability to gain or hold ground, and (3) their efficiency in terms of casualties incurred. If the Combat Power Ratio of Force A with respect to Force B is greater than 1, then the Result Value for Force A should be greater than that for Force B. In the event of a different relationship between Combat Power Ratio and Result Values, or if the Result Value differential is not consistent with "normal" relationships of Combat Power Ratios and Result Values, further exploration is necessary to explain the discrepancy, which is usually due to behavioral considerations.

1. COMPILE DATA

a. Quantitative

General
  (a) Weapons characteristics
  (b) TO&Es, both sides

Specific (this engagement)
  (a) Numbers of troops, wpns, etc.
  (b) Losses
  (c) Distances (front, depth, advance)

b. Qualitative

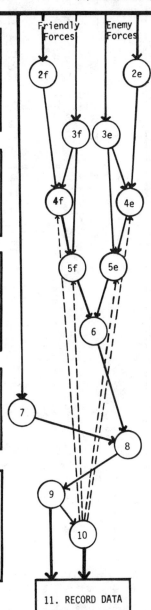

Friendly Forces   Enemy Forces

2. CALCULATE PROVING GROUND WEAPONS EFFECTIVENESS (OLI) VALUES

Enter characteristics of each into OLI calculation formulae to obtain a value for each individually and by categories.

3. DETERMINE VARIABLES

From narrative ascertain applicable environmental & operational variables discerned. Take values from tables or formulae.

4. CALCULATE FORCE STRENGTH

Apply all relevant environmental variables to the OLI values of weapons inventories in each category. Add results to derive Force Strength (S).

5. CALCULATE COMBAT POWER

Apply all relevant operational variables to Force Strength (S), to obtain Combat Power (P).

6. CALCULATE RELATIVE COMBAT POWER

If $P_f/P_e > 1$, friendly side should theoretically have been successful; if $P_f/P_e < 1$, enemy side should have been successful.

7. CALCULATE ACTUAL OUTCOME

Calculate outcome value (R) for each side from sum of mission accomplishment, spatial effectiveness (gaining or holding ground), and casualty effectiveness. If $R_f - R_e$ is positive, friendly side was successful; if negative, enemy side was successful.

8. COMPARE THEORETICAL AND ACTUAL OUTCOMES

If $P_f/P_e > 1$, $R_f - R_e$ should be positive;
If $P_f/P_e < 1$, $R_f - R_e$ should be negative.

9. ANALYSIS

a. Is comparison consistent with relevant historical experience?
b. Plot P_f/P_e and $R_f - R_e$ results, & compare to "Normal Battle Line."
c. If a & b appear seriously inconsistent, review data & narrative for hint of discrepancy.

10. APPLY NEW OR REVISED FACTORS

If new factors (as for surprise), or revised factors (based on Step 9c) are calculated, enter in Step 4 (rarely) and/or Step 5, and continue Steps 6-9 as before.

11. RECORD DATA

Figure 4-2
THE QJM PROCEDURE

Figure 4-3
APPLICATION OF QUANTIFIED JUDGMENT MODEL TO ENGAGEMENTS

		Tables or (Formulae)	Engagement: , Vietri		, Pozzilli		54, Velletri	
	Symbol		Forces: Br 46 ID	G HGoer PzD	US 45 ID	G 3 Pz GD	US 1 Armd D	G 362 ID
			Posture: HD	A	A	FD	A	FD
WEAPONS EFFECTIVENESS-STRENGTH*								
Infantry								
Lethality (Proving ground) (W_s,W_{mg},W_n)	—	—	27,227	21,376	37,416	8,201	17,456	16,669
Terrain	r_u	1	0.9	0.9	0.7	0.7	0.9	0.9
Result	—	—	24,504	19,238	26,191	5,741	15,710	15,002
Artillery								
Lethality (Proving ground)	W_g	1	35,619	56,110	29,409	17,881	30,034	18,881
Terrain	r_{vg}	2	0.9	0.9	0.8	0.8	0.9	0.9
Weather	h_{wg}	3	1.0	1.0	1.0	1.0	1.0	1.0
Season	Z_{wg}	4	0.9	0.9	1.0	1.0	1.0	1.0
Air Superiority	W_{yg}	—	1.1	0.9	1.1	0.9	1.1	0.9
Result	—	—	31,737	40,904	25,880	12,874	29,734	15,277
Armor								
Lethality (Proving ground)	W_i	—	9,022	9,678	16,800	5,719	69,383	16,608
Terrain	r_{vi}	1	0.8	0.8	0.3	0.3	0.8	0.8
Weather	h_{wi}	2	1.0	1.0	0.8	0.8	1.0	1.0
Result	—	—	7,218	7,742	4,032	1,373	55,506	13,286
Close Air Support								
Lethality (Proving ground)	W_y	—	1,011	4,333	910	8,600	2,328	0
Terrain	r_{vy}	1	1.0	1.0	1.0	1.0	1.0	—
Weather	h_{wy}	2	1.0	1.0	0.5	0.5	1.0	—
Season	Z_{wy}	3	1.0	1.0	0.9	0.9	0.9	—
Air Superiority	W_{yy}	4	1.1	0.9	1.1	0.8	1.1	—
Result	—	—	1,112	3,900	450	3,096	2,305	0
Total (Σ)	s	(11)	64,569	71,784	56,553	23,084	103,255	43,565

MOBILITY FACTOR		Step						
Personnel (N)								
Trucks (J)								
Armor (W_t)								
Air Superiority (m_r)	M	(6)	—	(1.134)	(0.742)	—	(1.567)	—
Weather	h_m	2	—	(1.0)	(0.8)	—	(1.0)	—
Terrain	r_m	1	—	(0.8)	(0.5)	—	(0.8)	—
Factor	m	(7)	1.0	1.109	0.897	1.0	1.454	1.0
VULNERABILITY FACTOR								
Personnel (N)	V	(8)						
Posture (u_r)								
Terrain (r_u)								
Relative Strength (S_a/S_r)			(0.147)	(0.218)	(0.217)	(0.158)	(0.090)	(0.149)
Air Superiority (v_r)								
Shoreline Vulnerability (v_s)								
Factor	v	(10)	0.853	0.782	0.783	0.842	0.910	0.851
OTHER OPERATIONAL FACTORS								
Terrain	r_u	1	1.45	1.0	1.0	1.55	1.0	1.45
Weather	h_u	2	1.0	1.0	0.8	1.0	1.0	1.0
Season	Z_u	3	1.0	1.1	1.1	1.0	1.1	1.0
Posture	u_e	5	1.3	1.0	1.0	1.6	1.0	1.6
Leadership	l_e	—	1.0	1.0	1.0	1.0	0.8	1.0
Training/Experience	t	—	0.764	0.897	0.727	0.948	0.820	1.0
Morale	o	7	1.0	1.0	1.0	1.0	1.0	0.9
Logistics	b	—	1.0	1.0	1.0	1.0	1.0	0.8
COMBAT POWER POTENTIAL	P		79,355	61,447	25,415	45,709	98,586	61,928
RELATIVE COMBAT POWER	P_t/P_e	(12)	1.29		0.56		1.59	
OUTCOME EVALUATION								
Mission Factor	MF	8	8.0	5.0	4.0	4.0	4.0	6.0
Spatial Effectiveness	E_{sp}	(14)	0.58	0.58	0.19	1.93	0.39	0.62
Casualty Effectiveness	E_{ca}	(15)	−1.03	−0.66	−0.46	1.41	−1.95	−2.70
Result Calculations	R	(16)	7.55	4.92	3.73	7.34	2.44	3.92
RESULT COMPARISON	R_r-R_e	(17)	2.63		−3.61		−1.48	

*Antitank (W_{at}) and Antiair (W_{ar}) weapons are included with artillery and infantry weapons.

53

The procedure is shown in flow chart form in Figure 4-2. Subsequent paragraphs provide examples of the application of this concept and procedure to some actual World War II engagements.

Model Engagement Examples

Figure 4-3 shows the QJMA calculation details of three 1943 engagements, all in Italy; Vietri, 12-14 September 1943; Pozzilli, 6-7 November 1943; and Velletri, 26 May 1944. The figure shows how the environmental variables are applied to the various weapons categories for each side, to arrive at a Force Strength value (S) for each. Next is shown the application of the two formular operational factors—mobility and vulnerability—and of the other operational variables. These convert the respective Force Strength values for each side into Combat Power Potential values (P), and then these are converted into Combat Power Ratios (P/P). Finally, the Outcome evaluation is shown, and then the comparison of the theoretical outcome (P/P) with the quantification of the actual outcome (R-R). A brief discussion of each of these three comparisons follows:

5. VIETRI.

This was the defense of the British 46th Division against a counterattack by the German Hermann Goering Panzer Division at the Salerno Beachhead on 12-16 September 1943. Including available naval gunfire support and air support, the P_f/P_e ratio is 1.52. (See Relative Combat Power line.) Thanks to the naval and air support, and to some tough fighting by the Tommies, the outcome $R_f - R_e$ is, as expected, positive, 2.63. (See Result Comparison line.)

23. POZZILLI.

This was an operation in the Volturno Campaign, 6-7 November 1943, by the American 45th Infantry Division against elements of the 3d Panzer Grenadier Division. The Germans were in prepared defenses in very rugged terrain in front of the Winter Line. The Combat Power Ratio of 0.72 suggests that the position was too strong to be attacked successfully, but the doughboys tried anyway—as they had been ordered to. As might be expected, the result was a repulse, as shown by the Result Comparison value of −3.61.

54. VELLETRI.

This was an assault on 26 May 1944, by the US 1st Armored Division against the German 362d Infantry Division, in a previously prepared fortified position during the Rome Campaign, just after the breakout from the Anzio Beachhead. General Ernest Harmon's division, with a power ratio superiority of 1.61, had every reason to expect success, particularly since the 362d had been badly mauled in the previous three days. However, the Result Comparison value of −1.48 reflects the fact that the 1st Armored Division was unable to make its expected breakthrough. This example, with results inconsistent with the prediction based on comparative combat power, is included here for three reasons:

1. First, there will be times when results and prediction will not agree (even if both are perfect reflections of what they are supposed to represent), simply because of the unpredictable nature of man and of human institutions. In this instance, the calculations of combat intensity[17] reveal that the determination and stubbornness of German defense and counterattacks were quite disproportionate to their calculable capabilities.

2. The example demonstrates the value of the model for analytical purposes. An apparent inconsistency such as is found here is bound to be questioned. Is it explicable? In this case it is. In addition to the unpredictable intensity and tenacity of the German defense, there was another intangible factor: surprise as a result of the unanticipated German readiness and effectiveness. It is impossible to say how much American overconfidence and the unexpected vigor of German defense and counterattacks contributed to the American failure, but application of the QJM formula to a number of surprise situations in World War II and more recent Arab-Israeli Wars has confirmed not only the importance of surprise, but also the consistently quantifiable results of surprise. (See page 63 for our hypotheses on this.)

3. Actually, the Power Ratio shown here may be too high, even before we consider the effects of surprise. General Harmon's memoirs suggest that there was a failure in command by one of his combat command commanders; thus a leadership degradation factor has been applied, but it may not be enough. Also, the terrain factor used may not properly represent the actual conditions, where gullies inhibited tank maneuver, despite the generally flat configuration of the land.[18]

SUMMATION—THE QJMA AS A THEORY OF COMBAT

The QJMA concept is based upon three comparisons. The first comparison is done by the Quantified Judgment Model—QJM—itself, comparing the combat power potentials of two opposing forces at the start of an engagement. The opposing combat power potentials—P_f for the "friendly" side, and P_e for the "enemy"—are derived by applying the effects of all identifiable variables to the OLI values representing the lethality of the

---

[17] See discussion of Combat Intensity, page 69.

[18] This is an example of the effects of "macro-terrain" features, a matter discussed by French analyst Colonel Maurice Bresson in research presented at the NATO Land Models Conference at Ottobrunn, Germany, in August 1974.

total weapons inventories of each side. This comparison is made by a ratio of the two opposing potentials—P_f/P_e. If P_f/P_e is greater than 1.0 then the friendly side should theoretically have been successful; if less than 1.0 then the enemy theoretically should have been the winner of the engagement, according to the information compiled from the records. If the comparison results in a ratio between 0.9 and 1.1, the differential between the two forces is not considered to be great enough to determine a theoretical winner, and the engagement is "unpredictable."

The second comparison is made by means of the Outcome or Result Model, in which the actual battlefield performance of the opposing sides, as determined from the records and as quantified by standard formulae, is compared on the basis of three performance criteria: (1) the extent to which each side accomplished its assigned or perceived mission; (2) effectiveness in gaining or holding ground, in terms of kilometers gained or withdrawn per day during an engagement; and (3) casualty effectiveness, calculated on the basis of number of casualties suffered per day by each side. One side's R value is subtracted from that of the other side. The side with the larger value in this comparison is determined to have been actually successful in the engagement. If, however, $R_f - R_e$ is between $+0.5$ and -0.5, then the engagement is "inconclusive."

It should be noted that—to assure a basis for consistent, standard outcome comparisons—whenever a battle lasts more than a day the casualty and movement elements of the Result values are calculated on a daily basis; i.e., so many casualties per day, and so many kilometers of advance or withdrawal per day.

An engagement normally ends when one side or the other has clearly gained, or has clearly failed to gain, its mission. Of course, when one side has failed to accomplish its mission, usually the other has been successful; however, there can be instances in which both sides substantially accomplish their missions. It is not likely that *both* would essentially *fail* in mission accomplishment. An engagement can end before mission accomplishment of the originally opposing forces has been determined, if the situation is substantially changed in mid-engagement, for instance, by the arrival of substantial reinforcements to one side or the other.

The third comparison is between the calculated results of the two models. If in the QJM the ratio P_f/P_e is greater than 1, then in the Outcome Model $R_f - R_e$ should be positive; if P_f/P_e is less than 1, $R_f - R_e$ should be negative. As will be seen in the following chapters, we usually find this consistency between QJM and Outcome calculations. When they are not consistent, however, we can be certain that the inconsistency is due to some exceptional combat phenomenon, which is usually explicable after further study and analysis. In fact, it has been through the exploration of the causes of such inconsistencies that the value of the QJMA as an analytical tool has been greatest.

5

Representing
World War II Combat

The work that we did in 1969, 1970, and 1971 in developing and refining the Quantified Judgment Model provided us with a capability that could quite faithfully represent combat situations and relative force capabilities in more than 90 percent of 60 engagements in Italy in 1943 and 1944. In 1971 a young officer in the Army's official combat simulation organization, Strategic Analysis Group (STAG), took the data which we had compiled for these 60 engagements and fed it into the computer program for the Army's "Atlas" theater-level model. He found that no matter how he tinkered with the data and with the model program, he could not get better than 68 percent correlation between the theoretical engagement outcomes predicted by "Atlas" and the actual outcomes as we had quantified them. We thought this was significant; nobody else paid any attention.

There were a number of reasons for this general disinterest, which will be discussed in a later chapter. But the principal reason that concerned us then—or at least the one that was most often cited by occasional critics —was that our developmental work on the 60 engagements was really a kind of "curve-fitting" exercise. In other words, if one has as many variables as equations (or battles), it is mathematically possible to adjust the variable values so that all will be made to fit. But this, the critics pointed out, provides no assurance that these variables would fit any additional battles, particularly if these were fought under different circumstances from those in Italy.

We had, indeed, been engaged in a kind of curve-fitting—within very rigid limitations in adjustment of variable values that had to remain consistent with professional military judgment. But more important, we began to realize that we and the mathematicians had different interpretations of the word "variables." (See p. 32) Historians and soldiers, however, are at a disadvantage in discussing mathematics and quantification with mathematicians. And so HERO got considerable praise for the quality of its historical research, but we also received a number of veiled and direct suggestions that we would do well to get out of the operations systems analysis business for which we had no qualifications, and stick to pure history, for which we were well qualified.

However, being stubborn, as well as convinced of the validity of an approach which based models of combat on real-world combat experience rather than on untested mathematical formulae, we persisted. In 1971 and 1972 we were able to enlarge our combat engagement data base as part of a study of World War II rates of advance of major German, Soviet, and American forces.[19] In that study we compiled data on operations which included two series of US corps operations in France from August to November 1944. During this study we were able to use the QJM to analyze eighteen engagements of US divisions and corps against German formations.

Soon after that we undertook another study, focusing this time on the use of obstacles and barriers in World War II,[20] which provided us with data for three more engagement analyses. One of these engagements was the offensive of the German XLVIII Panzer Corps at Kursk, in July 1943, the first compilation we had made of Eastern Front data in sufficient detail to warrant analysis by means of the QJM. Another was an operation in Italy in late 1944. The third was an attack of a German division in the Battle of the Bulge, December 16-18, 1944.

These two studies, then, provided us with 21 sets of engagement data for what I now term the "Validating Data Base," as opposed to the "Development Data Base," which comprised the original 60 engagements in Italy. Using the identical procedures, formulae, and tables of variables which had been developed to represent warfare in Italy in 1943 and 1944, by mid-1973 we were able to obtain with the 21-engagement Validating Data Base results that were practically identical to those of the Development Data Base. Although there was a higher proportion of unpredictable outcomes (due mainly to the fact that the US XII Corps attacked consistently in Lorraine in November 1944 with a very slender numerical preponderance over the defending Germans), there was only one instance of inconsistency between predicted result and actual outcome (a German attack in the 1944 Ardennes offensive), and that example is fully explicable by the surprise which the Germans achieved in that offensive.

Appendix B contains a consolidated summary of HERO's QJM Engagement Data Base. The first 81 examples in this consolidated statistical comparison show the theoretical results and actual results of these 81 World War II engagements (60 in the Development Data Base, 21 in the Validating Data Base; 61 in Italy, 19 in northwest Europe, and 1 in

---

[19] *Opposed Rates of Advance of Large Forces in Europe (ORALFORE)*, HERO, 1972.

[20] *Historical Evaluation of Barrier Effectiveness*, HERO, 1974.

Russia). In all of these the P/P value reflects an average German combat effectiveness superiority factor of about 23 percent.

It should be noted that all but one of the results in the Validating Data Base were achieved for engagements on terrain quite different from that to be found in Italy, and under circumstances frequently varying from those of the Italian Campaign. Series 500 engagements (as identified in Appendix B) are operations of the US XX Corps and 7th Armored Division during breakout and pursuit operations in northern France in August 1944; series 600 engagements are from the bitterly contested Seille-Sarre offensive by the US XII Corps in November and early December 1944.

This validating exercise provided us with a substantial basis for confidence that the QJM method, as well as its input values for weapons and variables, is a remarkably accurate reflection of World War II combat circumstances and combat processes.

Figure 5-1 is a plot of these 81 engagements, with the Combat Power Ratio plotted along the abscissa (P_f/P_e to the right of the Y-axis, P_e/P_f to the left), and the Result Value plotted along the ordinate ($R_f - R_e$ above the X-axis, $R_e - R_f$ below). In other words, every plot to the right of the Y-axis is a predicted Allied success, to the left a predicted German success; everything above the X-axis is an actual Allied success, below an actual German success. Thus, if the theoretical outcomes predicted by the method were always consistent with the actual outcome, all of the plots would fall in the upper right or lower left quadrants. Since, however, as shown in Appendix B, there were six of the 81 engagements in which the actual outcome was different from the theoretically predicted outcome, we would expect that six plots would fall into the upper left or lower right quadrants. The examples discussed in the previous chapter above are identified. It will be noted that the inconsistent results for No. 54, Velletri, put it in the lower right quadrant. It should also be noted that the plotted results for the Validating Sample fall into the same general pattern as those for the Development Data Base.

Note also the "normal battle line." This represents (at least to a non-professional mathematician) the mean curve for the plotted locations; half of the plotted points are on one side of the line, half on the other. This line shows the values of $R_f - R_e$ that would normally be expected for any given values of P_f/P_e. Only after this line had been drawn did it become evident that it ran from the intersection of abscissa and ordinate at a slope which suggests that a value of 2.0 for P_f/P_e in a "normal battle" would correspond to an $R_f - R_e$ value of $+5.0$ and a P_e/P_f value of 2.0 (which is the same as a P_f/P_e value of 0.5) would in a "normal battle" plot as 5.0 for $R_e - R_f$ (or -5.0 for $R_f - R_e$). It has been found that when the results of an engagement plot considerably off this line, and particularly when they plot out of the expected quadrant, reasons for the discrepancy should be sought. For instance, the discrepancy for the Battle

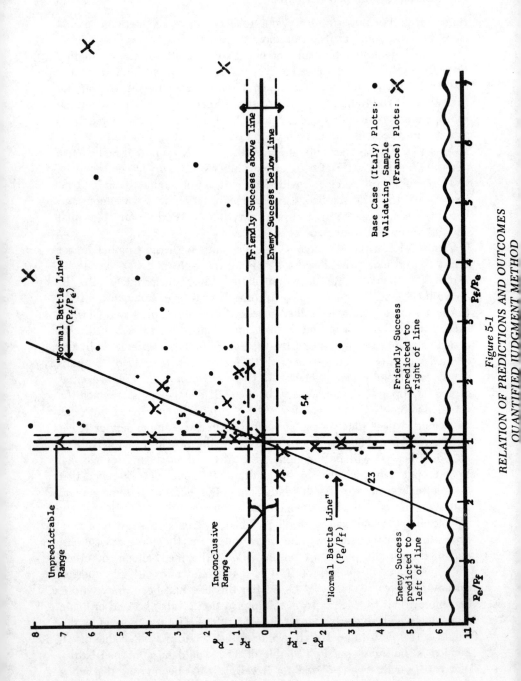

Figure 5-1

RELATION OF PREDICTIONS AND OUTCOMES

QUANTIFIED JUDGMENT METHOD

60

of Velletri shown on Figure 4-3, and discussed on pp. 54-55, is shown visually by the plot marked 54 in the lower right quadrant of Figure 5-1. As will be demonstrated in a subsequent chapter, when we take into consideration the factor of surprise, that point 54 will shift left, very close to the Normal Battle Line, in the lower left-hand quadrant.

The relationship between P/P and R−R along the Normal Battle Line can be represented mathematically in the following simple expressions:

$$(R-R)/5=(P/P)-1, \text{ or } P/P=(R-R)/5+1 \qquad (18)$$

This formula, representing a "normal battle" was to be very useful in our subsequent research.

Problems

During the process of developing the model, three very significant problems had to be dealt with. Two of these, although we didn't know it originally, were interrelated; the relative combat effectiveness of different national forces, and the representation of the effects of air weapons on the ground battle. The third problem—and again we didn't at first recognize what we were dealing with—was the disruption created by combat surprise.

EFFECTS OF AIRPOWER, AND GERMAN PROWESS

Despite the complaints of our airmen that we were not giving due consideration to the effects of air weapons, we seemed to be getting a pretty good fit for most engagements, and were not distressed when a few failed to fit into the pattern. After all, human behavior will vary from time to time and place to place. Suddenly, however, it became disconcertingly obvious that the deviations from the norm were most evident in those battles in which Allied airpower was not employed, or in which its involvement was slight—usually due to bad weather. At the same time another phenomenon became evident in our results. Where the Allied power superiority in the P_f/P_e ratio was very great, the result was usually (but not always) an Allied success. Where the Allies' P_f/P_e ratio was slight or marginal, the Germans were usually successful, or the outcome was inconclusive (an outcome value between $+0.5$ and -0.5); where the P_f/P_e ratio suggested an indeterminate outcome (a value between 0.9 and 1.1), the Germans were invariably successful, as they were when the P_f/P_e ratio was in their favor.

We had started out with an assumption that the Germans probably had something like a 10 percent combat effectiveness advantage over the less experienced British and Americans at the time of the Salerno landings. But we also assumed that (discounting the inevitable differences that will exist among units due to leadership and other indefinable causes) by mid-1944 the Allies would, on the average, have closed this experience-capability gap. Our results now indicated that this was not the case.

Suddenly, answers for these various discrepancies fell into place within our theory of combat. We had been getting reasonably consistent results for most of our engagements because our underestimation of German combat effectiveness had been offset by an underestimation of the effect of predominantly greater Allied air strength. We listed both the power ratio and outcome values in order of descending magnitude, and drew a line through the middle of the indeterminate engagements (on the P/P listing) and through the middle of the inconclusive outcomes (on the R-R listing), and found that these midpoints did not match. We found, however, that we could bring these two midpoints into close conformity with each other by applying a 1.2 relative combat effectiveness value (CEV) factor to show the German superiority, and by doubling the values we had been applying for the effects of air weapons. We didn't like one of the two conclusions which this adjustment forced upon us— that 100 Germans were roughly the combat equivalent of 120 Americans or British—but we could not ignore the fact that our numbers demonstrated that this was so. Our airmen, of course, felt justified by the other conclusion: that air weapons had about twice as much effect on ground combat outcomes as we ground soldiers had initially been willing to recognize.

This decision substantially reduced the number of engagements of our Development Data Base that did not fit the theory of combat represented by our two basic formulae and the factors for variables of combat. As noted above, only five out of sixty, less than 10 percent, did not fit.

EVALUATION OF GERMAN COMBAT EFFECTIVENESS SUPERIORITY

The QJMA analyses of the engagements of the Validating Sample showed that the same 20 percent German ground effectiveness superiority was also evident from the results of 19 engagements in northern France in July-December 1944. At the same time it became evident from the Kursk example that German combat effectiveness superiority over the Russians in 1943 must have been more than 100 percent. (These findings have been confirmed and reaffirmed by other research described below.)

An interesting fact emerged from a preliminary effort to investigate the reason for the consistent German ground combat superiority. A rough comparison of fighting strength versus overhead for German and American infantry divisions was made, based on tables of organization of 1943-44.

In an American infantry division 50.26 percent of its personnel strength was directly connected with manning or serving weapons in normal combat situations; in a German infantry division, using the same basis of calculations, the percentage was 59.83 percent. This suggests that part of the overall German superiority probably resulted from better utilization of manpower. The remainder could possibly be the result of such factors as more experience, greater mobility, better doctrine, more effective battle drill, superior leadership, or inherent national characteristics. A serious analysis of the reasons for this greater German effectiveness is an important research requirement.[21]

Surprise

At the outset of this chapter I stated that one of the three principal problems encountered in evaluating the preliminary QJM analyses of World War II data was the perturbation in the data created by combat surprise. This was not immediately obvious.

In several of the engagements included in the data base, the quantified value of the outcome seemed disproportionate to the calculated relative combat power of the opposing forces. In further analysis of most such instances it was found that the outcome had been influenced by the fact that one side or the other achieved some degree of tactical surprise.

One of the worst of several poor showings of the British 56th Division can be seen in Appendix B in the results for Engagement No. 39 (Moletta River II, 16-19 February 1944), where, with massive combat superiority, the division barely held off a diversionary or holding attack by the understrength German 65th Infantry Division. In endeavoring to analyze these results, we were forced to recognize that a substantial contribution to the German successes must have been from the surprise that the 65th Division achieved. This led to a very tentative exploration of whether or not it might be possible to quantify the effects of surprise.

Surprise, we theorized, produces at least three major effects which can be represented in the QJM model:

1. The mobility of the surprising force is enhanced by permitting optimum disposition of troops before the attack;

2. The vulnerability of the surprised force is increased by the surpriser's ability to place fire unexpectedly and accurately;

3. The vulnerability of the surprising force is decreased (although probably less significantly than for the previous two effects) through pre-planning and pre-positioning.

[21] See T.N. Dupuy, "The Current Implications of German Military Excellence," *Strategic Review*, V. IV, No. 4, (Fall, 1976), and *A Genius for War, The German Army and General Staff*. 1807-1945 (Englewood Cliffs, 1977), both *passim*.

Tentative values for these factors were derived. Those in Table 9 (Appendix A, p. 231) are only slight modifications of the original values, based upon twenty or more examples. When the factors were applied to Engagement No. 39, the massive combat potential superiority of the 56th Division was reduced to less than 0.1, quite consistent with the inconclusive outcome which actually took place in that engagement (see first example in Figure 5-2).

Figures 5-3, 5-4, 5-5 and 5-6 show the application of this hypothesis to four other engagements. In two of the five engagements shown, surprise magnified an already existing combat superiority of the attacking force; in one a presumably shattered defender surprised and defeated a more powerful attacker; in the other two (including Engagement No. 39) attackers used surprise to achieve the necessary power ratio preponderance required for success. It should be noted that of these five examples three were in the original 60 engagement data base, one (a German secondary attack in the 1944 Ardennes Offensive, or Battle of the Bulge) was in the World War II Validating Sample, and one was in the Middle East Wars. In all of these engagements the relative combat effectiveness of the opposing units was considered; in the World War II examples this was represented either by calculated values which will be discussed later, or the standard German 20 percent superiority over the Allies; for the Arab-Israeli Wars it was represented by an Israeli 90 percent superiority over the Egyptians, which later research has shown to have actually been between 75 percent and 98 percent.

Thus, the general validity of this thesis, and the significance of the effect of surprise on mobility and vulnerability, have been established for both World War II and the Arab-Israeli Wars. In a subsequent chapter we will discuss refinements of the thesis. There are, however, undoubtedly other effects of surprise, and further research should be undertaken to attempt to ascertain these.

Operational Analysis

Quite early in the process of developing the QJMA it became obvious that the methodology and its two basic formulae provide a powerful composite tool for analysis of military experience and exploring combat processes. The development of the hypothesis on the effects of surprise provides a striking example of this fact. It is possible that this applicability to analysis will prove to be the most significant contribution of the QJMA to modern military thinking. It has been our experience that the method continually opens new vistas into the fundamental nature and processes of combat, as will be amply demonstrated.

Discussed briefly below are some of the insights emerging from our early QJMA analyses of World War II engagements.

Table 5-2
MOLETTA RIVER II, 16-19 FEBRUARY 1944
(Engagement No. 39)

	Allied	German (Surpriser)	Comparison	
Manpower	9,761	21,478	1/2.20	
Firepower (OLI, in thousands)	89.97	56.24	1.60/1	
Combat power (reflects variable factors of engagement)	124.97	17.31	7.22/1	
Modified combat power (reflects combat effectiveness indices)	64.15	12.29	5.22/1	
Result (reflects mission accomplishment, ground gained/-lost, and casualties)	4.86	5.03	−0.17	(German success)
Ratio theoretically consistent with result			1/1.03	
Revised combat power (reflects surprise factors)	56.75	57.95	1/1.02	
Effect of Surprise			1/5.32	(1.02 × 5.22)

Table 5-3
ANZIO BREAKOUT, 23-25 MAY 1944
(Engagement No. 51)

	American (Surpriser)	German	Comparison	
Manpower	16,215	12,815	1.27/1	
Firepower (OLI, in thousands)	157.39	67.98	2.32/1	
Combat power (reflects variable factors of engagement)	123.91	75.55	1.64/1	
Modified combat power (reflects combat effectiveness indices)	85.50	61.20	1.40/1	
Result (reflects mission accomplishment, ground gained/lost, and casualties)	7.77	−0.52	8.29	(American success)
Ratio theoretically consistent with result			2.66/1	
Revised combat power (reflects surprise factors)	173.58	54.50	3.05/1	
Effect of Surprise			2.18/1	(3.05/1.40)

Table 5-4
VELLETRI, 26 MAY 1944
(Engagement No. 54)

	American	German (Surpriser)	Comparison	
Manpower	14,620	12,327	1.19/1	
Firepower (OLI, in thousands)	113.52	52.16	2.18/1	
Combat power (reflects variable factors of engagement)	117.63	73.52	1.60/1	
Modified combat power (reflects combat effectiveness indices)	81.16	53.67	1.51/1	
Result (reflects mission accomplishment, ground gained/lost, and casualties)	2.44	3.92	−1.48	(German success)
Ratio theoretically consistent with result			1/1.30	
Revised combat power (reflects surprise factors)	51.29	57.15	1/1.11°	
Effect of Surprise			1/1.68	(1.11 × 1.51)

°Exceptional German leadership and substandard American leadership on this date should raise this ratio closer to 1/1.30.

Table 5-5
ARDENNES—SAUER RIVER, 16-17 DECEMBER 1944
(Engagement No. 81)

	American	German	Comparison	
Manpower	8,634	10,000	1/1.16	
Firepower (OLI, in thousands)	40.88	42.10	1/1.03	
Combat power (reflects variable factors of engagement)	55.12	16.96	3.25/1.00	
Modified combat power (reflects combat effectiveness indices)	39.68	15.26	2.60/1	
Result (reflects mission accomplishment, ground gained/lost, and casualties)	5.10	6.59	−1.49	(German success)
Ratio theoretically consistent with result			1/1.30	
Revised combat power (reflects surprise factors)	27.28	31.38	1/1.15	
Effect of Surprise			1/2.99	(1.15 × 2.60)

Table 5-6
SUEZ CANAL CROSSING, 6 OCTOBER 1973
(Engagement No. 73-1)

	Egyptian (Surpriser)	Israeli	Comparison	
Manpower	30,750	4,005	7.68/1	
Firepower (OLI, in thousands)	375.05	92.12	4.07/1	
Combat power (reflects variable factors of engagement)	159.19	156.77	1.02/1	
Modified combat power (reflects combat effectiveness indices)	159.19	235.16	1/1.48	
Result (reflects mission accomplishment, ground gained/lost, and casualties)	7.49	1.49	6.00	(Egyptian success)
Ratio theoretically consistent with result			2.20/1	
Revised combat power (reflects surprise factors)	370.95	218.93	1.69/1	
Effect of Surprise			2.50/1	(1.69 × 1.48)

AIR AND NAVAL GUNFIRE SUPPORT IN AMPHIBIOUS OPERATIONS

Only a very preliminary approach has thus far been made to QJMA evaluation of the importance of air and naval gunfire support in amphibious operations. The probable results have been calculated for two engagements at Anzio and four at Salerno—all German counterattacks against an Allied beachhead—if close air and naval gunfire support had not been available.

In the face of mounting German pressure against the gap which existed between the US XI Corps and the British X Corps at the Salerno beachhead, beginning 11 September the Fifth Army Commander, General Mark Clark, rushed reinforcements into the center of the line, and his supporting air forces concentrated a massive effort in front of the same area. The engagements have been analyzed for the effects of support by stripping out the OLI values of close air support and naval gunfire support. Two of the four Salerno engagements for which this was done were in the central area of the beachhead, about which the Allies were deeply concerned. The calculations show, however, that the heavily reinforced Allied ground forces in this central area possessed sufficient strength with their own resources to have retained favorable P_f/P_e ratios, even with naval and air support eliminated.

This was not so, however, on the extreme left of the Allied beachhead, where in Engagements Nos. 4 and 7 the British 46th Division was facing a violent counterattack by the Hermann Goering Panzer Division, reinforced. The QJMA calculations for one engagement between these divisions confirm historical assessments that without naval gunfire support the 46th Division would probably have been pushed into the sea. As it was, Allied destroyers' five-inch guns proved to be effective antitank weapons, picking off the German tanks as they emerged over the escarpment and headed down the open slopes toward the beaches.

A similar analysis was made of Engagement No. 38, which was the German main effort of 16-19 February 1944 at Anzio against the 45th Division. This supreme effort to smash the beachhead was stopped with the combined help of naval gunfire and close air support. The QJM suggests that, even with close air support, had it not been for naval gunfire the Germans would probably have been able to reach the beaches, with a result that could have been disastrous to the Allies.

ASSESSMENT OF PERFORMANCE
IN RELATION TO PLANS

The above discussion shows how a technical analysis of the effects of naval gunfire and close air support is also in part operational analysis, both stimulated and facilitated by the QJMA.

From all such operational and technical analyses flow almost automatically evaluations of force performance in relation to plans and in relation to capability. For instance, in Engagement No. 5 the bitter struggle of the British 46th Infantry and German Hermann Goering Panzer Divisions, far from the center of the Salerno Beachhead, where Allied attention was focused, demanded a review of the German perception of the Salerno Battle. While Allied historical works have paid little attention to the fact, it became clear from reviewing German documents that the principal concern of the German commanders at Salerno had been the security of the Tenth Army's strategic right flank. This led to a main effort by the Hermann Goering Division, with only secondary German attention to probing the strongly reinforced Allied center, where General Clark had expected the main effort.

The analyses of engagements in late May 1944, during the Rome Campaign, demonstrate an exceptional German effort to hold open the withdrawal routes for the right wing of the Tenth Army, south and west of Cassino. Again a review of German documents suggests that General Clark's shift of the axis of his advance from northeasterly (up the Tiber Valley) to north (toward Rome), assured the success of Field Marshal Kesselring's desperate efforts to save the shattered remnants of his Fourteenth Army and the threatened right wing of his Tenth Army. This is not a new thesis, but the demonstrated level of German effort, as shown by the QJMA analyses, provides a quantified confirmation hitherto unavailable.

Similar operational analyses are stimulated by the QJMA results for engagements during the overwhelming Allied drive across northern France in August 1944. These engagement analyses, combined with other HERO assessments of the results of Allied air interdiction at this same time, suggest that had the Allies made a concentrated thrust on a relatively narrow single army front, the Germans would have been unable to withstand it. I am now convinced that had this been done the Allies could have at least reached the Rhine by September 1944. Beyond that, of course, one can only speculate, but certainly under such circumstances a German Ardennes offensive in December would have been impossible.

COMBAT INTENSITY

It has long been evident that there is a hitherto indefinable factor, intensity of combat, which affects not only the number of casualties suffered by both sides in an engagement, but other aspects of the outcome as well. By plotting the relationship between casualties and strengths for 212 military forces in 106 engagements, HERO has obtained some curves which suggest what normal combat intensity has been in modern combat for forces of varying sizes and combat circumstances. (See Figure 5-7)

Establishment of this or a comparable scale of values for Combat Intensity could have been accomplished without the Quantified Judgment Method (although it is doubtful that it would have been). It has become evident, however (as will be discussed below), that this new quantification of an important but elusive aspect of combat can be related usefully to other values which come directly from the QJMA.

FACTORS INFLUENCING RATES OF
ADVANCE (FEBA MOVEMENT)

A HERO feasibility study, in which the QJMA was applied to some but not all of the combat data,[22] reached the following conclusions: (1) it is feasible to determine historical rates of advance of large forces in combat and to identify the operational and environmental factors influencing those rates of advance; and (2) it is likely that force ratios, whether calculated by QJM or otherwise, do not influence rates of advance, but that sustained advances are probably not possible unless a threshold force ratio superiority has been achieved. The report also suggests a method—based upon QJMA procedures—for calculation of "normalized" advance rates for standard tactical situations, which can then be modified to reflect specific operational and environmental circumstances. (A preliminary set of such rates is to be found in Appendix A.)

[22] ORALFORE.

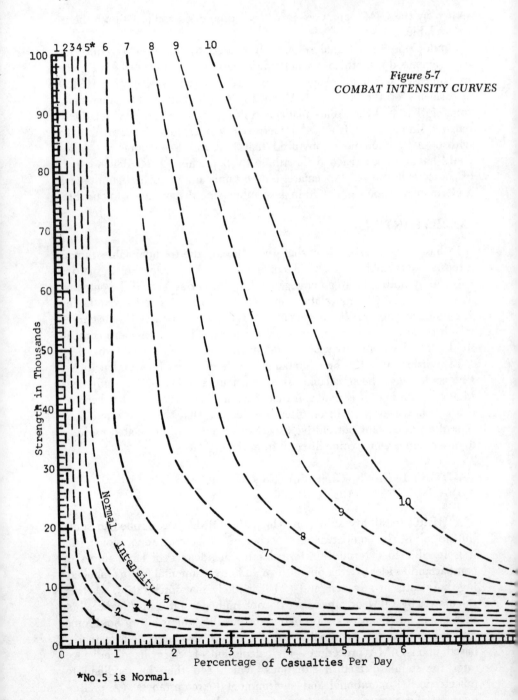

Figure 5-7
COMBAT INTENSITY CURVES

*No.5 is Normal.

6

Representing
Air Support
in World War II

Theoretical Effects of Air Weapons

RELATING AIR WEAPONS TO THE GROUND BATTLE

As we have seen, the QJMA concept is based upon a comparison of
the combat power potentials of two opposing forces at the outset of an
engagement. The starting point for determination of combat power potentials is calculation, in OLI units, of the total weapons firepower available to each side. This is a straightforward, readily conceptualized
process.

There is no problem in determining the total OLI values for all of the
weapons arrayed against each other, if we follow the procedures for OLI
calculations presented in Chapter 2. There is no problem, that is, with
respect to weapons on the ground. They are there, in use or available for
use, and (unless destroyed or abandoned in the battle) will remain there
until the end of the engagement. But there is a problem—in fact two
major problems—when we try to incorporate air support weapons into
this concept.

The first of these problems is that aircraft, and the ordnance they carry,
are actually present over the battlefield for only a fraction of the duration
of an engagement—a matter of minutes, or at most an hour or two, per
day during an engagement. Complicating that problem is the fact that
the length of time the aircraft is present in the battle area depends—
amongst other things—upon the distance of the aircraft's base from the
battlefield.

The other major conceptual problem is that the presence of an aircraft
on an airfield within range of a battle area does not mean that it is
necessarily available to provide direct support to the ground forces in
the engagement. The air commander may decide that the best use for
some or all of his aircraft is in the air-superiority role, employing them

71

either against the hostile air force in the air, or in attacks on enemy air bases. Or the air commander, usually in consultation with a higher-level ground or combined force commander, may decide to employ a significant number of his available aircraft on interdiction tasks, against the supplies or lines of communication of the enemy ground forces. Of course in either of these cases the aircraft so employed are at least indirectly supporting the ground battle, either by preventing enemy air from attacking the supported forces, or by making it difficult for the enemy to get supplies or reinforcements to his ground troops opposed to our own. As we shall see, it is possible to consider these indirect support aircraft missions in the QJM, but so far as the actual ground engagement is concerned, the firepower of such indirect support aircraft cannot be included in the total weapons or firepower inventory on the battlefield.

It has been necessary to take an arbitrary approach to the first of these two problems: that of relating the effects of fleetingly present aircraft firepower with the effects of the ground weapons available on the ground 24 hours per day. The OLI values calculated for aircraft, by the procedures for mobile fighting machines presented in Chapter 2, are considered to represent the value of an aircraft for one sortie, whether the specific individual aircraft appears once or several times a day over the battlefield. In fact, once this fundamental decision was made, the OLI calculation process for aircraft was adjusted to give results that proved to be consistent in the first 60-Engagement Developmental Data Base, and it has given equally good results since.

Related to this was the assumption that any single aircraft sortie over the battlefield was worth the full calculated OLI value, regardless of how distant the aircraft's base might be, and regardless of how long it appeared over the battlefield. This assumption could be challenged on various technical grounds, but is supported by common-sense logic. Air commanders will not commit aircraft unless they can reach and attack targets on the battlefield, and will always strive to provide the maximum possible support. Even when aircraft bases are close to the battlefield, this advantage will be utilized to increase the number of sorties, not to increase the duration of sorties beyond a relatively brief optimum time for delivering ordnance.

An arbitrary but logical approach also resolved the second problem—that of relating the value of potential airpower to the practicalities of different missions in accordance with air doctrine. An exception was made to the rule that all available ground weapons should be considered in the firepower calculation, whether or not they were likely to be employed. Regardless of the number of aircraft on bases theoretically in range of the battlefield, in the QJM we included the OLI weapons values only for close support sorties actually flown in support of engaged ground troops.

Having established these rules for calculation of air support, we were able to integrate aircraft OLIs with ground weapons OLIs to arrive at overall firepower inventories for each engagement analyzed. We then reviewed the results of these calculations, to assess the realism with which the model dealt with the effects of air weapons on World War II battlefields. We undertook this assessment in four different respects: close air support; interdiction; interaction of air and ground weapons; and overall effects of airpower. The relevant data is assembled in Figure 6-1.

CLOSE AIR SUPPORT

The effect of close air support was analyzed by attempting to assess what changes in outcome could have been expected in the various engagements if neither side had received close air support. This was done by recomputing the model for each engagement with close air support values eliminated. Then the recomputed values of P_f/P_e were compared with the original unmodified values to ascertain whether the combat power preponderance of either side had been reversed, or had been so modified as to change the Combat Power Ratio. In two engagements (27 and 41 in the figure), the combat power preponderance had been reversed, although in both instances to an "unpredictable" value. However, since Engagement 27 had had inconclusive results with a P_f/P_e value of 1.03, there can be no doubt that it would have been a German success with a P_f/P_e of 0.98. The change for Engagement 59 was comparable, but not so conclusive.

In some of the other engagements it is found that the value of P_f/P_e is so changed by the elimination of close air support that, in the light of the known outcome of the engagements, the result would have been certain or likely to change. In Engagement 6, for instance, the Allied margin of success was a very slight one, despite a P_f/P_e of 5.54. With a new P_f/P_e of 3.52 the outcome might well have changed. In Engagement 13 the outcome was inconclusive, with a P_f/P_e of 1.48. By eliminating the German close air support we get a value of 1.66; thus we can assume that German close air support had definitely been responsible for preventing an Allied success. In Engagement 42 the ratio had been 1.73, resulting in an inconclusive engagement; without Allied air support the ratio is 1.54, thus permitting an assumption that Allied close air support had been definitely responsible for preventing a German victory.

Thus we find that close air support had definitely been responsible for preventing one side or the other from winning in three engagements (13, 27, and 42), had possibly been responsible for the Allied successes in two others (6 and 42), and may have been responsible for preventing a German success in one more (59). Air support was present for one or both sides of 54 engagements; we can conclude that in Italy in 1943 and 1944

Figure 6-1
ANALYSIS OF AIR SUPPORT SIGNIFICANCE*

Eng No.	Actual Combat Power Potential Allied	German	Relative Combat Power & Outcome P_f/P_e Allied Succ	Fail	Close Air Effort in OLI Allied	German	Modified Combat Power Allied	German	Modified P_f/P_e	Changed Outcome Y	N	14-Day Average Interdiction Effort
6	108,296	34,405	3.15	—	15,750	2,429	92,546	31,976	2.89		N	—
4	79,355	61,447	1.29	—	1,093	3,338	78,242	58,099	1.35		N	—
5	154,471	27,893	5.54	—	64,093	2,215	90,378	25,678	3.52	?	—	—
7	87,557	43,017	2.04	—	1,823	807	85,734	42,210	2.03		N	—
8	53,804	37,028	1.45	—	2,603	1,575	51,201	35,453	1.44		N	—
9	52,925	37,449	1.41	—	6,214	1,592	46,711	35,857	1.30		N	—
10	62,690	28,976	2.16	—	0	0	62,690	28,976	2.16		N	—
12	54,828	30,088	1.79	—	909	109	44,919	29,979	1.50		N	—
13	29,425	19,937	1.48	1.48	0	2,229	29,425	17,708	1.66	Y		—
14	54,804	25,827	2.12	—	215	1,161	54,589	24,666	2.21		N	—
15	61,528	24,106	2.55	—	1,378	0	60,150	24,106	2.50		N	—
16	44,672	33,827	1.32	—	660	3,113	44,012	30,714	1.43		N	—
17	35,351	31,337	1.13	—	416	77	34,935	31,260	1.12		N	—
19	30,679	25,671	1.20	—	0	0	30,679	25,671	1.20		N	—
20	23,090	23,366	0.99	0.99	0	0	23,090	23,366	0.99		N	—
18	38,173	26,666	1.43	—	1,190	0	36,983	26,666	1.39		N	—
21	55,377	27,483	2.02	—	3,095	2.877	52,242	24,606	2.12		N	—
28	18,977	18,506	1.03	1.03	885	0	18,042	18,506	0.98	Y		—
27	23,049	19,459	1.18	1.18	741	0	22,308	19,459	1.15		N	—
29	21,123	16,661	1.27	—	1,636	0	19,487	16,661	1.17		N	—
30	37,849	24,442	1.55	—	0	961	37,849	23,481	1.28		N	3,074
31	124,404	49,194	2.53	—	3,945	3,168	120,459	46,026	2.62		N	3,219
33	62,525	57,146	1.09	—	1,445	869	61,080	56,277	1.09		N	3,214
34	65,120	53,094	1.23	—	523	424	64,597	52,670	1.23		N	2,249
35	37,368	14,668	2.55	—	373	151	36,995	14,517	2.55		N	2,249
38	189,123	115,323	1.64	—	58,697	5,474	130,426	109,849	1.19		N	1,640
39	81,007	13,620	5.95	5.95	1,680	278	79,327	13,342	5.95		N	1,640
40	140,856	34,792	4.05	—	4,761	1,367	136,104	33,425	4.07		N	1,555
41	58,819	51,610	1.14	—	8,726	0	50,013	51,610	0.97	?	—	5,991
42	49,071	28,360	1.73	1.73	5,397	0	43,674	28,360	1.54	Y		5,991
43	41,534	38,232	1.09	—	1,151	0	40,383	38,232	1.06		N	6,268
44	57,073	28,117	2.03	—	1,726	0	55,347	28,117	1.97		N	6,268
46	36,032	18,506	1.95	—	1,264	0	34,768	18,506	1.88		N	6,024
45	51,287	13,829	3.71	—	0	0	51,287	13,829	3.71		N	6,038
47	51,792	9,679	5.35	—	239	410	51,553	9,269	5.56		N	5,550
48	43,430	8,842	4.91	—	186	0	43,244	8,842	4.89		N	5,980
49	47,421	29,038	1.63	—	365	0	47,056	29,038	1.62		N	5,561
50	39,842	33,374	1.19	—	620	0	39,222	33,374	1.18		N	5,561
51	94,914	66,227	1.43	—	5,022	0	89,892	66,227	1.34		N	5,561
52	70,601	48,139	1.47	—	2,035	0	68,566	48,139	1.42		N	5,561
53	40,668	32,145	1.27	—	229	0	40,439	32,145	1.26		N	5,169
55	54,294	42,651	1.27	—	0	0	54,294	42,651	1.27		N	4,173
57	55,992	31,220	1.79	—	0	215	55,992	31,005	1.81		N	4,305
59	101,505	92,418	1.10	1.10	711	352	100,794	92,066	1.09	?	N	4,539
60	105,422	42,209	2.50	—	193	0	105,229	42,209	2.49		N	4,344

*Includes only Allied successes and Inconclusive engagements. However, German air support did not significantly influence the outcome of any German successes, and had a clearly discernible effect only on Engagement No. 13, an Inconclusive engagement.

74

		Interdiction Analysis				Overall Airpower Analysis						
	OLI Value of	Effect of Eliminating Interdiction				Overall Air Component of Allied OLI	Effect of Eliminating All Air Power					
Log Degradation Factor	Interdiction Effect	Modified German OLI	Modified P_t/P_e	Changed Outcome Y	N		Modified Allied OLI	Modified German OLI	Modified P_t/P_e	Changed Outcome Y	N	Allied Posture
—	—	—	--	—	—	27,572	86,635	37,887	2.29	—	N	HD
—	—	—	—	—	—	14,403	71,587	64,754	1.11	—	N	HD
—	—	—	—	—	—	77,963	83,443	32,613	2.56	Y	—	HD
—	—	—	—	—	—	14,425	79,433	48,511	1.64	—	N	HD
—	—	—	—	—	—	13,359	45,463	41,191	1.10	—	N	A
—	—	—	—	—	—	16,785	41,425	41,142	1.01	?	—	A
—	—	—	—	—	—	7,896	54,794	32,924	1.66	—	N	A
—	—	—	—	—	—	10,987	39,880	35,018	1.14	—	N	A
—	—	—	—	—	—	7,738	25,556	21,577	1.18	Y	—	A
—	—	—	—	—	—	10,689	49,352	29,903	1.65	—	N	A
—	—	—	—	—	—	11,751	54,963	29,292	1.88	—	N	A
—	—	—	—	—	—	9,875	39,404	35,321	1.12	—	N	A
—	—	—	—	—	—	8,790	30,748	35,447	0.87	Y	—	A
—	—	—	—	—	—	6,545	27,406	28,943	0.95	?	—	A
—	—	—	—	—	—	5,683	20,248	26,207	0.77	Y	—	A
—	—	—	—	—	—	10,003	32,576	31,072	1.05	?	—	A
—	—	—	—	—	—	12,560	47,509	29,338	1.62	—	N	A
—	—	—	—	—	—	7,934	14,517	22,030	0.66	Y	—	A
—	—	—	—	—	—	7,640	18,858	22,908	0.82	Y	—	A
—	—	—	—	—	—	7,497	16,256	19,891	0.82	Y	—	A
0.80	5,696	30,138	1.26	—	N	16,474	32,460	34,566	0.94	Y	—	A
0.895	7,628	56,822	2.19	—	N	30,090	111,200	62,912	1.78	—	N	HD
0.90	9,780	66,926	0.93	Y	—	23,186	55,099	72,037	0.76	Y	—	HD
0.925	6,356	59,450	1.10	—	N	17,119	59,477	64,146	0.93	Y	—	HD
0.925	1,649	16,317	2.29	—	N	8,334	33,839	19,322	1.75	—	N	HD
0.955	7,399	122,722	1.54	—	N	91,570	117,689	135,459	0.87	Y	—	HPD
0.955	2,269	15,889	5.09	?	—	16,975	72,809	22,407	3.25	Y	—	HPD
0.955	2,620	37,412	3.77	—	N	25,302	127,143	46,372	2.74	—	N	PD
0.84	5,870	57,480	1.02	?	—	26,708	43,959	63,536	0.69	Y	—	A
0.84	3,702	32,062	1.53	Y	—	19,382	38,532	37,203	1.04	Y	—	A
0.82	6,766	44,998	0.92	Y	—	17,929	35,377	50,004	0.71	Y	—	A
0.82	4,151	32,268	1.77	—	N	16,426	50,072	37,542	1.33	—	N	A
0.83	3,070	21,576	1.67	—	N	10,835	31,517	24,826	1.27	—	N	A
0.83	3,704	17,533	2.93	—	N	13,242	46,518	22,302	2.09	—	N	A
0.83	3,042	12,721	4.07	—	N	11,447	47,470	16,804	2.82	—	N	A
0.80	2,731	11,573	3.75	—	N	10,567	39,419	15,398	2.56	—	N	A
0.80	5,623	34,661	1.37	—	N	15,121	42,489	39,227	1.08	—	N	A
0.80	6,296	39,670	1.00	?	—	15,738	34,811	44,081	0.79	Y	—	A
0.80	11,561	77,788	1.22	—	N	32,331	82,018	85,652	0.96	?	—	A
0.80	9,014	57,153	1.24	—	N	25,869	58,156	64,563	0.90	Y	—	A
0.81	7,267	39,412	1.03	?	—	16,189	36,092	43,758	0.82	Y	—	A
0.81	6,246	48,897	1.11	—	N	15,891	49,471	53,719	0.92	Y	—	A
0.81	4,642	35,862	1.56	—	N	13,167	51,729	40,124	1.29	—	N	A
0.81	12,687	105,105	0.97	?	—	31,940	95,690	110,209	0.87	Y	—	A
0.79	7,323	49,532	2.13	—	N	24,830	96,572	58,189	1.66	—	N	A

close air support clearly determined the outcome of three engagements, or 5.6 percent, and possibly determined the outcome for three more, for a total of 11.2 percent whose outcomes *probably* were influenced by the presence of German or Allied close air support.

INTERDICTION

For purposes of the QJMA, air interdiction is assumed to include attacks on all ground targets more than 10,000 meters from the front lines, except for attacks on ground installations of the hostile air forces, and on field artillery in position, with the range of interdiction extending as far back as (but not including) the enemy industrial base. It is assumed that interdiction has three principal effects upon the military force being interdicted: its supply capability is diminished by destruction of supplies and inhibitions on their movement; its capability of shifting troops engaged in combat, or of moving reserves into combat, is impaired; command and control are impaired through damaged communications and consequent disruption and confusion.

Later in this chapter is presented a method for quantifying the effects of air interdiction upon the logistical capability (and thus upon the combat effectiveness) of a force subjected to such interdiction, in this case the Germans in the Anzio and Rome campaigns. The method was applied to the 31 engagements of those campaigns.

There is no evidence that air interdiction had a significant direct effect upon any of the operations in the Salerno or Volturno campaigns, although all German operations in Southern Italy were affected by damage done to the railroad system during the Sicilian campaign. During those campaigns there was no sustained Allied air interdiction effort. The German records suggest that there was a definite harassing effect from Allied air interdiction, and that certain temporary supply problems occurred, apparently at least in part as a result of air interdiction. But there was never any need for such drastic measures as massive and continuous diversion of tactical vehicles to supply purposes, as occurred as a result of the Allied air offensive in Operations "Strangle" and "Diadem."

No effort has yet been made to ascertain or quantify the effect of air interdiction upon mobility or upon command and control. Thus that part of Figure 6-1 which shows the effects of interdiction in degrading combat effectiveness represents *only* the effects through reduced logistical capability. The table shows the calculated degradation effect of air interdiction upon German logistical capability, and how this affected both the German OLI and the relative combat power ratio. The results indicate that in the 26 engagements that were Allied successes, or that were inconclusive, had there been no Allied air interdiction the Germans certainly would have won three (or 9.7 percent). In five other instances, while the sense of the P_f/P_e ratio was not changed by eliminating the logistical effects of interdiction, nonetheless the value of the ratio was changed sufficiently so that the Germans probably would have won. Bearing in mind the fact that only one of the three effects of interdiction upon combat capability has been assessed, it is interesting that this incomplete effect appears to have been decisive in approximately 25 percent of the engagements in which interdiction effects were discernible. In fact, it was probably more influential.

INTERACTION OF AIR
AND GROUND WEAPONS

In the QJM the effects of airpower on ground action are reflected in eight different ways. One of these affects the ground attacking force, regardless of air superiority; three directly affect the side with air superiority; and four affect the side without air superiority. These are listed below:

1. The force strengths (S) of both sides are increased directly by the OLI value of direct air support aircraft;
2. Relative mobility is enhanced for the side with air superiority;
3. Vulnerability is reduced for the side with air superiority;
4. The effectiveness of artillery is enhanced for the side with air superiority;
5. Vulnerability is increased for the side with*out* air superiority;
6. Artillery effectiveness is reduced for the side with*out* air superiority;
7. Direct air support is degraded for the side with*out* air superiority;
8. Supply capability is degraded by air interdiction.

Most of these effects increase the relative combat power of the side with air superiority. For the side without air superiority, only the direct air support actually provided tends to increase its overall combat power.

It is instructive to see what the model says about the overall significance of the presence of superior airpower (all eight of the elements listed above) in operations in Italy in 1943 and 1944. Of the 60 engagements of the Italian data base, 38 were US successes and seven were inconclusive. These are the 45 engagements listed in Figure 6-1. In 21 of the Allied successes, Allied ground combat strength was so superior to the Germans' that even with the elimination of the air component of combat potential, the P_f/P_e ratio would not have been less than unity. In 20, however (and possibly as many as 24), the elimination of the total air component of the OLI would have so reduced the P_f/P_e ratio that an enemy success was either predictable or else very likely. In most of these the combat power ratio was reduced from greater than one to less than unity; in several of the inconclusive engagements the ratio remained greater than unity, but was so reduced that Allied success would have been extremely unlikely.

Figure 6-1 suggests, therefore, that even though *close* air support did not greatly influence battle outcomes, the *overall* contribution of available air support to the American ground combat capability was overwhelming in its effect. In at least 44 percent of the American successes and inconclusive engagements, and perhaps up to 53 percent, airpower provided the margin which provided victory or prevented defeat.

Effects of Interdiction— Operation STRANGLE

In one study we had an opportunity to explore the ability of the QJM to analyze the effects of air interdiction. The reasons that had earlier led us to use the Italian campaign as a basis for studying the general relationship of air support were even more compelling for the analysis of the effects of interdiction on ground operations.

BASIC ASSUMPTIONS

The attempt to relate air interdiction efforts to hostile ground combat capability was based on four general assumptions:

1. There are three distinguishable components of the effects of air interdiction:
    a. Degradation of supply capability;
    b. Inhibition of movement of the engaged combat force and of reserves; and
    c. Delays, confusion, and disruption, particularly in electronic and other means of communication, and in the exercise of command and control.

2. The magnitude of an interdiction effort (in sorties, tons, or some combination) can be related quantitatively to the supply capability of the force being interdicted.

3. Inferences regarding the quantitative significance of the other interdiction effects may be drawn from measurements of the effects of air interdiction upon supply capability.

4. Effects of interdiction are cumulative; they become significant only after two weeks.

THE SITUATION

Figure 6-2 is a map showing the general situation on part of the Italian Front from March to June, 1944. The principal historical events in 1944 having a significant relationship to our analysis of air interdiction were as follows:

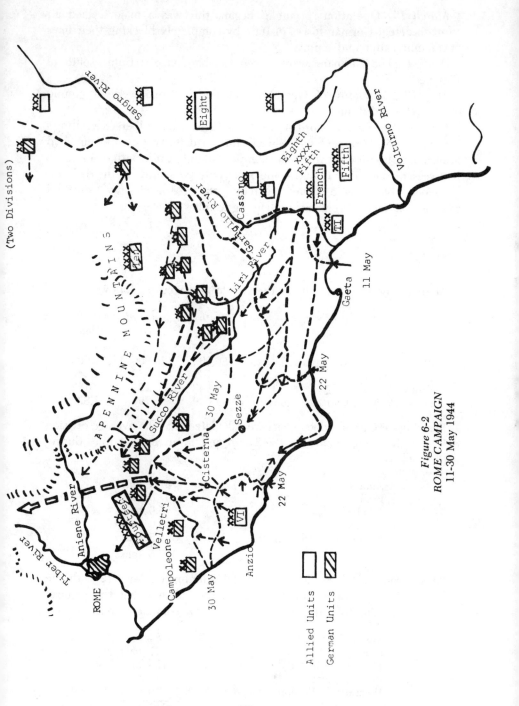

Figure 6-2
ROME CAMPAIGN
11-30 May 1944

Allied Units

German Units

March 19 Operation "Strangle" began; this was a major Allied air effort to defeat German forces in Italy by completely blocking their lines of communication and supply.

April 4 The Germans were forced to abandon rail traffic south of Florence.

May 12 Beginning of Operation "Diadem," a major Allied ground offensive toward Rome.

On the key date of April 4, 1944, Field Marshal Albert Kesselring's German Army Group C (Southwest) informed its two component field armies that, because of Allied air interdiction, rail traffic south of Florence had ceased; the Army Group could meet only two-thirds of the daily requirements of the field armies. Therefore, the field armies were directed to divert "all tactical vehicles" for hauling supplies.

THE DATA

At that time the strengths of the two armies were as follows:

	Tenth Army	Fourteenth Army	Total
Divisions	10	8	18
Personnel Strength (approx.)	150,000	120,000	270,000
Artillery Guns	701	539	1,240
Tanks	42	127	169
Truck Carrying Capacity (tons)	1,030	790	1,820

Based upon German documents we calculated that the average division daily supply requirements for the Tenth and Fourteenth Armies during early 1944 were:

Ammunition	37.5 tons
Fuel	37.5 tons
Food	25.0 tons
Fodder	15.0 tons
Weapons & Equipment	2.5 tons
Total	117.5 tons

During the period of intense combat beginning on May 12 with the Allies' ground offensive, the German records indicate that the requirements per division for a day of the most intensive combat were as follows:

Ammunition	84 tons
Fuel	47 tons
Food (unchanged)	25 tons
Fodder (unchanged)	15 tons
Weapons & Equipment (est.)	10 tons
Total	181 tons

An approximate average struck between these two sets of figures, one for very light combat, the other for very intensive combat, was assumed to provide a reasonably accurate figure for daily division requirements during active operations:

Ammunition	61 tons
Fuel	43 tons
Food (unchanged)	25 tons
Fodder (unchanged)	15 tons
Weapons & Equipment	7 tons
Total	151 tons

Thus, the requirements for a division slice of either of the two German armies was about 150 tons for an average day of combat in mid-1944.

QUANTIFYING THE DATA

On April 4, in a period of light combat, the average daily supply requirements of the 18 divisions of the two field armies were 2,115 tons. (See Figure 6-3.) The Army Group could meet only two-thirds of these requirements, or 1400 tons. The tactical vehicles of the armies therefore supplied the remaining 715 tons per day, using for this purpose about 40 percent of the entire operational transport capacity of the two armies, which was some 1,820 tons. Once the Allied offensive began neither army could continue to provide such a proportion of its tactical vehicles for routine supply purposes without severe detriment to combat capability. We can assume that, through various expedients, a diversion of perhaps 10 percent of the armies' transport was possible, without seriously impairing combat efficiency. Naturally such diversions would have been made, and undoubtedly were made, particularly to obtain essential ammunition and fuel. Therefore, it is reasonable to conclude that a total of 1,582 tons (1,400 + 182) was deliverable to the armies (at the cost of negligible adverse effect on tactical capabilities) or a total of about 88 tons per division, or a total delivery of 1,582 tons.

Figure 6-3
GERMAN COMBAT SUPPLY REQUIREMENTS AND TRUCK CAPACITIES
Tenth and Fourteenth Armies
March-May 1944

(1)	"Quiet period" average daily supply requirements, March-April	2,115 tons
(2)	Active combat average daily supply requirements, May-June	2,718 tons
(3)	Army group administrative truck carrying capacity, approximately	1,400 tons
(4)	Tenth and Fourteenth Armies tactical truck carrying capacity	1,820 tons
(5)	Tactical truck capacity diverted to supply, 4 April	715 tons
(6)	Total tactical and administrative truck capacity available without combat efficiency degradation for active combat $[(3)+.1\times(4)]$	1,582 tons
(7)	Shortage for active combat $[(2)-(6)]$	1,136 tons

Since the active combat requirements for the Army group were 2,718 tons, there was a daily shortage of 1,136 tons. Thus the supply deliveries were probably approximately 58.2 percent of requirements during relatively active, or average, combat. This is shown graphically on Figure 6-4.

Figure 6-4

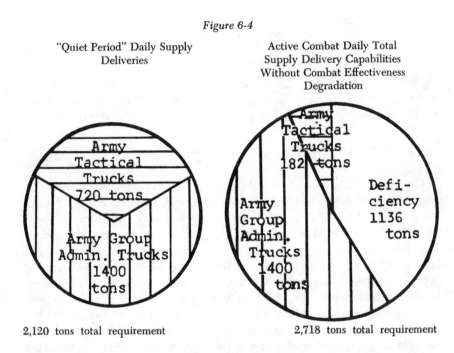

"Quiet Period" Daily Supply
Deliveries

Active Combat Daily Total
Supply Delivery Capabilities
Without Combat Effectiveness
Degradation

Army
Tactical
Trucks
720 tons

Army Group
Admin. Trucks
1400
tons

Army
Tactical
Trucks
182 tons

Army
Group
Admin.
Trucks
1400
tons

Defi-
ciency
1136
tons

2,120 tons total requirement   2,718 tons total requirement

Historical experience indicates that combat power is not substantially diminished by small supply deficiencies. Strengths prescribed in TO&Es are normally calculated to make the most effective use of a given number of men, machines, and weapons. Thus *any* deficiencies in consumable or replacement supplies should *theoretically* have a directly degrading effect upon combat effectiveness. In practice, however, human response to challenge or adversity is such that, by various expedients, well-trained and experienced troops can operate at close to maximum effectiveness even with reduced amounts of supplies and equipment. We assumed that this capability applies as long as a unit receives at least 65 percent of its normal supply requirements. The falloff in fighting power thereafter was assumed to be roughly linear (i.e., a unit receiving 60 percent of its supplies would have a 5 percent degradation; one receiving 50 percent of its supplies would have a 15 percent degradation; etc., to a maximum 65 percent degradation). Since cannibalization, hoarding, and various kinds of improvisation will always permit some residual fighting power, the factor b, representing logistical capability, may be expressed in a scale from 0.35 if no supplies are received to 1.0 if at least 65 percent of requirements are received.

Some additional allowance should be made to provide for flexibility in the allocation of supply deficiencies among the component units of a military force. It must be presumed that such a force can so arrange for logistical redistribution that sufficient supplies can be allocated to selected component units as required for local offensive action. In such circumstances, with the attacker possessing the initiative, it is assumed that only half of the calculated supply degradation rate would apply to the unit on the offensive.

The effect of interdiction on supply capability, therefore, can be expressed as follows:

$b = 1$, when deliveries are 65 percent of requirements or more;

However, when deliveries are less than 65 percent of requirements, separate factors will be required for units on the defensive (b_d), and on the offensive (b_a):

$$b_d = .35 + \frac{\text{deliveries (in tons)}}{\text{requirements (in tons)}} \tag{19}$$

$$b_a = b_d + .5(1 - b_d) \tag{20}$$

Returning, then, to the situation of April 4, 1944 (the date of the German report of cessation of rail traffic south of Florence), we can now calculate a logistical factor b based upon a supply situation in which deliveries were meeting only 58.2 percent of requirements (or a deficiency of 41.8 percent, which is 6.8 percent more than that which causes a drop off in effectiveness). Under normal defensive circumstances, in which the side with air superiority retains the initiative, by use of Formula (19) above we can calculate that b_d is .932, suggesting that (as far as supply is concerned) German combat effectiveness had been reduced to about 93.2 percent of normal. In selected circumstances, however, by accumulating supplies for local offensive action, and then seizing the initiative, German units could temporarily achieve an offensive capability, with b_a calculated at .966, using Formula (20); in such circumstances, therefore, we assume that (again, as far as supply is concerned) combat effectiveness temporarily could be increased from 93.2 percent to 96.6 percent.

The records reveal that the Allied air interdiction effort during the remainder of "Strangle" and during Operation "Diadem" increased in intensity after April 4, and through to the conclusion of the Rome Campaign. Evidence as to the continuing effectiveness of this interdiction is abundant in both German and Allied records. That German combat effectiveness was degraded by this continuing interdiction effort is undeniable. In order to quantify the extent of this degradation, however, certain assumptions are necessary.

The Allied air interdiction effort in Italy, which had been intensive during the critical period of the Anzio operation, in late January and early February, had dwindled somewhat by late February and early March, partly because of weather, and partly because of other operational considerations. Operation "Strangle," the concerted Allied air effort to reduce German combat effectiveness through interdiction, began in mid-March. By April 4, as we have noted earlier, the cumulative effects of the Allied air effort had forced the Germans to cease all rail supply south of Florence. (See Figure 6-5 for a summation of the Allied effort in Operation "Strangle" up to April 4.) Since this was almost exactly two weeks after the beginning of Operation "Strangle," we obtained rather direct confirmation of the assumption that a cumulative effort of approximately two weeks is required for an air interdiction operation to be fully effective. Consequently such a two-weeks effort is represented in Figure 6-5 for the period from March 21 through April 3. The efforts of heavy, medium, and light bombers and of fighter bombers are calculated by applying to the number of sorties flown against interdiction targets the OLI value for each sortie as calculated in Chapter 2. It should be noted, however, that any other unit of comparison can be used, without in the slightest altering the methodology or the results (save possibly for comparisons of the relative effects on air interdiction and close support, as shown below).

In our analysis we used firepower measurements in OLI units which can be, of course, related to combat power of ground forces. The table shows the daily OLI values of the interdiction effort of the USAAF's XIII Air Force, and of RAF units supporting the US Fifth Army. These averaged 14,202 OLI units per day. Available data indicates that the RAF units supporting the British Eighth Army contributed approximately 25 percent of the total of the air interdiction effort in Operations "Strangle" and "Diadem." Thus, the average daily effort for the entire Mediterranean Air Force during this fourteen-day period is calculated to be 17,752 OLI units per day. This was the interdiction effort which accomplished the degradation of German supply capabilities revealed by the German report of April 5, 1944.

As noted above, in the face of this Allied air effort the Germans were providing only 58.2 percent of the average active combat logistical requirements of the German armies, or a total of about 1,581.9 tons per day, or a shortage of 1,136.1 tons per day during active combat operations. If a shortage of 1,136.1 tons was a 41.8 percent deficiency, then a shortage of 951.3 tons was a 35 percent deficiency. The difference between these two shortages was 185.8 tons. Thus, by April 4, 1944, if active combat

Figure 6-5

SCALE OF ALLIED AIR INTERDICTION EFFORT[1]
OPERATION STRANGLE, BY 4 APRIL 1944

A/C Type	Heavy Bomber		Med. Bomber		Light Bomber		Fighter-Bomber				XII AF Daily OLI Total	XII AF 14-Day Cum Total	14-Day Average Daily Total
							P-47		A-36/P-40				
OLI/Sortie	460		200		97		61		51				
	S°	OLI	S°	OLI	S°	OLI	S°	OLI	S°	OLI			
Mar 21	—	—	146	29,200	—	—	11	671	15	765	30,636	182,061	13,004
22	21	9,660	72	14,400	—	—	—	—	27	1,377	25,437	198,813	14,201
23	—	—	72	14,400	—	—	—	—	48	2,448	16,848	213,519	15,251
24	—	—	21	4,200	—	—	17	1,037	36	1,836	7,073	197,888	14,135
25	—	—	17	3,400	—	—	—	—	—	—	3,400	176,190	12,585
26	—	—	70	14,000	—	—	31	1,891	20	1,020	16,911	193,101	13,793
27	—	—	67	13,400	—	—	42	2,562	156	7,956	23,918	204,575	14,613
28	—	—	70	14,000	—	—	—	—	60	3,060	17,060	192,966	13,783
29	25	11,500	—	—	—	—	8	488	52	2,652	14,640	202,806	14,486
30	—	—	—	—	—	—	20	1,220	72	3,672	4,892	206,678	14,763
31	—	—	—	—	—	—	—	—	—	—	—	197,856	14,133
Apr 1	—	—	69	13,800	—	—	36	2,196	48	2,448	18,444	199,034	14,217
2	—	—	71	14,200	—	—	45	2,745	80	4,080	21,025	202,369	14,455
3	—	—	35	7,000	24	2,328	43	2,623	108	5,508	17,459	215,643	15,403
14-day average OLI XII AF Interdiction													14,202**

[1]For USAAF XII Air Force, and RAF units supporting US Fifth Army only. This comprised approximately 80% of the total Allied air interdiction effort for Operations STRANGLE and DIADEM.

°Sorties

**MAF 14-day daily average: 17,752.

85

Figure 6-6
INTERDICTION COMPUTATION VALUES
Italy, March-June 1944

Basic German Data

		Tons	%
(1)	Average daily combat supply requirements	2,718	100
(2)	Minimum daily deliveries required for full combat effectiveness	1,767	65
(3)	Critical tonnage level $[(1)-(2)]$	951.3	35
(4)	Supply deficiencies as of 4 April 1944	1,136.1	41.8
(5)	Combat efficiency degradation as of 4 April 1944 $[(4)-(3)]$	184.8	6.8

Basic Allied Data

	OLI
Average daily interdiction effort 21 March-4 April 1944	17,752

operations had begun that day, the critical daily shortage, or amount of shortage exceeding 951.3 tons, would have been 184.8 tons. (See Figure 6-6.)

The data, and the line of approach presented above, lead to the conclusion that there must be a direct relationship between a total daily Allied OLI interdiction effort of 17,752 and the critical shortage of 184.8 tons which degraded German supply capabilities by 41.8 percent, and reduced combat capabilities by 6.8 percent. In order to find out the effects of more or less intensive air interdiction efforts upon German logistical capabilities, it was next necessary to ascertain what level of effort would have been required to reduce the German supply capability by exactly 35 percent, or to the verge of a significantly critical situation.[23] Of an almost infinite variety of possible calculations, the following empirically derived formula appears to provide a satisfactory basis for determining this critical level of interdiction effort:

$$x-y=(T/3)^2 \tag{21}$$

when x is the OLI value for the actual effort, y is the OLI value to reduce

[23] There are a variety of ways in which one could calculate the effects of shortages upon the German forces, using the 65-35% assumption, or any other assumption regarding significance of shortages. The most obvious alternative method of calculation is by proportional relationships, either direct or by various square and square-root relationships. After trying a number of these, we used the method shown herein, since it appeared to give results most acceptable to historical and military experience. For the purposes of that particular study, the precise numbers were far less important than development of a method which would later be susceptible of refinement to provide greater precision.

German supply capability by precisely 35 percent, and T is the critical supply tonnage shortage which results from an OLI effort of x.[24]

Applying this formula to the situation which existed on April 4, 1944, we have:

$$17{,}752-y=\left(\frac{184.8}{3}\right)^2$$

$$y=13{,}957 \text{ or } 14{,}000 \text{ (for the level}$$
$$\text{of precision we need)} \qquad (22)$$

Thus, it is calculated that, under the circumstances which existed in Italy in late March and early April 1944, a 14-day sustained Allied air interdiction effort with an average daily OLI value of 14,000 would have resulted in a German daily supply shortage of 951.3 tons in a period of active combat operations. Any increase in the OLI value of the interdiction effort, therefore, would have a significant effect on German combat capabilities, and the extent of this effect could be ascertained by calculating the critical tonnage shortage resulting from the effort, by use of Formula (22).

APPLYING THE QUANTIFICATION

As noted above, the figures derived are directly relatable *only* to the German situation as it existed in Italy in late March and early April 1944. This situation, insofar as it related to German supply requirements, apparently did not change significantly during the early phases of ground action in Operation "Diadem," or the Rome Campaign, at least through the time when the Germans evacuated Rome, on June 4, 1944. Although there is less basis for an assumption that the German supply situation from late January through early March (at the time of the Anzio Operation) was approximately the same as in late March, such an assumption is important in attempting to relate the effects of the intensive Allied air interdiction effort of that period to the ground operations at Anzio. Figure 6-7 presents the figures for air interdiction, and—by using formula (22)— the calculations of German critical shortages and the factor for degradation of combat capability as a result of supply shortages (b), for the period of the Anzio engagements. Figure 6-8 provides the same data for the early phases of Operation "Diadem," up to the fall of Rome, in May-June 1944.

---

[24] This may be an oversimplification of a most complex combination of elements, including road and railroad nets, supply levels, distribution of targets, and tonnage on targets. This requires much further exhaustive analysis in order to achieve confidence in this relatively simple relationship of interdiction effort to supply capability.

Figure 6-7
AIR INTERDICTION EFFORT AND CALCULATED LOGISTICAL EFFECTS
Anzio Campaign, January-March 1944

A/C Types	Heavy Bomber 460		Med. Bomber 200		Light Bomber 97		P-47 61		A-36/P-40 51		XII AF Daily Total	14-Day Cum. XII AF Only	14-Day Av Daily Total MAF	Critical Tonnage Interdicted	Logistics Factor (b)
OLI/Sortie	S°	OLI	S°	OLI	S°	OLI	S°	OLI	S°	OLI					
Jan 21	78	35,880	136	27,200	—	—	—	—	55	2,805	65,885	321,121	28,672	364	.87
22	146	67,160	173	34,600	—	—	—	—	84	4,284	106,044	405,967	36,247	448	.84
23	159	73,140	158	31,600	36	3,492	—	—	52	2,652	110,884	511,651	45,683	534	.80
24	—	—	—	—	—	—	—	—	28	1,428	1,428	511,855	45,701	534	.80
25	—	—	55	11,000	—	—	—	—	112	5,712	16,712	522,343	46,638	542	.80
26	—	—	—	—	—	—	—	—	38	1,938	1,938	508,413	45,394	532	.80
27	—	—	216	43,200	—	—	—	—	80	4,080	47,280	551,511	49,242	564	.79
28	40	18,400	154	30,800	—	—	—	—	72	3,672	52,872	599,583	53,534	597	.78
29	106	48,760	135	27,000	—	—	—	—	44	2,244	78,004	618,995	55,267	610	.78
30	—	—	125	25,000	—	—	—	—	20	1,020	26,020	623,595	55,678	613	.77
31	—	—	—	—	—	—	—	—	44	2,244	2,244	592,751	52,924	592	.78
Feb 1	—	—	45	9,000	—	—	—	—	28	1,428	10,428	559,251	49,933	569	.79
2	—	—	166	21,200	—	—	—	—	35	1,785	22,985	572,905	51,152	578	.79
3	—	—	—	—	—	—	—	—	6	306	306	540,930	48,297	555	.80
4	—	—	—	—	—	—	—	—	—	—	0	475,045	42,415	506	.81
5	—	—	24	4,800	—	—	—	—	16	816	5,616	374,617	33,448	418	.85
6	—	—	57	11,400	24	2,328	—	—	68	3,468	17,196	280,929	25,083	316	.88
7	—	—	69	13,800	—	—	—	—	38	1,938	15,738	295,239	26,361	334	.88
8	—	—	43	8,600	—	—	—	—	80	4,080	12,680	291,207	26,001	331	.88
9	—	—	—	—	—	—	—	—	52	2,652	2,652	291,921	26,064	332	.88
10	—	—	—	—	—	—	—	—	12	612	17,172	261,813	23,736	296	.89

88

Date															
11	—	—	—	—	—	—	—	—	—	—	0	208,941	18,656	204	.93
12	39	17,940	—	—	—	—	—	—	48	2,448	20,388	151,325	13,511	—	1.00
13	—	—	16	3,200	—	—	—	—	70	3,570	6,770	132,075	11,792	—	1.00
14	29	13,340	24	4,800	24	2,328	16	976	31	1,581	23,025	152,856	13,648	237	1.00
15	—	—	18	3,600	48	4,656	—	—	46	2,346	10,602	153,030	13,663	254	.91
16	180	82,800	35	7,000	48	4,656	5	305	48	2,448	96,904	226,949	20,263	254	.91
17	—	—	24	4,800	47	4,559	—	—	16	816	10,480	237,123	21,172	263	.91
18	—	—	—	—	—	—	—	—	—	—	0	237,123	21,172	248	.90
19	—	—	48	9,600	—	—	—	—	31	1,581	11,181	242,688	21,669	222	.91
20	—	—	39	7,800	—	—	—	—	—	—	7,800	233,292	20,830	315	.92
21	—	—	—	—	—	—	—	—	16	816	816	218,370	19,497	311	.89
22	—	—	24	4,800	—	—	36	2,196	8	408	74,404	280,094	25,008	289	.89
23	—	—	—	—	—	—	—	—	—	—	0	277,442	24,772	290	.89
24	—	—	—	—	—	—	12	732	—	—	732	261,002	23,304	260	.89
25	—	—	—	—	—	—	—	—	9	459	459	261,461	23,345	249	.90
26	—	—	—	—	—	—	—	—	—	—	0	241,073	21,524	210	.91
27	—	—	—	—	—	—	6	366	—	—	0	234,303	20,920	190	.92
28	—	—	—	—	7	679	—	—	—	—	366	211,644	18,897	—	.93
29	—	—	—	—	—	—	—	—	—	—	679	201,721	18,011	—	1.00
Mar 1	—	—	—	—	—	—	—	—	—	—	0	104,817	9,359	—	1.00
2	38	17,480	—	—	—	—	—	—	—	—	0	99,337	8,869	—	1.00
3	—	—	50	10,000	—	—	—	—	12	612	28,092	122,429	10,931	—	1.00
4	—	—	—	—	—	—	—	—	—	—	0	111,248	9,933	—	1.00
5	—	—	—	—	—	—	—	—	7	357	357	103,805	9,270	—	1.00

•Sorties

89

Figure 6-8
AIR INTERDICTION EFFORT AND CALCULATED LOGISTICAL EFFECTS
Rome Campaign, May-June 1944

| A/C Types | Heavy Bomber | | Med. Bomber | | Light Bomber | | Fighter-Bomber | | | | XII AF | 14-Day Cum. | 14-Day Av Daily | Critical tonnage | Logistics |
| | 460 | | 200 | | 97 | | P-47 61 | | A-36/P-40 51 | | Daily | XII AF | Total | Inter- | Factor |
OLI/Sortie	S°	OLI	S°	OLI	S°	OLI	S°	OLI	S°	OLI	Total	Only	MAF	dicted	(b)
May 10	—	—	146	29,200	—	—	127	7,747	129	6,579	43,526	335,706	29,974	379	.86
11	—	—	66	13,200	—	—	79	4,819	91	4,641	22,660	357,754	31,942	402	.85
12	67	30,820	179	35,800	—	—	169	10,309	86	4,386	81,315	384,588	34,338	428	.84
13	29	13,340	135	27,000	—	—	130	7,930	68	3,468	58,738	411,571	36,747	452	.83
14	31	15,640	124	24,800	—	—	159	9,699	114	5,814	55,953	439,775	39,266	477	.82
15	—	—	21	4,200	—	—	140	8,540	63	3,213	15,953	418,765	37,390	459	.83
16	—	—	84	16,800	—	—	149	9,089	39	1,989	27,878	417,303	37,259	457	.83
17	—	—	95	19,000	—	—	112	6,832	36	1,836	27,666	423,724	37,833	463	.83
18	—	—	82	16,400	—	—	99	6,039	16	816	23,255	430,697	38,455	470	.83
19	—	—	167	33,400	—	—	73	4,453	—	—	37,853	450,903	40,259	486	.82
20	—	—	—	—	—	—	11	671	—	—	671	435,604	38,893	474	.83
21	—	—	34	6,800	—	—	122	7,442	92	4,692	18,934	446,684	39,883	482	.82
22	179	82,340	24	4,800	—	—	131	7,991	115	5,865	100,987	538,236	48,057	554	.80
23	—	—	—	—	—	—	47	2,867	—	—	2,867	509,158	45,461	532	.80
24	—	—	131	26,200	—	—	—	—	24	1,224	27,424	493,056	44,023	520	.81
25	—	—	84	16,800	—	—	73	4,453	—	—	21,253	491,649	43,897	518	.81
26	—	—	309	61,800	—	—	111	6,771	24	1,224	69,795	480,129	42,869	509	.81
27	—	—	254	50,800	—	—	165	10,065	60	3,060	63,925	492,316	43,957	519	.81
28	—	—	145	29,000	—	—	148	9,028	128	6,528	44,556	480,919	42,939	510	.81
29	—	—	122	24,400	24	2,328	129	7,869	79	4,029	38,626	503,592	44,964	528	.80
30	—	—	168	33,600	—	—	116	7,076	53	2,703	43,379	518,093	46,258	539	.80
31	—	—	—	—	—	—	81	4,941	—	—	4,941	496,365	44,318	523	.81
June 1	—	—	107	21,400	—	—	176	10,736	25	1,275	33,411	506,522	45,225	531	.80
2	—	—	201	40,200	—	—	173	10,553	28	1,428	52,181	520,850	46,504	541	.80
3	—	—	181	36,200	—	—	197	12,017	24	1,224	49,441	568,620	50,770	575	.79
4	—	—	151	30,200	—	—	168	10,248	66	3,366	43,814	594,500	53,080	593	.78
5	—	—	296	59,200	—	—	189	11,529	85	4,375	75,104	568,617	50,769	575	.79

°Sorties

90

As indicated earlier in this chapter, it is believed, from results obtained in applying this methodology to the engagement data base by means of the Quantified Judgment Method, that it at least approximately reflects the nature of the relationship between an air interdiction effort and the resulting degradation of the logistical and combat capabilities of the opposing force. Corroboration of this, and increased confidence in the methodology, however, will require its application to other combat data, which if possible should include not only operations in World War II, but other, more recent combat operations (as opposed to artificial simulations).

EVALUATION OF RESULTS

Figure 6-9 presents a comparison of the close support efforts, the air interdiction efforts, and the air interdiction logistical effects for each engagement of the Anzio and Rome Campaigns which is analyzed in the Development Data Base.[25] Because of the difficulty of equating sorties of such varied aircraft as heavy bombers, medium bombers, light bombers, and different kinds of fighter bombers, and because of the varieties of weapons loadings and effects for the various sorties within types, both the close support and interdiction efforts are shown in OLI unit values only.

In analyzing the figures presented in this tabulation, it must be remembered that these relate only to operations in Italy in the spring of 1944. It must also be realized that the figures for interdiction efforts and interdiction results reflect what happened in a systematic and carefully prepared interdiction campaign, in which the Allied superiority in airpower resources was overwhelming in both relative and absolute terms. It must further be realized that, while certain types of aircraft are quite versatile in terms of performing in both the close support and interdiction roles (and all types could and did perform in each role to some extent), for the most part the bombers were employed—and best employed—in the interdiction role, while the priority of fighter bomber efforts was generally in the close support role. Finally, these are results based upon a tentative and unproven analytical methodology.

With these qualifying considerations in mind, the following seem to be the most important results revealed by Figure 6-9.

[25] It is possible that the actual air interdiction efforts per engagement were slightly less than shown, since there was, on the average, less than one German division engaged in each of these actions. However, upon consideration of such matters as varying levels of combat efforts among divisions, depending upon the intensity of effort, and applicability of some of the air interdiction effort to non-engaged German units in reserve, it is not believed practical to attempt to refine this value further.

Figure 6-9

COMPARISON OF CLOSE SUPPORT EFFORT, INTERDICTION EFFORT AND INTERDICTION RESULTS

			Close Support Effort			Interdiction Effort			Interdiction Results	
Dates	Eng. No.	No. of Days	OLI Value	Total OLI per Engagement	(Less Engagements Nos. A7 & A9)	14-Day Average Daily Int. Effort in OLI Values	Interdiction Effort Per Ger. Division	Approx. Average Interdiction Effort per Engagement	Effect of Interdiction on German OLI	Total Degradation Effect per Engagement
Jan. 25	30	2	0	0		46,638	2,591	5,182	5,606	11,212
27	31	3	2,627	7,881		49,242	2,736	8,208	7,384	22,152
29	32	3	210	630		55,267	3,070	9,210	14,750	44,250
Feb. 3	33	2	998	1,976		48,297	2,683	5,366	9,706	19,412
7	34	3	324	972		26,361	1,465	4,368	6,331	18,993
7	35	1	245	245		26,361	1,465	1,465	1,641	1,641
9	36	2	28,360	56,720		26,064	1,448	2,896	6,359	12,718
11	37	2	0	0		18,656	1,036	2,072	2,651	5,302
16	38	4	33,408	133,632		20,263	1,126	4,504	7,218	28,872
16	39	4	834	3,336		20,263	1,126	4,504	2,246	8,984
21	40	2	3,021	6,042		19,497	1,083	2,166	2,568	5,136
May 12	41	2	5,156	10,312		34,338	1,908	3,816	6,398	12,796
12	42	2	3,559	7,118		34,338	1,908	3,816	3,853	7,706
14	43	2	674	1,348		37,390	2,077	4,154	7,142	14,284
14	44	2	1,174	2,348		37,390	2,077	4,154	4,151	8,302
16	45	3	0	0		37,259	2,070	6,210	3,719	11,157
17	46	3	714	2,142		37,833	2,102	6,306	3,070	9,210
20	47	3	140	420		38,893	2,161	6,483	2,978	8,934
22	48	3	109	327		48,057	2,670	8,010	2,731	8,193
23	49	2	253	506		45,461	2,526	5,052	5,623	11,246
23	50	2	450	900		45,461	2,526	5,052	6,296	12,592
23	51	3	6,581	19,743		45,461	2,526	7,578	11,561	34,683
23	52	3	1,228	3,684		45,461	2,526	7,578	8,636	25,908
25	53	3	106	318		43,897	2,439	7,317	7,267	21,801
26	54	2	654	1,308		42,869	2,382	4,764	7,544	15,088
27	55	2	0	0		43,957	2,442	4,884	9,996	19,992
26	56	3	0	0		42,869	2,382	7,146	6,246	18,738
28	57	3	0	0		42,939	2,386	7,158	4,634	13,902
29	58	4	6,145	24,580		44,964	2,498	9,992	5,520	22,080
29	59	3	457	1,371		44,964	2,498	7,494	12,663	37,989
June 3	60	2	138	276		50,770	2,821	5,642	7,323	14,646
Totals		80		270,365	(80,013)			172,547		507,919
Per Day				3,379.6	(1,081.3)			2,156.8		6,349.0

a. When the massive close support efforts provided in support of the desperate defense of the Anzio Beachhead are included in the totals (Engagements 36 and 38), we find that the average daily effort for interdiction was approximately two-thirds the average daily close support effort (2,156.8 to 3,379.6 in OLI values). However, a more normal comparison, from which these two extraordinary close support efforts are eliminated, suggests that on a longer-term comparison basis, the average daily interdiction effort was double that of the average daily close support effort (2,156.8 to 1,081.3).

b. The average daily interdiction result in these engagements, in terms of degradation of German combat capability through logistical deficiencies, was three times as great as the Allied combat power expended to achieve this degradation (6,349 to 2,156.8).

c. This leads to the conclusion that the Allied air effort in the interdiction role, measured in OLI values, was three times as effective as the same effort expended in close support; this multiple of three is evident whether we include the massive efforts of Engagements 36 and 38, or not (in the one case two-thirds the effort achieves double the results; in the other, twice the effort achieves six times the results).

Confidence in the comparison presented in Figure 6-9 must be somewhat less definite than in the data and conclusions shown in and resulting from Figures 6-7 and 6-8. This is in part because of the inherent difficulties in determining the relative influence on, and interaction among and between, air and ground weapons in land combat. Some basis for confidence can be found in the high correlation which we have found to exist between the theoretical outcomes of historical engagements, and the actual outcomes. However, in order to have real confidence in the methodology, a larger data base from other operational circumstances than Italy in 1943-44 will be essential.

To the extent the comparisons of Figure 6-9 and the conclusions drawn therefrom are valid, it is possible to apply the first general assumption (p. 78) to the problem of ascertaining the general order of significance of air interdiction in all of its implications, and not just for its effect on hostile logistical capabilities.

The total effect of air interdiction, according to that assumption, is roughly divisible into three major components: (1) degradation of hostile supply capability; (2) inhibitions against movement of engaged combat forces and of reserves; and (3) delays, confusion, and disruption, particularly in the exercise of command and control. No effort has yet been made to ascertain the relative impact of each of these components upon hostile combat effectiveness, but there is some reason to believe that the total effect of Allied air interdiction on German combat capability in Italy in early 1944 was about double the logistical degradation effect. Thus, for the Anzio and Rome campaigns, we could calculate that the total effect of a sustained interdiction effort of 1,000 OLI units per day reduced hostile capability by an average of 6,000 OLI units in an average engagement day. This, in turn, suggests that a sustained interdiction campaign yielded six times as much result as a close support effort, per OLI unit expended. Offsetting this to some as yet unestimated extent is the enhancement of close support effect through interaction with ground weapons effects.

7

Behavioral Variables
in World War II

Explaining the Application of Behavioral Variables

"FUDGE FACTORS"

When members of the HERO staff attempt to describe the QJM, and demonstrate its applicability to World War II data—or any other operational data—they sometimes find it difficult to explain why, when, and how we apply the two major behavioral variables which the model is currently capable of representing: surprise and combat effectiveness. The effects of these two significant behavioral factors cannot be perceived or appreciated unless the observer sees what the combat power ratio would be without the factors. But once this is shown an immediate—and, we have discovered, lingering—doubt is implanted into the observer's mind. He suspects that the HERO analyst applies these factors selectively—using them as "fudge factors" as one distinguished retired general once called them—only when he needs them to make the formulae work out correctly.

In fact, in some instances the relevance of these factors was discovered only when the preliminary analysis, which ignored them, gave peculiar results. In each case this called for a review of sources, data and calculations, and the oversight was discovered in the process of this review. As a result, the factor or factors were included, and new (and usually better) results were recorded.

But, in general, when the HERO analyst knows that surprise was achieved by one side or another in an engagement, he automatically includes a factor for surprise, selecting the appropriate factor on the basis of his assessment of the record. In an engagement between two units for which average combat effectiveness values of the opposing sides are known, those CEVs are entered into the equation. And, in those cases where we do not have an average CEV figure for one or both forces in an engagement, but do have consistent national force effectiveness comparisons, then we use the CEV resulting from a comparison of the national relationships.

RELATIVE COMBAT EFFECTIVENESS VALUES

To return to the graph, Figure 5-1, the P/P value used for those plots includes the unit CEVs, or else has an arbitrary 1.2 CEV for Germans to reflect their average superiority over the Americans and British—and a 2.68 value for the one example with Russian participation. (Of that, more later.) The plots in that graph do *not* reflect the quantification of surprise.

In looking at that graph, it is interesting to note the locations of the six instances in which there is no connection between the actual outcome and the theoretical outcome. We would expect that they would be about equally divided between the upper left and lower right quadrants. However, all six plot in the lower right quadrant, suggesting that the average German combat effectiveness with respect to the Western Allies was probably somewhat higher than previously calculated; i.e., somewhat higher than 20 percent. (However, the overall results are still so good and consistent that it was decided that we would not yet tinker with the earlier combat effectiveness calculations; that is left for future refinements of the QJM.)

The graph also provides us with another visual evidence of the consistent German combat effectiveness superiority over the Americans and British. While the plots cluster along the "Normal Battle Line," in the upper right quadrant, a number trail away to the right. The Allied combat superiority over the Germans in the engagements represented by these plots did not produce results as decisive as the power differential would have led us to expect. In reviewing the record of these engagements that plot far to the right of the Normal Battle Line, we see that in many of those battles Allied commanders were overcautious, or failed to pursue vigorously; in other words, they failed to exploit their combat power advantages and the opportunities that these presented. We do not find many such plots to the left of the Normal Battle Line in the lower left quadrant; in other words, the Germans generally made the most of their much more limited opportunities for success.

SURPRISE

Among the plots in the lower right quadrant of Figure 5-1 are those for Engagements No. 54 and 81. Number 54 was Velletri, where (as we know) the American 1st Armored Division suffered a bloody setback at the hands of the German 362d Infantry Division; the data for this engagement was shown in Figure 4-3 and also in Figure 5-4, where the effects of surprise are shown. As already discussed, the apparently anomalous results of the QJM analysis of this engagement were explicable in terms of surprise.

Engagement No. 81 was the assault of the German 212th Volks Grenadier Division over the Sauer River on December 16-18, 1944, on the extreme left wing of the Ardennes Offensive which most Americans know as the Battle of the Bulge. As shown in the data in Figure 5-5, the combat power of the defending US 4th Infantry Division was such that theoretically the German attack across an unfordable stream should not have been successful. However, we know that it *was* successful, and that the Germans, surprising the Americans, pushed slowly but steadily ahead for two days, until the arrival of reinforcements, mostly from the American 10th Armored Division, changed the circumstances so much that there was a new engagement.

We know, of course, that the principal reason for the initial German success all along the Ardennes Front was the fact that they were able to surprise the Allies completely. When we crank into the data for Engagement No. 81 the factor for major surprise, which we postulated to explain similar anomalies in the Italian campaign, we find the 212th Volks Grenadier Division's combat power sufficiently increased to provide a combat power ratio predictive of success. This example gave us greater confidence in the hypotheses upon which the original surprise variable factors had been based.

Score: Casualty Inflicting Capability

But what about the German combat effectiveness superiority? What clear-cut evidence did we have of this as a verifiable phenomenon, other than as a by-product of our original "curve-fitting" process, and its handy applicability as a "fudge factor"?

In fact, as military historians, we were able to confirm this consistent German combat effectiveness superiority through an entirely different approach: that of assessing casualty-inflicting capability. This measure of combat effectiveness had first made itself apparent to us through a study of statistics of the American Civil War.

SCORE EFFECTIVENESS IN THE CIVIL WAR

Thomas Livermore's famous book, *Numbers and Losses in the Civil War*,[26] is the basic source for statistics of that war. In his two-sided sets

[26] Thomas L. Livermore, *Numbers and Losses in the Civil War* (Bloomington, 1957), reprint.

of statistics for 48 major battles, he showed not only the proportion of casualties (in his words, "hit *in* 1,000"), but also a relationship between the casualties of one side and the strength of the other side—in his words, again, "hit *by* 1,000." Livermore's figures for these 48 battles are consolidated in Figure 7-1, converting his "hit in 1,000" to an overall percentage casualty rate, and his "hit by 1,000" into another percentage figure which I call "score."

Figure 7-1
AMERICAN CIVIL WAR SCORE EFFECTIVENESS,°
CONSOLIDATED STATISTICS 48 BATTLES

	Total Numbers Engaged	*Total Casualties*	*% Casualties*	*Score/100*	*Score Effectiveness*
Union	1,575,033	176,550	11.21	11.88	11.88
Confederate	1,243,538	187,124	15.05	14.20	10.92°°

°From Livermore, *Numbers and Losses.* . . .
°°Corrected for predominantly defensive posture; factor 1.3 is based on WW I and WW II data.

No one has given very serious attention to Livermore's "hit by" figures, since in each case they are the result of interactions between forces of varying sizes, under different circumstances, with all kinds of leaders, in several postures of defense and offense, in all kinds of weather, and on all kinds of terrain. So, what can the figures tell us?

Well, if we take an actuarial approach to history, we can assume that in 48 battles most of these differences cancel out, with the exception of the predominantly defensive posture of the Confederate armies. (The "posture" of a force is the nature of the preparation and organization of its offensive or defensive attitude.) Thus, the fact that more frequently attacking Union forces were more exposed to hostile firepower than the more frequently defending Southerners (often behind protective cover, as at Fredericksburg, Cold Harbor, and Petersburg), accounts, at least in part, for the fact that on the average 100 Southerners inflicted casualties on 14.2 Northerners, while 100 Union soldiers were able to inflict only 11.88 casualties on the Confederates. For comparable circumstances in World War II, where the Germans were essentially, but not always tactically, on the defensive, it has been determined that this posture effect was, on the average, about 1.3. Applying that to Livermore's raw figures, we get what we call a "Score Effectiveness" value, for Confederates and for Union troops. Lest the results arouse the ire of professional Confederates, let me hasten to point out two things: first, the average defensive posture factor for the Civil War, while certainly greater than 1, may not have been as great as the 1.3 factor I have found operative in World War

II. Second, the very slightly lower casualty-inflicting capability of the Southerners as suggested here, and which I happen to think is about right, does not allow for the generally inferior quality of Confederate weapons.[27]

CASUALTY TRADEOFFS IN THE WORLD WARS

In World War I, as shown in Figure 7-2, the Germans mobilized military forces totaling about 11 million men, and suffered almost exactly 6,000,000 casualties. Against Germany alone, the Allies mobilized approximately 28 million, more than two-and-a-half times as many. Allied casualties in combat against Germany (and ignoring losses against Austria-Hungary, Turkey, and Bulgaria) totaled about 12 million. Thus on the average each mobilized German soldier killed or wounded slightly more than one Allied soldier; it took almost five Allied soldiers to incapacitate one German. However, since the Germans were predominantly on the defensive, they had an advantage which, as I have pointed out, could be represented in World War II by an average factor of 1.3. Applying this factor, then, we find that on an equal, or normalized basis, there was an overall German superiority of four-to-one in inflicting casualties.

Figure 7-2
BASIC STATISTICS OF THE WARS AGAINST GERMANY
WORLD WARS I & II

	Mobilized	Casualties		Score	Score Effectiveness
		Numbers	%		
World War I (51 mos)					
Allies (vs Germany)	28.0 mil	12.0 mil	43	0.21	0.21
Germany	11.0 mil	6.0 mil	55	1.09	0.84
World War II (68 mos)					
Allies (vs Germany)	40.4 mil	23.0 mil	57	0.25	0.25
Germany	12.5 mil	10.1 mil	81	1.84	1.42

The statistics are similar for World War II. The Allies mobilized approximately 40.4 million troops against 12.5 million Germans. Allied military losses against Germany were about 23 million (most of these Russians); German casualties were 10.1 million. This means that one in four Allied soldiers inflicted a casualty on the Germans, while each German averaged nearly two Allied casualties. When we correct the German score effectiveness rate to allow for defensive posture, it is still 1.42

[27] The almost identical Score Effectiveness values for Union and Confederate forces is not surprising, of course, and demonstrates the usefulness of analyzing Civil War operations with respect to considerations unrelated to modern military technology.

Figure 7-3
AGGREGATED STATISTICS OF FIFTEEN WORLD WAR I BATTLES

Date	Battle	Duration (Days)	Opposing Forces
1. 1914, Aug 14-23	The Frontiers	10	German Armies, West French Armies
2. 1914, Aug 26-29	Tannenberg[2]	4	German Eighth Army
			Russian Second Army
3. 1914, Sep 5-10	The Marne	6	German Armies, West French Armies
4. 1914, Sep 9-14	Masurian Lakes[2]	5	German Eighth Army
			Russian First Army
5. 1914, Nov 11-25	Lodz	15	German Ninth Army Russian Army Group, N.W.
6. 1915, Feb 7-21	Winter Battle[2]	15	German Eighth & Tenth Armies
			Russian Tenth Army
7. 1915, May 2-4	Gorlice-Tarnow[2]	3	German Eleventh Army
			Russian Third Army
8. 1915, Sep 25-Nov 8	Champagne II	45	German Third Army French Second Army (+)
9. 1916, July 1-Oct 31	Somme I	123	German Second Army British Fourth & French Sixth Armies
10. 1917, April 9-24	Arras	15	German Sixth Army British Third Army
11. 1917, April 16-30	Aisne II (Nivelle Offensive)	15	German Seventh Army (+) French Fifth & Sixth Armies (+)
12. 1917, July 31-Nov 6	Ypres III	98	German Fourth Army British Fifth & Second Armies
13. 1918, Mar 21-Apr 9	Somme II	20	German Ruprecht Group British Fifth, Third & Fourth Armies
14. 1918, Apr 9-30	Lys	22	German Sixth & Fourth Armies British First Army
15. 1918, Sep 26-Nov 11	Meuse-Argonne	47	German Gallwitz Group US First and Second Armies

[1]Postures: A—Attack; HD—Hasty Defense; PD—Prepared Defense; FD—Fortified Defense. Drawn battles are shown by indicating both success and failure.

[2]Russian casualties are shown *including* prisoners (*underlined*), and without prisoners (not underlined).

Posture[1] Suc	Fail	Strength	Casualties	Casualties Per Day	Percent Cas/Day	Score	Score Effectiveness
A		1,200,000	200,000	20,000	1.67	2.50	2.08
	A	1,390,000	300,000	30,000	2.16	1.44	1.20
A		187,000	13,212	3,303	1.77	16.04	13.37
						4.68	3.90
	A	160,000	120,000	30,000	18.75	2.06	1.72
			35,000	8,750	5.47		
	A	900,000	300,000	50,000	5.56	4.63	3.86
A		1,200,000	250,000	41,666	3.47	4.17	3.48
A		288,600	40,000	8,000	2.77	8.66	7.22
						3.47	2.89
	A	273,000	125,000	25,000	9.16	2.93	2.44
			50,000	10,000	3.66		
A	A	260,000	60,000	4,000	1.54	2.44	2.03
A	A	400,000	95,000	6,333	1.58	1.00	0.83
		250,000	40,000	2,667	1.67	5.60	
						2.67	
	HD	300,000	210,000	14,000	4.67	0.89	
			100,000	6,667	2.22		
A		175,000	25,000	8,333	4.76	38.10	38.10
						11.43	11.43
	PD	300,000	200,000	66,667	22.22	2.78	1.85
			60,000	20,000	6.67		
FD		190,000	60,000	1,333	0.70	1.70	1.06
	A	500,000	145,000	3,222	0.64	0.27	0.27
FD		250,000	500,000	4,065	1.63	2.18	1.36
	A	600,000	670,000	5,447	0.91	0.68	0.68
FD		120,000	75,000	5,000	4.17	4.67	2.92
	A	276,000	84,000	5,600	2.03	1.81	1.81
FD		480,000	40,000	2,667	0.56	1.64	1.03
	A	1,000,000	118,000	7,867	0.79	0.27	0.27
FD		200,000	200,000	2,041	1.02	1.53	0.96
	A	380,000	300,000	3,061	0.81	0.54	0.54
A	A	870,000	190,000	9,500	1.09	1.15	1.15
FD	FD	550,000	200,000	10,000	1.82	1.73	1.08
A	A	500,000	175,000	7,955	1.59	1.39	1.39
FD	FD	400,000	152,500	6,932	1.73	1.99	1.24
	FD	380,000	126,000	2,681	0.71	0.73	0.46
A		600,000	130,000	2,766	0.46	0.45	0.45

casualties inflicted by each mobilized German, a rate more than five times as great as that of the Allies.

The reader may or may not find these gross national performance statistics interesting, and he may or may not find them persuasive. But what about battlefield performance? Let's examine a statistical summary of the grim facts. First for World War I.

SCORE EFFECTIVENESS IN WORLD WAR I

Using approximate and aggregated figures, as shown in Figure 7-3 for fifteen of the most important battles of World War I—ten on the Western Front, five on the Eastern Front—the score effectiveness of the Germans against the Allies has been calculated.

A summary of the overall statistics for these fifteen battles (Figure 7-4) shows that the Germans had a four-to-one score effectiveness superiority over the combined Allies; against the Western Allies, British and French, this was only a three-to-two superiority, but against the Russians it was nearly eight-to-one.

Figure 7-4
WORLD WAR I SCORE EFFECTIVENESS
(Consolidated Statistics, 15 Battles)

I.   Overall

		Total Numbers Engaged	Total Casualties	Average % Casualties /Day	Score Effectiveness
Allies	} 15	8.329 mil	3.099 mil	4.864	1.801
Germans		6.250 mil	2.044 mil	2.039	7.462
W. Allies	} 10	6.896 mil	2.349 mil	1.483	1.588
Germans		5.090 mil	1.866 mil	1.868	2.369
Russians	} 5	1.433 mil	0.750 mil	11.628	2.226
Germans		1.160 mil	0.178 mil	2.381	17.648

The breakdown by nations is shown on Figure 7-5. Against the British, the German score effectiveness superiority averaged 1.49 to 1; against the French it was 1.53 to 1 (almost identical); against us, in the Meuse-Argonne, the German divisions that our own intelligence reports described as "tired and depleted," had a score effectiveness advantage of 1.04 to 1. Overall, in the ten selected battles on the Western Front, the Germans' advantage was 1.49 to 1. These figures have been adjusted to allow for the increased effectiveness of defensive firepower, so that they suggest that on the offensive as well as defense two German soldiers could on the average fight three Allies to a standstill.

Figure 7-5
Comparative Statistics by Nation

	Score Effectiveness	
French	1.92	or 1/1.53
Germans	2.94	
Russians	2.23	or 1/7.93
Germans	17.65	
British	1.51	or 1/1.49
Germans	2.24	
Americans°	0.67	or 1/1.04
Germans°	0.70	

°One battle only: Meuse-Argonne

The statistics are less reliable for the Eastern Front, and it is difficult to know how to include in the calculations the tremendous and exceptional hauls of prisoners which the Germans took at Tannenberg, Masurian Lakes, the Winter Battle, and Gorlice. Including the Russian prisoners, German score effectiveness superiority was close to 7.9 to 1.

SCORE EFFECTIVENESS IN WORLD WAR II: THE WESTERN FRONTS

Our detailed engagement analyses in the development and validation of the QJMA permitted us to give consideration to all identifiable variables that were likely to affect number of casualties. Furthermore, having calculated precise OLI proving ground values for weapons, we were able to relate casualties directly to firepower, rather than to the less precise numerical manpower strengths which we used for our more general comparisons of Civil War and World War I data. To get a standard, normalized score effectiveness value, to reflect the casualty-inflicting capability of a force under all possible combat circumstances, we were able to incorporate the effects of vulnerability and posture into the calculation.[28]

Again the results were successful, in that numerical relationships were consistent with known, historical facts. The only problem was that deviations from normal values seemed sometimes to be excessively large or excessively small. A dampening effect was achieved by employing the square root, resulting in the following equation:

$$SE_t = \sqrt{\frac{Cas_e}{.001 \times S_t \times v_t \times u_t}}$$

(23)

[28] It is probable that consideration should also be given to the effects of season and weather. Calculated score effect values have tended to be somewhat higher in summer and in good weather than in winter and in bad weather.

SE$_f$ stands for Score Effect (and since it is also a measure of effectiveness, it is also called Score Effectiveness);

Cas$_e$ stands for the number of hostile casualties inflicted by side f
v$_f$ is the friendly vulnerability factor
u$_f$ is the friendly posture factor
S$_f$ is the friendly force strength, firepower modified by environmental variables

An analysis of Score Effectiveness in 72 divisions and 8 corps engagements of World War II in Italy and Northern France in 1943 and 1944 is shown in Figure 7-6. A summary of these statistics shows that the Germans had the same kind of score effectiveness superiority over us and the British as they had had over the Western Allies in World War I. And, as in World War I, this was true on the offensive as well as on the defensive, it was as true on the relatively few occasions when the Germans had numerical superiority as it was in the more normal circumstances of numerical inferiority. It was true in the few instances when they had effective close air support; it was true in the normal situation where we had complete air superiority. The numbers tell the story.

Figure 7-6
WORLD WAR II SCORE EFFECTIVENESS
(Consolidated Statistics 78 Engagements, 1943-44)

I.   Overall

	Total Numbers Engaged	Total Casualties	Average % Casualties /Day	Score Effectiveness
W. Allies	1,783,237	47,743	1.251	1.449
Germans	940,198	48,585	1.827	2.247

II.   Comparative Statistics by Posture

	W. Allies	German	German	Preponderance
Attack				
Success	1.47	3.01	yes	2.05/1
Failure	1.20	2.27	yes	1.89/1
Defense				
Success	1.60	2.23	yes	1.39/1
Failure	1.37	2.28	yes	1.66/1
Average:	1.45	2.25	yes	1.55/1

The statistical averages for German Score Effectiveness superiority in the Western Front battles selected for World War I, and the engagements in this data base, are remarkably close to each other; 1.5 to 1 for World War I, and 1.6 to 1 for World War II. This provides a very useful tool for assessing the relative combat effectiveness of opposing forces. It will be noted that Score Effectiveness superiority is greater than Combat Effectiveness superiority; relative Score Effectiveness Values (SEVs) seem usually (but not always) to be something like the square of the CEV.

The QJMA results bear out historical evidence that some divisions on both sides performed consistently better than others on the same side, as shown by the relationships of P_f/P_e and $R_f - R_e$. When we compare the performance of these same divisions in terms of Score Effectiveness, we obtain strikingly similar results.

One problem in making an assessment of combat effectiveness from engagement outcomes is the fact that the margin of success actually achieved in an engagement is not necessarily a reflection of the real difference in effectiveness between the two opposing units. It is directly influenced by the use a commanding officer makes of his manpower, time, and space. If a commander accomplishing his mission decides to move cautiously in order to avoid unnecessary casualties, the margin of victory as shown in the $R - R$ value may be less than the matching normal battle line value for the P/P combat power ratio of the two forces. On the other hand, a commander in a hopeless situation may decide to disengage suddenly and completely, and the resulting outcome differential will be greater than would be expected from the combat power ratio and the normal battle line.

, Figure 7-7 represents a preliminary and tentative effort to use the data from QJM analyses to determine the relative combat effectiveness of most of the Allied and German divisions which participated in the 81 engagements of the consolidated World War II data base. Listed in that figure are all divisions and corps which participated in three or more of the 81 engagements. For each engagement of these divisions the P/P value was calculated (including any factors for surprise) and the $R - R$ value was converted to an Effective P/P value (or PR/PR) by means of Formula (18) on p. 61. The CEV—relative combat effectiveness—of each division with respect to its opponent in that engagement was then determined by dividing the PR/PR ratio by the originally calculated P/P. A tentative average CEV was then calculated for each division. The tentative CEV for each division was then applied against the opposing engagement CEVs calculated for each of that division's opponents, and then a refined average CEV was calculated for each division.

It is these refined average CEVs which are listed in Figure 7-7. Also listed are the average engagement Score Effectiveness values for each division. These Score Effectiveness values have then been converted to factors ranging from a low of .85 to a high of 1.0, and then applied against the calculated CEVs. The result, as shown in the last column of Figure 7-7, is a relative numerical ranking of all of the divisions— American, British, and German. Since the values are all less than 1.0, (the Score Effectiveness degradation factors were designed to assure this)

Figure 7-7
AVERAGE DIVISION COMBAT EFFECTIVENESS
WORLD WAR II: 81-ENGAGEMENT DATA BASE

Division/Corps	Number of Engagements	Average Weighted CEVs	CEVs as %	Average Score Effectiveness	Score Effectiveness Weighted Factor	Average Relative Effectiveness in %
US						
1st Armored	3	0.86	70	2.80	.98	69
3d Infantry	4	0.86	70	1.75	.93	65
4th Armored	8	0.73	64	2.02	.94	60
39th Infantry	5	0.81	68	1.57	.92	63
45th Infantry	11	0.72	63	1.73	.93	59
85th Infantry	6	0.79	67	1.91	.94	63
88th Infantry	4	1.14	84	2.40	.96	81
XII Corps	5	0.90	72	2.96	.99	71
XX Corps	3	0.65	60	1.42	.91	55
US Averages		0.829	68.7	2.06		65.1
British						
1st Infantry	8	0.82	68	2.15	.95	65
5th Infantry	3	0.61	58	2.40	.96	56
7th Armored	3	0.83	69	1.20	.90	62
46th Infantry	6	0.96	75	1.25	.90	68
56th Infantry	9	0.60	57	1.31	.91	52
British Averages		0.764	65.4	1.66		60.6
Allied Averages		0.806	67.5	1.92		63.5
German						
Herman Goering Pz	5	1.49	99	2.65	.97	96
Pz Lehr	4	1.02	76	2.01	.94	71
3d Pz Gren	17	1.17	84	2.65	.97	81
4th Para	5	0.93	72	2.59	.97	70
11th Panzer	4	1.31	90	5.10	1.09	98
15th Pz Gren	11	1.12	81	3.14	1.00	81
16th Panzer	7	1.07	79	2.84	.98	77
29th Panzer	3	0.82	66	2.54	.97	64
65th Infantry	6	0.98	74	2.41	.96	71
94th Infantry	8	1.38	94	3.05	.99	93
361st Infantry	3	0.95	.73	4.52	1.07	78
362d Infantry	3	0.98	74	2.74	.98	73
XIII SS Corps	5	1.03	77	3.96	1.00	80
German Averages		1.096	79.9	3.09		79.5

these can be considered as percentage rankings, or at least as relative rankings in terms of percentages.

These results ignore the effects of airpower (or lack thereof), which were assumed to have been cancelled out, and of weather and terrain. Nevertheless, the values generally reflect evaluations consistent with those made by British, American, and German historians and confirmed by veterans of each campaign.

The generally poor and unpredictable performance of the British 56th Infantry Division in Italy in 1943-44 is evident from the record of nine engagements in the data base. It was reassuring to learn that higher British headquarters in Italy in 1943 and 1944 assessed the division in similar terms.

On the other hand, both the American 3d Infantry Division and the German 3d Panzer Grenadier Division were held in high regard by their corps commanders and their opponents. It is apparent that the lower assessment in Figure 7-7 results from the fact that several of the analyzed engagements of these divisions took place after long periods of intense and protracted combat in very bad weather. The significance of this distortion unquestionably can be determined at some future time, since Score Effectiveness and Intensity of Combat values will permit evaluation of the effects of sustained combat and a steady casualty drain.

It did not at first seem reasonable that the US 88th Infantry Division should have such a high combat effectiveness. However, Major General James C. Fry, a regimental commander and later assistant division commander of the 88th, in his book, *Combat Soldier*,* points out that the Germans by early 1945 were classing the 88th as a "shock troops" division.

A review of the data in Figure 7-7 reveals an interesting fact that sheds further light on the comparison of the US 3d Infantry with the US 1st Armored and the 88th Infantry Divisions. The 1st Armored and the 88th —along with the 85th—were the only divisions in the list for which we have data only for the Rome Campaign in Italy, in May and June 1944. Thus we have only good weather data for these divisions.

Although weather is accounted for in the QJM calculations, possibly the consistently better weather in Italy in May and June of 1944 should be given even greater weight than it has been. But more research is necessary to determine the full meaning of this phenomenon.

THE EASTERN FRONT

The German superiority over the Russians in World War II has not been analyzed as systematically as that with respect to the Western Allies, nor even as extensively as for World War I. It is evident, however, that

*James C. Fry, *Combat Soldier* (Washington, DC, National Press, 1968).

that German superiority was still much greater in the East than in the West, although not so much so as in World War I.

Figure 7-8 shows some of the statistics for the Oboyan sector of the Battle of Kursk, July 4-16, 1943. The data shown, based mainly upon Soviet secondary sources, was checked carefully against German data on microfilm in the National Archives. In only one respect was there any significant difference between the Soviet and German figures; the Soviets assessed the German casualties as almost three times greater than the data recorded in the German files, and showed German tank losses about five times greater than the German figures. Since there was no reason for the Germans to falsify the records, and since we have found their casualty and loss figures always quite reliable in other theaters, we have taken their figures for these losses rather than the Soviet assessments.

Figure 7-8
BATTLE OF KURSK (OBOYAN SECTOR) 1943, JULY 5-11, INCL.

	Soviet Sixth GRD Army First Tnk Army	German XLVIII Pz Corps	Ratio
Manpower	90,000	62,000	1.45/1.00
			(1.00/0.69)
Tanks & Assault Guns	931	522	1.78/1.00
Artillery Pieces	647	310	2.09/1.00
Air Support Sorties (est)	3,150	1,575	2.00/1.00
Proving Ground Firepower (OLI/1000)	698	553	1.26/1.00
Actual Combat	1,344	661	2.03/1.00
Power (OLI/1000)			(1.00/0.49)
Outcome	4.26	5.83	−1.57 (Ger)
EFF Combat Power (OLI/1000)			1.00/1.31
CEV			1.00/2.68
Casualties	23,387	4,384	5.33/1.00
Casualties/Day	3,341	626	5.33/1.00
% Casualties/Day	3.71	1.01	3.67/1.00
Score Effectiveness	0.82	2.83	1.00/3.45
Tank Losses	450	141	3.19/1.00

It should be realized that the XLVIII Panzer Corps was attacking even though it had a 2-3 numerical inferiority, instead of the 3-1 superiority that conventional military wisdom says is required for successful attacks. And the Germans were attacking into what was probably the most heavily fortified area the world had seen since November 1918, against an enemy alerted by good intelligence. Yet despite numerical inferiority, Soviet alertness, and the strength of the Russian defenses, over a seven-day period the Germans advanced about 35 kilometers, and were finally halted only when the Russians committed an entire new army in their sector, thus creating a new combat situation and a new engage-

ment. In order to achieve the success they had won before Russian reinforcements changed the battle, the Germans had to have a combat effectiveness superiority of 168 percent, or a CEV factor of 2.68, or in other
words, 100 Germans in the Battle of Kursk were approximately the
combat equivalent of 268 Russians.

This is a startling figure, of course, and much greater than the German
CEV of about 1.2 with respect to the Western Allies. If, however, we look
at Figure 7-5 and the German Score Effect superiority of 7.9, we find
that this superiority is not at all inconsistent with the comparisons we
noted in World War I between the Russians and the Germans. The Score
Effectiveness differential in the Battle of Kursk seems somewhat lower
than usual, in relation to the CEV, but this is probably explicable by the
exceptional strength of the defenses, which greatly reduced Russian
vulnerability.

In more recent studies HERO has had an opportunity to undertake
more analyses of German-Soviet battles on the Eastern Front. Thus, in
addition to a major sector of the Battle of Kursk, we have data and QJM
analyses of the breakthrough of the German First Panzer Group into the
Ukraine in June 1941, the Soviet offensive at Leningrad which broke the
German siege of that city in January 1943; and a sector of the Soviet
Kharkov-Belgorod Offensive of August 1943, which is sometimes called
the Kursk Counteroffensive. The analyzed QJM data for these four engagements is summarized in Figure 7-9.

Figure 7-9
WORLD WAR II SOVIET-GERMAN OPERATIONS

	Operation	N_r/N_g	Fire-Power	Basic P/P	Surprise/ Disruptn	Refined P/P	Effective PR/PR	German CEV	CEV Average
1.	Ukraine '41	1.14	0.85	1.22	0.88°	1.07	0.30	3.58	
2.	Leningrad '43	4.00	4.83	2.21	—	2.21	1.51	1.47	
3.	Kursk-o '43	1.45	1.27	2.04	—	2.04	0.76	2.68	
4.	Belg-Khrkv	4.67	5.03	2.38	—	2.38	1.57	1.52	2.31

°Effects of Surprise First Day—0.38; Average for Five Days—0.88

There is an interesting phenomenon evident in this data summary. The
calculations demonstrate that there was a major German combat effectiveness superiority over the Russians in all four of these battles. But that
superiority over the Russians was much greater in all battles in which the
Germans were on the offensive and successful than in those in which they
were unsuccessful. There is no comparable phenomenon to be found in
the Western Front data compilations. The reasons for this phenomenon
have since been discovered but not until we were analyzing other data in
another war. (See p. 123.)

Figure 7-10
SOVIET-GERMAN FORCE COMPARISONS
EASTERN FRONT, 1944

	Russian	German	Ratios
Field Force Strength	6,100,000	3,500,000-	1.74/1-2.44/1
(Consideration of German		2,500,000	
Defensive Posture) Combat			
Effectiveness			1.34/1-1.88/1°
Total Battle and Non-Battle			
Casualties	7,000,000	1,800,000	
Non-Battle Casualties	2,000,000 (est)	700,000	
Battle Losses	5,000,000 (min)	1,100,000	4.55/1.00
Battlefield Exchange Ratio per man			
(3.5 mil Germans)	0.18	1.4	1.00/7.78
(Consideration of German			
Defensive Posture) Score			
Effectiveness			1.00/5.98

°Estimated @ 2.35 for Kursk, July 1943

Figure 7-10 shows a comparison of Soviet and German forces in 1944. The Russians were not only growing in strength, they were improving in combat effectiveness. At the same time the Germans were scraping the bottom of their manpower barrel, and the effectiveness of their forces was declining. Yet they still had a CEV factor between 1.3 and 1.9, and their Score Effectiveness value was almost 6 times that of the Russians.

We should not forget, however, that the Russians won the war—with considerable logistical assistance from us. They won, at least in large part, because they recognized the German qualitative superiority, and with grim determination made effective use of their superior numbers to offset the qualitative difference.

8

Projecting Future Combat

As a result of work on the QJM through mid-1973, it was obvious that we had a model of combat that could reliably represent combat in World War II between the Western Allies and the Germans, and which could also represent combat between the Germans and Russians in that war. We were slightly less confident (but only slightly) of our representation of Eastern Front battles because we could not be so sure of the data. German data was from primary sources and reliable; Soviet data was from secondary sources, and when comparisons were possible seemed reliable save for some evidence of exaggeration of German loss figures.

At about this time we were beginning to get some official expressions of interest in the model, and were frequently asked if it could be used for predictive purposes. I was cautious in my responses to this—perhaps too cautious, some people suggested. I could say that we had full confidence in it for World War II and earlier at least to the Battle of Austerlitz, in 1805. Not only could it represent Napoleon's most renowned victory, it could portray his climactic defeat at Waterloo, and it could reproduce the Battles of Antietam and Gettysburg in the Civil War and the German Somme Offensive of 1918 in World War I. (See Chapter 11.)

The work done up to that time (mid-1973) on World War II and earlier conflicts suggested that although there were constant changes in the combat power values of weapons in war, there seemed to be little if any change in the other—environmental and operational—variables. Thus, I told my questioners, if we could be sure that we could adapt our OLI methodology of measuring weapons effects to post-World War II technology in order to calculate proving ground values of modern weapons, then we could have reasonable confidence in the predictive capability of the QJM.

During early 1973, by coincidence, we had an opportunity to test the adaptability of the OLI methodology to the weapons technology of the 1970s. Two officers of a Pentagon wargaming group were undertaking a comparison of the various systems used to represent weapons effects in the different wargames, models, and simulations[29] in use by the Department of Defense and the military services. They asked if we at HERO

[29] For our purposes, the words "wargame," "model," and "simulation" are considered to be roughly synonymous.

could calculate the OLI values of the principal weapons then deployed in Europe by NATO and the Warsaw Pact.

Indeed we could! Even though we could expect no reimbursement for the effort.

In the process of doing these calculations, we substantially revised and expanded the OLI formulae, but with no change in the fundamental philosophy or approach. Thus, without application of the Dispersion Factor, the Theoretical Lethality Indices (TLIs) which we calculated for weapons of the 1970s are directly relatable to the TLIs of all other weapons back through history. Figure 8-1 shows the considerations now included in the updated OLI methodology.

Figure 8-1
WEAPONS CHARACTERISTICS CONSIDERED

Towed or Carried Weapons
 Rate of Fire
 Potential Targets Per Round (Power or Area of Burst)
 Range (or Muzzle Velocity)
 Accuracy
 Reliability
 Effect of Electronic Guidance for Missiles and Rockets°
 Effect of Self-Propelled Mobility
Additional, Mobile Fighting Machines
 Battlefield Mobility (related to Speed)
 Radius of Action, or Endurance
 Protection, or Punishment-Absorbing Capability
 Rapidity of Fire Responsiveness°
 Fire Control Effectiveness°
 Ammunition Supply for Main Armament°
Additional, For Special Weapons
 Amphibious Capability°
 Helicopter Vulnerability°
 Target Availability for AA and AT Weapons°

°New

At a symposium in mid-1973 the two officers presented the OLI data we had given them as one of seven or eight sets of weapons "measures of effectiveness" then currently in use in official Department of Defense models and simulations. They carefully refrained from drawing any comparative conclusions, but it was obvious that for each category of weapon the OLI values were close to the mean of professional judgment; and they were the only one of the several sets of measures of effectiveness for which this was true.

Whether or not the OLIs are reasonably faithful representations of effectiveness values of current weaponry, it was evident from this presentation that the OLIs were at least as good as any other method of weapons representation then in use.

At this time, also, we had an opportunity to apply the QJM, with the 1970s weapons OLIs, in a brief classified study comparing NATO and Warsaw Pact forces in hypothetical combat in Europe.[30] The terms of reference for this study were as follows:

1. Using our recently updated OLI methodology, to calculate the weapons effectiveness values of all currently available weapons on both sides;

2. To compile consolidated inventories of the weapons available to typical, currently deployed NATO divisions (we considered only American, British, and West German) and Pact divisions (we considered only Soviet, East German, and Polish);

3. To compare the theoretical combat power and mobility characteristics of selected NATO and Pact divisions; and

4. To match opposing forces in hypothetical combat situations under varying circumstances of terrain and weather.

We had, of course, done much of the work required for the first task in our recent work in preparing OLI values for our two Pentagon friends, although some of this had to be redone to fit the data provided us for this new study. Much of this data came from classified documents. However, the results of the study were so interesting that we repeated many of the calculations, using weapons data from Jane's *All the World's Weapons Systems*, and organizational data from such unclassified professional journals as *Army* Magazine and *The Strategic Review*. We undertook this unclassified version only for Soviet divisions—tank and motorized rifle—and American divisions—standard infantry and mechanized. The figures used here, illustrating the results of that study, all come from the unclassified version.

Figure 8-2 contains the OLI values for most of the American weapons then deployed with NATO combat forces. Figure 8-3 contains similar OLI values for the corresponding Soviet weapons. It is interesting that none of these unclassified values differed by more than 20 percent from the values calculated from the classified sources. Furthermore, the consolidated OLI values for the inventories of the weapons of the four divisions included in the unclassified version were all within 5 percent of the consolidations calculated in the classified study.

Figure 8-4 includes those consolidated inventory totals for the four divisions. It also shows the comparative mobility characteristics of the divisions, using the QJM sub-formula for mobility. Note how the combination of many vehicles and much firepower with a relatively small

[30] "Feasibility Study for Net Assessment of Effectiveness of NATO-Warsaw Pact Forces by Means of the Quantified Judgment Method." HERO, 1974.

Figure 8-2.
SAMPLE US WEAPONS° PROVING GROUND VALUES

	OLI
Rifle, M-16, 5.56 mm	0.35
Machine gun, M-66, .30 cal.	1.0
Machine gun, M-2	1.7
Mortar, 81 mm, M-125, SP	50
Mortar, 4.2″, M-106, SP	80
RR, 90 mm	79
RR, 106 mm	112
LAW	62
TOW, SP	176
Howitzer, 155 mm, SP	235
Howitzer, 8″, SP	212
Missile, Chaparral	158
AA Gun, SP, 20 mm, Vulcan	86
Rocket, Honest John (HE)	107
Tank, M-600A1	797
ARV, M-551	381
Helicopter AH-IG	509

°Sources, US FM 101-10-1, July 1971; Jane's *Weapons Systems,* 1973-1974.

Figure 8-3.
SAMPLE SOVIET WEAPONS° PROVING GROUND VALUES

	OLI
Rifle, AK-47, 7.62 mm	0.32
Machine gun, RPK 7.62	0.66
AAMG ZPU-4, 14.5 mm	35
AA Gun ZSU-23-4, 23 mm	179
Grenade Launcher, ATRPG-7	31
ATGM-AT-3, Sagger	70
Gun AT, M-55, 100mm	205
Mortar, 120 mm	68
MRL, 122 mm, BM-21	559
Howitzer, 122 mm, M-1938	227
Gun-Howitzer, 152 mm, D-20	236
SCUD, SSM	86
GRAIL, SAM, SA-7	34
SAM, SA-4, TEL	328
Tank, Med, T-54	405
Tank, Med, T-55	573
Tank, Med, T-62	767
Tank, Lt, PT-76	160

°Sources, Jane's *Weapons Systems,* 1973-1974.

number of men gives a very high mobility value to the Soviet tank division.

In carrying out the fourth study task we set up a total of 36 hypothetical engagements, about half in the northern zone of Allied Forces, Central Europe, in other words on the North German Plain, where both British and West German forces are deployed. The other half were sited in the more mountainous region of southern Germany, the zone of operation of US forces, and some West German units. Figure 8-5 is an unclassified version of seven of these hypothetical engagements—matching only American and Soviet forces.

All seven of the engagements of Figure 8-5 are predicted successes for the attacker, five being Soviet attacks, two being American counterattacks.

Figure 8-4
PROVING GROUND COMPARISON, US AND SOVIET "TYPE" DIVISIONS

	Weapons Inventory OLI	Weapons Inventory Normalized	Mobility Factor	Mobility Normalized	Firepower/Man
US					
Armored Div	369,188	2.08 (1)	21.20	1.65 (2)	21.89 (2)
Mechanized Div	304,162	1.71 (2)	16.83	1.31 (3)	18.37 (3)
Soviet					
Tank Div	263,554	1.48 (3)	26.25	2.05 (1)	31.32 (1)
Mtrzd Rifle Div	177,568	1.00 (4)	12.83	1.00 (4)	16.94 (4)

Figure 8-5
PROJECTED OUTCOMES, SAMPLE ENGAGEMENTS

US Force	Posture	Soviet Force°	Posture	Good Weather P_t/P_e	Moderate Rain P_t/P_e	Good Weather River Crossing P_t/P_e
South Germany						
Armored Div	PD	Tank Army (1)	A	0.75	0.96°°	0.82
Armored Div	PD	Tank Corps	A	0.88	1.07°°	1.04°°
Mchnzd Div	A	Mtzd Rifle Div	HD	1.02	0.72°°	0.92°°
Corps (AD, MD)	A	Tank Army (1)	HD	1.30	1.02°°	1.18
North Germany						
Mchnzd Div	PD	Comb Arms Army	A	0.64	0.75	0.70
Corps (AD, MD)	PD	Tank Army (2)	A	0.94	1.13°°	1.02°°
Mchnzd Div	A	Mtzd Rifle Div	HD	1.36	0.97°	1.24

°Tank Army (1): 3 Tank Divisions, 1 Motorized Rifle Division
Tank Army (2): 3 Tank Division, 2 Motorized Rifle Divisions
Tank Corps: 3 Tank Divisions
Combined Arms Army: 1 Tank Division, 3 Motorized Rifle Divisions
°°Change in predicted outcome.

Thus, in most of these instances, whether in flat or rugged terrain, the combat power of the attacker was significantly greater (by at least 10 percent) than that of the defender. This is demonstrated by the Combat Power Ratio (P/P).

Our terms of reference, however, required us to consider differing weather circumstances, as well as differing terrain circumstances. And when we applied the different environmental and operational variable values for weather to Force Strength and Mobility, the results were significantly changed from what they had been with good weather values. This is shown by the next to the last column in Figure 8-5. In six out of seven cases the inclusion of the weather factors changed a predicted attacker success to an indeterminate outcome (P/P between 0.9 and 1.1), or to a clearcut defender success (P_{atk}/P_{def} or 0.9 or less). The principal reason for this, of course, was that the generally attacking Soviet forces, with their highly mobile tank divisions, had their effectiveness more hampered by bad weather than the American divisions—at least in the eyes of the QJM.

This result—which had not been foreseen, although possibly it should have—led us to go one step beyond the terms of reference of the study. We decided to make a simple weapon-for-weapon comparison of the effects of posture, weather, and terrain on the proving ground values of some of the principal Soviet and American weapons. The result of that comparison is to be found in Figure 8-6. The extremely wide range of values for each of these weapons—particularly the tanks—under differing circumstances of combat, reveals how dangerous it is to endeavor to use firepower scores—unmodified by environmental and operational variables—as a basis for comparison of the effectiveness of two military forces.

Figure 8-6
EFFECTS OF VARIABLES ON SOVIET AND US WEAPONS

	Soviet Weapons					US Weapons				
	AT-3° Sagger (Portable)	SAM SA-4	Gun How 152mm	Tank T-55	Tank T-62	AT Wpn TOW	AA Wpn Chaparral	How 155mm	Tank M60-A1	ARV M-551
Proving Ground Values	70	328	236	573	767	176	158	235	796	381
Offensive Values										
Flat Terrain, Sunshine	63	328	236	516	691	157	158	235	717	343
Rugged Terrain, Sunshine	49	262	188	172	231	123	126	188	239	114
Flat Terrain, Moderate, Rain	44	295	212	180	243	111	142	211	251	120
Rugged Terrain, Moderate, Rain	34	234	169	102°°	123°°	86	113	169	131°°	55°°
Defensive Values										
Flat Terrain, Sunshine	104	541	389	852	1,138	261	261	388	1,182	566
Rugged Terrain, Sunshine	107	571	410	284	379	268	275	409	391	187
Flat Terrain, Moderate, Rain	104	541	389	425	571	261	261	388	591	283
Rugged Terrain, Moderate, Rain	107	571	410	166°°	245°°	268	275	409	229	110

°Sagger on BMP: 207.
°°Used as artillery.

117

9

Reliably Representing
the Arab-Israeli Wars

In 1973, while we were adapting the QJM to post-World War II weapons, the course of events in the Middle East provided us with a modern war, fought with modern weapons—the very weapons for which we had recently calculated OLI values. Naturally we were anxious to have an opportunity to test the QJM on data from that war—the October War of 1973, known to the Israelis as the Yom Kippur War, and to the Arabs as the War of Ramadan.

THE DATA PROBLEM

But data—or at least reliable data—was not easy to obtain. The author of this book, who has devoted much of his adult life to studying and writing about military history, soon was engaged in a diligent search for Middle East data, not only for use with the QJM, but also in studies for the Pentagon, and as a topic for books and articles on the historical significance of the war. In fact I was already under contract to write a book about the previous Arab-Israeli Wars, and had visited the Middle East a little more than a year before the war. In four subsequent trips I collected data from as many official and unofficial sources as possible in Israel, Egypt, Jordan, Syria, and Lebanon.

Military security barriers were formidable in all of these countries, which understandably did not wish to reveal any of their military secrets for publication. On the other hand, all of the participants had things to be proud of about their performance in the war, and all had reasons for wanting to have their side of the story at least understood by a serious military historian who was bent upon publishing a book about that war and the previous wars.

In October of 1975 both the Israelis and the Egyptians sponsored international symposia to commemorate their rather different images of the war—one in Jerusalem in mid-month, one in Cairo toward the end of the month. By the time these two conferences were over, I felt that I had enough data to undertake serious QJMA analyses of the October War, and its predecessor, the 1967 Six-Day War. In fact, my colleagues and I had already begun some tentative QJM analyses, which I had discussed with military friends in Egypt and Israel, and which had provoked comments and reactions enough to enable me to refine the data further, and to write detailed narratives of all of the main engagements of the wars.

For a number of reasons we gave first priority to analyzing the October War engagements. In the first place, we were struck by a remark made in 1974 by a senior US Army general, who was in a position to know what he was talking about. "Not a one of the models currently in use by the Army," the general told me, "can replicate *any* of the battles of the October War." That was a challenge that had to be met.

We first looked at three battles on the Sinai Front: (1) the Egyptian crossing and consolidation on October 6 and 7; (2) the ill-fated Israeli counterattack of October 8; and (3) the equally ill-fated Egyptian offensive of October 14. Figure 9-1 shows the principal data for the battle of the 6th-7th, as I had discussed it at some length in the fall of 1975 with Egyptian staff officers.

Figure 9-1
SUEZ CANAL ASSAULT, OCTOBER 6-7, 1973
COMPARISON AVAILABLE FORCES ON EAST BANK

	Egyptians (Off)	Israelis (Def)	Ratio
	Elms 5 Inf Divs	1 Inf Bde (-)	
	Misc Commando,	1 Armd Bde	
	Engr, Arty, AA	Misc Arty, AA	
Troops	62,000	12,000	5.17-1.00
Tanks	500	280	1.79-1.00
Artillery Tubes	960	44	21.82-1.00
Close Air Support Sorties	150	90	1.67-1.00
Firepower Score° (OLI 1,000)	788.10	218.40	3.61-1.00
P/P (without CEV)	334.51	372.70	1.00-1.14
P/P (Israeli 1.5 CEV)	334.51	559.05	1.00-1.67
Surprise Considered (WW II Factors)			
P'/P' (without CEV)	779.59	347.32	2.24-1.00
P'/P' (Israeli 1.5 CEV)	779.59	520.99	1.50-1.00

°Includes AA, AT and c. 200 Egyptian tanks on West Bank.

One thing that had become evident to me in my study of the Arab-Israeli Wars was a consistent ground combat effectiveness superiority of the Israelis over the Arabs, obviously similar to the equally consistent superiority of the Germans over their enemies in World War II. I did not as yet have any idea what the quantitative value of this superiority was, but estimated that it was 50 percent or greater. My Egyptian friends were willing to admit that there was a measure of Israeli combat effectiveness superiority, but could not accept my estimate of 50 percent. So, in discussions with them we used a figure of 25 percent, comparable to the German superiority over the Western Allies in World War II. It soon became evident, however, that 25 percent was too low, so Figure 9-1 reflects our early calculations using the 50 percent estimated.

PRELIMINARY ANALYSIS

My Egyptian friends agreed, of course, that they had achieved surprise, and so we included the values for major surprise which had been developed in the original QJM analyses of the Italian campaigns of 1943 and 1944. Figure 9-1 shows the calculation of relative combat power first without applying the 1.5 factor for Israeli combat effectiveness, then with it, and it shows both of these same calculations with and without surprise. It will be seen that even without the inclusion of the combat effectiveness factor, but allowing for the Israeli advantage of a fortified defense, and the Egyptian disadvantage of crossing a major water obstacle, the greatly outnumbered Israelis (including the reinforcements that arrived late on the 6th) had a calculated combat power greater than that of the much larger Egyptian forces that crossed the Canal that day. Israeli preponderance is, of course, greater where the 1.5 CEV factor is included.

When, however, the factor of surprise was entered in the calculation, the Egyptians had a clear cut advantage—with or without the Israeli CEV preponderance—quite consistent with the successes they actually won on those days. To me these results meant that the Israeli defensive concept for the Bar Lev Line was sound, and that they had been defeated only because the Egyptians had achieved surprise. The Egyptians agreed with my conclusion.

Not long after this I had a chance to discuss this analysis with a prominent Israeli general, who had been one of the principal commanders on the Sinai Front during the war. He expressed considerable interest, but pointed out to me that at no time on the 6th or 7th had the Israelis been able to concentrate as many as 280 tanks at the front. By the time the two reserve armor brigades with about 190 tanks had reached the Bar Lev Line, the original 100 tanks that had been just behind the line had almost all been lost to Egyptian Saggers and RPG-2s. "It was really an entirely new battle on the 7th," he remarked.

I was somewhat chagrined that I had not realized this without the Israeli general's help. One of the fundamental concepts of the QJM from the beginning has been that an engagement lasts until one side or the other either clearly has, or clearly has not, achieved its mission, *or* when major losses or the arrival of reinforcements so changes the situation that a new engagement has obviously begun. Clearly, with the arrival of the two Israeli reserve brigades near the front during the night of

October 6-7, there was a new engagement. Figure 9-2 shows a recalculation of the October 6 Engagement.

Figure 9-2
SUEZ CANAL ASSAULT, OCTOBER 6, 1973, 1400-2000
COMPARISON AVAILABLE FORCES ON EAST BANK

	Egyptians (Off)	Israelis (Def)	Ratio
	Elms 5 Inf Divs	1 Inf Bde (-)	
	Misc Commando,	1 Armd Bde	
	Engr, Arty, AA	Misc Arty, AA	
Troops	30,750	4,005	7.68-1.00
Tanks	c. 30	100	1.00-3.33
Artillery Tubes	960	44	21.82-1.00
Close Air Support Sorties	50	30	1.67-1.00
Firepower Score° (OLI 1,000)	375.05	92	4.07-1.00
P/P (without CEV)	159.19	157	1.02-1.00
P/P (Israeli 1.5 CEV)	159.19	235	1.00-1.48
Surprise Considered (WW II Factors)			
P'/P' (without CEV)	371	146	2.67-1.00
P'/P' (Israeli 1.5 CEV)	371	219	1.69-1.00

°Includes AA, AT and c. 200 Egyptian tanks on West Bank.

Figure 9-3 shows the principal results of the analyses of the early major battles on the Sinai Front on October 6, 7, 8, and 14. Actually each of these battles (except that of the 8th) had been two engagements, one on the front of the Egyptian Second Army north of the Great Bitter Lake, and one on the front of the Egyptian Third Army, south of the lakes. Thus Figure 9-3 shows seven engagements. (See the map, Figure 9-4.)

Figure 9-3
1973 WAR, SUEZ-SINAI FRONT
ANALYSES OF EARLY ENGAGEMENTS

		Oct	N_a/N_i	W_a/W_i	Basic P/P	Supr/ Disrptn	Refined P/P	Result	Effective PR/PR	Israel CEV	Average
1.	Suez Canal (N)	6	6.62	2.96	0.98	2.39	2.34	6.39	2.28	1.03	
2.	Suez Canal (S)	6	7.57	2.98	1.06	2.36	2.50	6.51	2.30	1.09	
3.	Egypt Bldp (N)	7	4.57	2.76	1.33	–	1.33	3.21	1.64	0.81	
4.	Egypt Bldp (S)	7	4.11	2.93	1.51	–	1.51	4.49	1.90	0.79	
5.	Kantara-Firdan	8	2.11	1.60	1.40	–	1.40	4.19	1.84	0.76	
6.	Egypt Off (N)	14	1.87	1.42	0.82	–	0.82	−9.05	0.36	2.30	
7.	Egypt Off (S)	14	2.03	1.93	1.34	–	1.34	−6.94	0.42	3.20	1.42

ANOMALIES AND HYPOTHESES

It will be seen that in Figure 9-3 we have followed the same procedure for comparing calculated P/P to effective PR/PR that has been followed in early analyses, as, for instance, that of the four Eastern Front

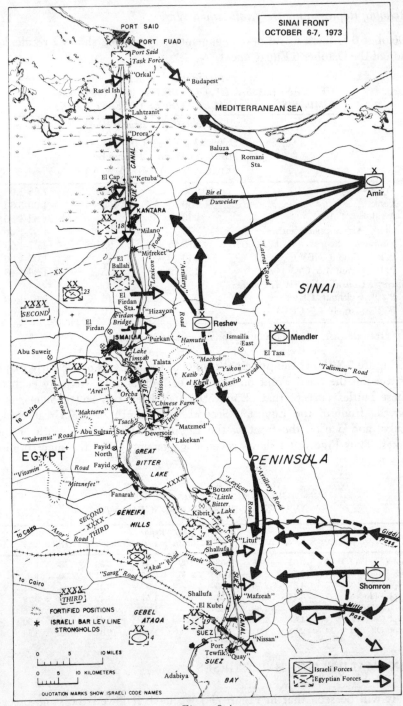

Figure 9-4

122

battles in Figure 7-9. The effect of surprise was included for the battles of the 6th and 7th (major surprise for the 6th, and substantial surprise for the 7th), but not for those of the 8th and 14th. The most interesting thing to emerge from this set of figures is that they suggest that there was little Israeli combat effectiveness superiority on October 6, and that the Egyptians were actually superior on the 7th and 8th. However, on the 14th the Israeli CEV value is close to 2.

We seriously doubted that there could have been any such fluctuations in Israeli combat effectiveness, even though the Egyptians—with far superior numbers—were victorious on three of those days. In contemplating these troublesome results, I suddenly remembered the four Eastern Front battles of World War II shown in Figure 7-9. In each of the October War battles in which the Egyptians showed a higher combat effectiveness than normal, they had held the initiative in operations which they had carefully planned and rehearsed. (This was as true on the 8th, when they were on the defense, as it had been on the 6th and 7th, when they were the attackers.) This was also true in the two World War II battles in which the Russians had apparently had a higher combat effectiveness than normal. Obviously, and quite logically, both the Egyptians and the Russians had received some sort of bonus in their combat power as a result of their special preparations for these battles, and for their possession of the initiative under these circumstances. The question was, what was the bonus, and how to calculate and represent it?

Going back to the similar discrepancies noted on the Eastern Front in World War II, I noticed that the difference in combat effectiveness of the participants on that front was of comparable magnitude—a differential in the vicinity of 100 percent or more for most battles. Suddenly three hypotheses fell into place to resolve these anomalies, and also to give consistent relationships between the value of surprise in World War II and in the Six-Day and October Wars.

Here are the hypotheses:

1. When a force with a lower CEV is operating in a well-planned, usually rehearsed, set-piece situation, the CEV differential is reduced by one-third.

2. The effects of surprise in the 1967 and 1973 Wars are approximately 133 percent of effects of surprise in World War II (interestingly consistent with a recent Soviet observation on the increased significance of surprise, and with an Israeli study on surprise).

3. Disruptive effects of surprise last for approximately three days; on the second day the effect is two-thirds that of the first day; on the third day the effect is one-third that of the first day.

Figure 9-5 shows the effect of the first and third of the new hypotheses on the Eastern Front Data of Figure 7-9. (The second hypothesis—increase in surprise since World War II—is, of course, not applicable.)

Note that in Figure 7-9 we had a range of calculated German CEVs ranging from 3.58 to 1.47, a difference of more than 200 percent. The high CEVs were for German offensives, the low ones were for Soviet attacks. I had thought that possibly the postures might be the key, until this study led to the formulation of the first hypothesis—the bonus which accrues to a force of lower CEV when it is able to operate within the parameters of a carefully prepared, usually rehearsed, set-piece battle. Applying that, and the value for lingering disruption for surprise, in Figure 9-5 we got CEVs ranging from 3.1 to 2.43, with those for 1943 clustering very closely to the average, 2.64.

When, as shown in Figure 9-6 we apply these same three hypotheses to the first seven engagements on the Suez Front in 1973, the peculiar CEVs which we saw in Figure 9-3 are greatly modified, and become quite consistent with each other, and with the World War II Eastern Front results in Figure 9-5.

PREPARING FOR A COMPREHENSIVE STUDY

We had a chance to examine the Middle East Wars further in a study done for the benefit of US Government agencies concerned with American policy in the Middle East, and with planning to meet various possible contingencies in that most volatile of regions.[31] Although we were authorized to use classified information—which would have made this a classified study—a review of the classified information led us to the conclusion that the unclassified data that HERO had been compiling for more than two years was at least as accurate and reliable.

The objective of the study was to analyze the engagements from each war, quantitatively (using the QJM) and qualitatively (as military historians), to ascertain the following:

a. Relative combat effectiveness of opponents for each engagement;
b. Patterns or differences in Arab relative CEVs;
c. Patterns or differences between Arab and Israeli performance in 1967 and in 1973;
d. Changes in Israeli and Arab relative CEVs, between offense and defense;
e. The significance of the presence or absence of air support;
f. The extent to which outcomes were influenced by other combat variables.

The major engagements of the 1967 War are shown in Figure 9-7.[32]

[31] *Comparative Analysis; Arab and Israeli Combat Performances, 1967 and 1973 Wars,* HERO, June 1976.

[32] For more details on these battles and their locations, see the author's *Elusive Victory, The Arab-Israeli Wars, 1947-1974,* New York, 1978, *passim.*

Figure 9-5
WORLD WAR II SOVIET-GERMAN OPERATIONS

Operation	N_r/N,	Fire-Power Factor	Set Piece Factor	Basic P/P	Surprise/Disruptn	Refined P/P	Effective German CEV P/P	CEV	Average
1. Ukraine '41	1.14	0.85	—	1.22	0.75°	0.92	0.30	3.10	
2. Lengrad '43	4.00	4.83	1.6	3.54	—	3.54	1.51	2.34	
3. Kursk-O '43	1.45	1.27	—	2.04	—	2.04	0.76	2.68	
4. Belg-Khrkv	4.67	5.03	1.6	3.81	—	3.81	1.57	2.43	2.65

*First Day—0.38; Second Day—0.59; Third Day—0.79; Average for five days—0.75

Figure 9-6
1973 WAR, SUEZ-SINAI FRONT
REVISED ANALYSES OF EARLY ENGAGEMENTS

With Hypotheses		N_a/N_i	W_a/W_i	Basic P/P	Set Piece	Surp/Disrptn	Refined P/P	Effective PR/PR	Israel CEV	CEV Average
1. Suez Canal (N)	6	6.62	2.96	0.98	1.33	3.19	4.16	2.28	1.83	
2. Suez Canal (S)	6	7.57	2.98	1.06	1.33	3.14	4.43	2.30	1.92	
3. Egypt Bldp (N)	7	4.57	2.76	1.33	1.33	2.46	4.35	1.64	2.65	
4. Egypt Bldp (S)	7	4.11	2.93	1.51	1.33	2.42	4.86	1.90	2.56	
5. Kantara-Firdan	8	2.61	1.60	1.40	1.33	1.73	3.22	1.84	1.75	
6. Egypt off (N)	14	1.87	1.42	0.82	—	—	0.82	0.36	2.30	
7. Egypt off (S)	14	2.03	1.93	1.34	—	—	1.34	0.42	3.20	2.32

The major engagements of the October 1973 War are shown on Figure
9-8. We organized our information about weapons into approximate
Tables of Organization and Equipment (TO&E) summaries for each
participant in each war, allocating known or estimated weapons inventories to known formations. Figure 9-9 gives an example of how we did
that for the Israeli forces in 1967.

We allocated known or estimated overall personnel and tank losses for
each participant in each war to the various engagements or battles. When
we had solid data, we used that. Otherwise, we distributed the known
overall losses among engagements on a basis that seemed to be consistent
with detailed historical scenarios prepared in the process of other research.
Figure 9-10 shows a typical example of battle casualties allocations for
the Israelis and Arabs on the Sinai Front in the 1967 War. Figure 9-11
shows a similar allocation of tank losses. Comparable data breakdowns
are shown in the study report for each front in each war, both personnel
casualties and armor losses.

Figure 9-7
ENGAGEMENTS, SIX-DAY WAR, JUNE 1967

No.	Date	Engagement
	Sinai Front	
67-1	June 5	Rafah
67-2	5-6	Abu Ageila-Um Katef
67-3	5-7	Gaza Strip
67-4	5-6	El Arish
67-5	5-6	Bir Lahfan
67-6	6	Jebel Libni
67-7	7	Bir Hama-BirGifgafa
67-8	7	Bir Hassna-Bir Thamada
67-9	7-8	Mitla Pass
67-10	8	Bir Gifgafa
67-11	8	Nakhl
	West Bank Front	
67-21	June 5-7	Jerusalem
67-22	5-6	Jenin
67-23	6-7	Kabatiya
67-24	6-7	Tilfit-Zababida
67-25	7	Nablus
	Golan Front	
67-31	9	Golan
67-32	9	Zaoura-Kala
67-33	9	Tel Fahar
67-34	9-10	Rawiya

Figure 9-8
ENGAGEMENTS, 1973 WAR

Number	Oct.	Engagement
	Suez-Sinai Front	
73-01	6	Suez Canal Assault (N)
73-02	6	Suez Canal Assault (S)
73-03	7	Second Army Buildup
73-04	7	Third Army Buildup
73-05	8	Kantara-Firdan
73-06	14	Egypt Offensive (N)
73-07	14	Egypt Offensive (S)
73-08	15-16	Deversoir (Chinese Farm II)
73-09	16-17	Chinese Farm II
73-10	18	Deversoir West
73-11	19-21	Jebel Geneifa
73-12	12-22	Ismailia
73-13	22	Shallufa I
73-14	23-24	Adabiya
73-15	23-24	Suez
73-16	23-24	Shallufa II
	Golan Front	
73-21	6-7	Ahmadiyeh
73-22	6-7	Kuneitra
73-23	6	Rafid
73-24	7-8	Yehudia - El Al
73-25	7-8	Nafekh
73-26	8-9	Mt. Hermonit
73-27	8	Mt. Hermon I
73-28	8-10	Hushniyan
73-29	8-10	Tel Faris
73-30	11-13	Tel Shams
73-31	11-12	Tel Shaar
73-32	13	Tel El Hara
73-33	15	Kfar Shams-Tel Antar
73-34	16	Naba
73-35	19	Arab Counteroffensive
73-36	21	Mt. Hermon II
73-37	22	Mt. Hermon III

Figure 9-9.

ESTIMATED ISRAELI ARMAMENT SUMMARIES, 1967

	Inf Bde	Meczd Bde	Armd Bde	1/12 Div — Armd Rgt	1/12 Div — Arty Rgt	1/12 Div — 1/36 Bde Misc Units	9 Arty Rgts	2 Armd Rgts	14 Inf/Para Bde	2 Meczd Bde	8 Armd Bde	Totals
Personnel	4,300	4,300	3,600	2,000	1,000	25,000	9,000	4,000	60,200	8,600	28,800	135,600
Pistol	430	430	360	200	100	2,500	900	400	6,020	860	2,880	13,560
Rifle	3,870	3,870	3,240	1,800	900	22,500	8,100	3,600	54,180	7,740	25,920	122,040
Machine Gun, lt	120	80	40	30	10	250	270	60	1,680	160	320	2,740
Machine Gun, hvy	80	60	40	30	20	420	270	60	1,120	120	320	2,310
Mortar, 81mm	20	10	—	—	—	—	—	—	280	20	—	300
Mortar, 4.2"	12	8	—	—	5	—	—	—	168	16	—	184
Bazooka	20	10	—	—	—	45	45	—	280	20	—	390
AT Missile SS-10/11	12	4	—	—	—	78	—	—	168	8	—	254
RR, 106mm	6	4	—	—	—	—	—	—	84	8	—	92
APC, Halftrack	50	200	20	12	3	126	27	24	700	400	160	1,437
AA, lt, 20mm	16	12	12	6	2	140	18	12	224	24	96	514
AA, lt, 40mm	—	—	—	—	4	76	36	—	—	—	—	112
Hawk	—	—	—	—	—	50	—	—	—	—	—	50
How, 105mm	—	—	—	—	—	—	(4)96	—	—	—	—	96
How, 155mm	—	—	—	—	—	—	(3)72	—	—	—	—	72
Gun, 155mm	—	—	—	—	—	—	(1)24	—	—	—	—	24
Gun, 175mm	—	—	—	—	—	—	(1)12	—	—	—	—	12
Tanks	10	30	90	40	—	—	—	80	140	60	720	1,000
AMX-113	—	10	(30)	(10)	—	—	—	(20)	—	20	(240)	150
M-48 (90)	10	20	(90)(60)	(30)	—	—	—	(80)(20)	—	(60)	(720)(480)	200
Super Sherman {	—	—	—	—	—	—	—	—	—	—	—	400
Centurion {	—	—	—	—	—	—	—	—	—	—	—	250
APC, Halftrack	50	200	20	75	100	125	27	24	700	400	160	1,436
Trucks	150	150	150	100	100	2,500	900	150	2,100	300	1,200	8,586
SP Mounts	30	30	38	19	25	200	225	38	420	76	304	1,263

Figure 9-10.
ESTIMATED ALLOCATION OF BATTLE CASUALTIES,
SINAI FRONT, JUNE 5-8, 1967, INCLUSIVE

Date	Engagements								Egyptian			Israeli		
June	Egypt	Israel	Egypt	Israel	Egypt	Israel	Egypt	Israel	Daily Eng	Misc	Cumulative	Daily Eng	Misc	Cumulative
5 (1)	(1) 3,000	(1) 500	(2) 1,000	(2) 200	(3) 250	(3) 45	(4) 250	(4) 85	3,000	—	3,000	500	—	500
6	—	—	—	—	(3) 500	(3) 20	—	—	1,500	—	4,500	300	30	860
	—	—	—	—	—	—	—	—	500	500	5,500	20	—	880
	—	—	—	—	—	—	—	—	500	—	6,000	50	—	930
(5)	(5) 500	(5) 50	(7) 600	(7) 45	(8) 600	(8) 30	—	—	1,700	1,500	9,200	115	10	1,045
(6)	(6) 500	(6) 40	—	—	—	—	—	—	600	—	9,800	60	—	1,105
8 (10)	(10) 500	(10) 40	(11) 684	(11) 24	—	—	(9) 600	(9) 60	1,184	1,900	12,884	64	15	1,194

Figure 9-11.
ESTIMATED ALLOCATION OF TANK LOSSES,
SINAI FRONT, JUNE 5-8, INCLUSIVE

Date	Engagements								Egyptian				Israeli			
June	Egypt	Israel	Egypt	Israel	Egypt	Israel	Egypt	Israel	Daily Loss	Cum Loss	Re-turn	Net Loss	Daily Loss	Cum Loss	Re-turn	Net Loss
5 (1)	(1) 70	(1) 15	(2) 40	(2) 19	(3) 60	(3) 4	(4) 80	(4) 13	70	70	—	70	15	15	—	15
6	—	—	—	—	(3) 30	(3) 4	—	—	180	250	—	250	36	51	—	51
	—	—	—	—	—	—	—	—	30	280	5	275	4	55	2	53
	—	—	—	—	—	—	—	—	30	310	—	305	11	66	—	64
(5)	(5) 30	(5) 11	(7) 30	(7) 5	(8) 30	(8) 10	—	—	90	400	18	377	25	91	6	83
(6)	(6) 30	(6) 10	—	—	—	—	—	—	100	500	—	477	16	107	—	99
8 (10)	(10) 100	(10) 11	—	—	—	—	(9) 100	(9) 16	100	600	27	550	11	118	9	105
(10.1)	(10.1) 100	(10.1) 4	—	—	—	—	—	—	100	700	10	640	4	122	44	61

We followed a similar procedure to estimate the amount of close air support (CAS) available for each engagement. Figure 9-12 shows the allocations of fighter-bombers by Israelis and Egyptians for each day of the 1967 War. Allocations of CAS sorties to engagements were then made as shown in Figure 9-13.

DATA ANALYSIS FOR 1967 WAR

Figure 9-14, "QJM Analysis Summary, 1967 War, Sinai Front," provides a summation of analyses of the eleven engagements on that front after the data had been organized, and shows how the hypotheses were applied.

As in previous examples, Column 1 is a list of the engagements.

Column 2 is a manpower strength comparison, Arab strength divided by Israeli strength; thus for the Battle of Rafah the two sides were virtually identical in numerical strength, 19,500 Egyptians opposed by 19,520 Israelis; at Abu Ageila the Egyptians, 18,450 strong, were outnumbered by 19,280 attacking Israelis.

Column 3 is the OLI firepower comparison; the total Egyptian "proving ground" firepower inventory available for the battle (including airpower) is divided by the total Israeli firepower (also including airpower).

Column 4 shows the basic combat power ratio, reflecting the effects of all variable factors except for those directly related to troop and command quality and behavior.

Column 5 shows the effects of surprise or postsurprise disruption; in all of these instances in the 1967 War the effects of surprise favored the Israelis, and thus the factors degrade Egyptian performance.

Column 6 is the recalculated combat power ratio, to include the effects of the surprise factor.

Column 7 (PR/PR) is the effective combat power ratio based upon the Outcome assessment.

Column 8, showing the relative combat effectiveness values (CEVs) of the Israelis with respect to the Egyptians, is derived by dividing Column 6 by Column 7; i.e., by dividing the combat ratio which should theoretically have existed (from what we know of the statistics of the battle) by the combat ratio which was actually demonstrated on the battlefield.

Column 9 shows the average Israeli CEVs for the first half of the campaign, for the second half, and overall.

Column 10, applying only to the Battle of the Gaza Strip where the principal defending force was a Palestinian division, converts the CEV for troops other than "standard" on the basis of a conversion factor, in which the Palestinian division is assumed to be half as good as an Egyptian division of the same size and weapons strength. While this

Figure 9-12
FIGHTER-BOMBER OPERATIONS, SINAI FRONT, 1967

	Israeli Availabilities*						Egyptian Availabilities**					
			Losses		Sorties				Losses		Sorties	
June	On Hand	In Com-mission	Day	Cum	Total	CAS	On Hand	In Com-mission	Day	Cum	Total	CAS
5	243	219	17	17	767	78	358	179	300	300	37	28
6	226	192	6	23	672	152	58	30	20	320	30	20
7	220	187	6	29	655	152	38	20	10	330	20	0
8	214	182	6	35	637	245	28	?	0	330	?	0
9	209	178	5	40	622	***						
10	204	173	0	40	607	***						

*Israeli in commission rate: 90% first day, 85% thereafter; 3.5 sorties per day; 50% CAS
**Egyptian in commission rate: 50%; one sortie/day; 75% CAS.
***Allocated to Golan Front.

Figure 9-13
ESTIMATED CLOSE AIR SUPPORT FIGHTER-BOMBER SORTIES
SUEZ-SINAI FRONT, JUNE 5-8, 1967, INCLUSIVE

Date	Available Sorties		Engagements							
June	'Egypt	Israel	Egypt	Israel	Egypt	Israel	Egypt	Israel	Egypt	Israel
5	28	78	(1) 18	(1) 46	(10) 0	(32) 0	— 10	— 38	— 0	— 38
	—	—			(2) 0	(2) 0	(3) 10	(3) 38	(4) 0	(4) 38
6	20	152	(5) 20	(5) 76	(7) 0	(7) 40	(8) 0	(8) 40		
7	0	152	(6) 0	(6) 52					(9) 0	(9) 20
8	0	245	(10) 0	(10) 123	(11) 0	(11) 122				

Figure 9-14
QJM ANALYSIS SUMMARY, 1967 WAR, SINAI FRONT

1	2	3	4	5	6	7	8	9	10	11
			Basic	Surp/	Refined	Effec- tive	Israeli	CEV		
	N_a/N_i	W_a/W_i	P/P	Drptn	P'/P'	PR/PR	CEV	Av.		
1. Rafah	1.00	0.65	0.84	0.50	0.43	0.25	1.73			
2. Abu Ageila	0.96	1.01	1.91	0.32	0.58	0.32	1.83			
3. Gaza Strip°	1.44	1.01	1.52	0.67	1.02	0.28	3.58°	2.07		(1.71)
4. El Arish	1.84	0.63	0.77	0.67	0.52	0.34	1.52			
5. Bir Lahfan	0.96	0.59	0.66	0.67	0.44	0.26	1.70		(1.79)	
6. Jebel Libni	0.96	0.65	0.80	0.67	0.53	0.31	1.72			
7. Bir Hama	1.14	0.78	0.80	0.83	0.67	0.31	2.16			
8. Bir Hassna	1.24	0.55	0.49	0.83	0.41	0.28	1.46			
9. Mitla Pass	3.03	1.81	0.81	0.83	0.67	0.37	1.82			
10. Bir Gifgafa	0.97	1.02	0.58	—	0.58	0.38	1.54			
11. Nakhl	0.98	0.51	0.55	—	0.55	0.28	1.96	1.78		
								1.91		(1.75)

°Palestinian division under Egyptian command.

Figure 9-15
QJM ANALYSIS SUMMARIES, 1967 WAR,
WEST BANK FRONT; GOLAN FRONT

1	2	3	4	5	6	7	8	9	10	11
			Basic	Surp/	Refined	Effec- tive	Israeli	CEV		
	N_a/N_i	W_a/W_i	P/P	Drptn	P'/P'	PR/PR	CEV	Av.		
21. Jerusalem	0.49	0.41	0.77	0.83	0.64	0.40	1.61	1.61°		
22. Jenin	0.57	0.39	0.62	0.85	0.53	0.44	1.21			
23. Kabatiya	0.77	0.69	1.18	0.90	1.06	0.58	1.82	1.52		
24. Tilfit- Zababida	1.02	0.58	0.85	0.90	0.77	0.44	1.76			
25. Nablus	0.80	0.41	0.56	0.95	0.53	0.41	1.31	1.54		
								1.54		
32. Zaoura-Kala	1.46	0.36	0.58	—	0.58	0.30	1.91°°		(2.48)	
33. Tel Fahar	1.52	0.36	0.76	—	0.76	0.30	2.54			
34. Rawiyeh	0.80	0.74	1.76	0.54	0.95	0.33	2.88			
								2.44		(2.63)

°June 5-7; not included in partial averages.
°°Israeli column takes wrong road; command failure; factor=0.77.

factor of 2.0 is arbitrary, it is consistent with substantial research into the relative quality of Arab forces, which is discussed further below. Thus the Israeli CEV of 3.58 at Rafah is converted to a value of 1.79 in terms of "standard" Egyptian troops. That the conversion factor is reasonably accurate is demonstrated by comparing this 1.79 figure to the 1.73 and 1.83 figures for Rafah and Abu Ageila, and to the revised average in Column 11, 1.75.

Column 11, then, provides revised average Israeli CEV figures with respect to the Egyptians, allowing for the conversion in Column 10.

Figure 9-15 shows similarly calculated Israeli CEV values for actions in which Israelis were opposed by Jordanians and Syrians. Column 10 applies a correction to allow for what would probably have been the CEV at Zaoura-Kala, had one Israeli column not taken the wrong road.

The calculations in these two figures show that the Israeli combat effectiveness superiority over the Egyptians was on the average 75 percent, or a CEV of 1.75; their superiority over the Jordanians was on the average 54 percent, or a CEV of 1.54; Israeli superiority over the Syrians was on the average 163 percent, or a CEV of 2.63; and Israeli superiority over the Palestinians was about 250 percent, or a CEV of 3.50.

Normalizing these relationships on the Palestinian performance provides the following interesting comparisons:

Israelis	3.50	(1.54)	(1.75)	(2.63)			
Jordanians	2.27	(1.00)			(1.14)	(1.71)	
Egyptians	2.00		(1.00)		(1.00)		(1.50)
Syrians	1.33			(1.00)		(1.00)	(1.00)
Palestinians	1.00						

DATA ANALYSIS FOR 1973 WAR

Figure 9-16, "QJM Force Quality Analysis Summary, 1973 War, Suez-Sinai Front," is the same kind of overall summary of quantitative analysis of the 1973 War as is found in Figure 9-14 for the 1967 War. There are some minor differences, however:

Column 5 is new. This provides a basis for assessing the effects of the first hypothesis; i.e., the extent to which an attacking force, qualitatively inferior to the defender, is able to improve itself by special prebattle preparations and rehearsals for what is called a "set-piece battle." This was the situation that existed when the Egyptians were crossing the Suez Canal, and continuing the attack, on October 6 and 7, and when they waited—fully prepared—for the expected Israeli counterattack, on October 8.

Column 6 is the same as Column 5 in Figure 9-10, but includes the effects of the set-piece factor as well as the factor for surprise or post-surprise disruption; Column 7 is the same as Column 6 in 9-10; Column 8 is the same as Column 7 in 9-12; and so forth, through Column 10.

Figure 9-16

QIM FORCE QUALITY ANALYSIS SUMMARY, 1973 WAR, SUEZ-SINAI FRONT

1	2	3	4	5	6	7	8	9	10	11	12	13	14
	N_a/N_t	W_a/W_t	Basic P/P	Set Piece	Surp/ Disrptn	Refined P/P	Effec- tive PR/PR	Israel CEV	CEV Average	Quality¹ Arab	Israeli	Mod Is CEV	CEV Average
1. Suez Canal (N)	6.62	2.96	0.98	1.33	3.19	4.16	2.28	1.83		2	2	1.83	
2. Suez Canal (S)	7.57	2.98	1.06	1.33	3.14	4.43	2.30	1.92		2	2	1.92	
3. Egypt Bldp (N)	4.57	2.76	1.33	1.33	2.46	4.35	1.64	2.65		2°	2	2.04	
4. Egypt Bldp (S)	4.11	2.93	1.51	1.33	2.42	4.86	1.90	2.56		2°	2	1.97	
5. Kantara-Firdan	2.61	1.60	1.40	1.33	1.73	3.22	1.84	1.75		2	2	1.75	
6. Egypt off (N)	1.87	1.42	0.82	—	—	0.82	0.36	2.30		2°	2	1.77	
7. Egypt off (S)	2.03	1.93	1.34	—	—	1.34	0.42	3.20		2°	2	2.46	1.94
8. Deversoir	1.34	1.43	2.08	—	0.35	0.73	0.55	1.34	2.19	2	2°	1.74	
9. Chinese Farm	1.28	1.08	1.54	—	0.57	0.88	0.47	1.87		2	2	1.87	
10. Deversoir W	1.12	0.70	0.97	—	0.78	0.76	0.43	1.76		2	2	1.76	
11. J. Geneifa	2.10	1.21	1.31	—	—	1.31	0.35	3.71		2-3	2	2.47	
12. Ismailia	1.40	0.91	1.16	—	—	1.16	1.06	1.09		1-2	2°	1.78	
13. Shaluffa I	1.58	1.01	1.14	—	—	1.22	0.27	4.48		3	2	1.82	
14. Adabiya	1.34	0.95	1.22	—	—	1.14	0.42	2.74		2-3	2	2.23	
15. Suez City	1.53	0.69	1.07	—	1.52	1.63	1.22	1.33		2	2°	1.73	
16. Shaluffa II	1.93	0.92	1.31	—	—	1.31	0.34	3.81	2.60	2-3	2	2.54	2.03
									2.40				1.98

*Command Failure; factor=0.77

¹QUALITY: 1=Elite (factor=1.5); 2=Average (factor=1.0); 3=Below Average (factor=0.5)

Columns 11 and 12 show the estimated effects of differences in force quality (as for Palestinians in Figure 9-10) and command failure (as the Israelis' taking the wrong road in Figure 9-15).

Column 13 shows modified Israeli CEVs that take into consideration the factors of Columns 11 and 12.

Column 14 shows the averages of the modified Israeli CEVs.

Figure 9-17 goes through the same process for the Golan Front.

As with the 1967 War, the refined analyses show remarkably consistent values in relative combat effectiveness of the opponents in each of the two sets of data: that for the Suez-Sinai Front, and that for the Golan Front. The analyses show that the Israeli combat effectiveness superiority over the Egyptians was on the average 98 percent, or a CEV of 1.98; Israeli superiority over the Syrians was 154 percent, or a CEV of 2.54; superiority over the Jordanians was 88 percent, or a CEV of 1.88; superiority over the Iraqis was 243 percent or a CEV of 3.43.

A normalized comparison, similar to that for the 1967 War, is shown below:

Israelis	3.43	(1.88)	(1.98)	(2.54)			
Jordanians	1.82	(1.00)			(1.35)		(1.05)
Egyptians	1.73		(1.00)			(1.28)	(1.00)
Syrians	1.35			(1.00)	(1.00)	(1.00)	
Iraqis	1.00						

We see that the Syrians had apparently improved between the two wars. In fact, however, the unique recent history of Syria tells us that we cannot draw any significant military operational conclusions from this data, although it has considerable politico-military implications.

The Syrians didn't do well in 1967. While the Israeli performance on June 9-10, 1967, was commendable, the results achieved were in part due to the fact that the Syrians withdrew without serious resistance. But, in scattered fighting the Syrians' performance was not good.

The reason for this is evident in the history of Syria between 1949 and 1967. There had been nine military coups d'etat, and after each coup the successful upstart had cleared out all potential rivals or enemies in the officer corps. The result was turmoil in the armed forces, with inevitable incompetence of the sort demonstrated in the 1967 War.

In late 1970, following a comparably poor Syrian performance against Jordan, there had been one more coup d'etat, led this time by the then Minister of War, Air Force General Hafez al Assad. The new President— a strong and able leader—swept the senior commanders away (evidence of the recent wars suggests that this could not have done serious harm), and put in his own men, who have remained in the military leadership of the country ever since. Thus an improvement in Syrian performance, a major improvement, was inevitable, no matter what the Israelis, the Egyptians, or anyone else had also done in the meantime.

Figure 9-17

QIM FORCE QUALITY ANALYSIS SUMMARY, 1973 WAR, GOLAN FRONT

1	2	3	4	5	6	7	8	9	10	11	12	13	14
	N_a/N_i	W_a/W_i	Basic P/P	Set Piece	Surp/ Disrptn	Refined P/P	Effective PR/PR	Israel CEV	CEV Average	Quality[1] Arab	Quality[1] Israeli	Mod Is CEV	CEV Average
21. Ahmadiyeh	3.96	1.03	0.34	1.52	2.37	1.22	0.47	2.57		2	2	2.57	
22. Kuneitra	4.89	1.66	0.60	1.52	2.77	2.53	1.35	1.87		2	2	1.87	
23. Rafid	3.94	0.91	0.38	1.52	3.14	1.81	1.74	1.04		1-2	2(B)	1.95	
24. Yehudia-El Al	3.49	0.84	0.35	—	2.43	0.85	0.45	1.89		1-2	2	2.36	
25. Nafekh	1.80	0.80	0.51	—	2.30	1.17	0.45	2.60		2	2	2.60	
26. Mt. Hermonit	5.99	1.25	0.41	1.52	1.91	1.19	0.57	2.10		2	2	2.10	
27. Mt. Hermon I	0.59	0.36	0.85	1.52	1.91	2.47	1.65	1.50		1	2	2.25	
28. Hushniyah	1.15	0.63	0.92	—	1.65	1.52	0.41	3.71	2.16	2	2	3.71	2.43
29. Tel Faris	1.33	0.84	1.32	—	1.68	2.22	0.43	5.17		2*	2	3.98	
30. Tel Shams	1.20	0.76	1.62	—	—	1.62	0.47	3.43		2	2	3.43	
31. Tel Shaar	1.46	0.83	1.46	—	—	1.46	0.45	3.26		2	2	3.26	
32. Tel El Hara	1.14	1.09	0.77	—	—	0.77	0.29	2.66		I*	2	1.52	
33. Kfar Shams	1.09	1.09	1.99	—	—	1.99	0.37	5.39		I*	2	3.07	
34. Naba	1.05	0.94	0.53	—	—	0.53	0.37	1.42		J	2	1.92	
35. Arab Cntroff	2.22	1.84	0.94	—	—	0.94	0.39	2.40		2-J-I	2	2.40	
36. Mt. Hermon II	0.83	0.60	1.61	—	—	1.61	1.55	1.04		1	2	1.56	
37. Mt. Hermon III	0.42	0.37	0.95	—	—	0.95	0.36	2.63	3.05	1(B)	2	2.63	2.64
									2.63				2.54

*Command Failure; factor=0.77

[1]QUALITY: Syrian: 1=Elite (factor=1.5); 2=Average (factor=1.0); I=Iraqi (factor=0.77); J=Jordanian (factor=1.35); (B)=Broken (factor=0.67)

Thus, the only consistent military comparison is that between the Israelis and the Egyptians in both wars. The comparisons are remarkably consistent and similar, but there is a small yet significant difference. We find that the Israeli CEV has increased by 13 percent, from 1.75 to 1.98. In other words the gap between the Egyptians and the Israelis had widened, not narrowed, as most of us had assumed.

COMPARATIVE ANALYSIS

Thus we have an apparent anomaly: Arab (Egyptian) performance in 1973 was better than in 1967, yet Israeli relative combat effectiveness was greater in 1973.

But the anomaly can be explained:

1. In 1967 the Israelis started with surprise; the Arabs never recovered;

2. In 1973 the Arabs started with greater surprise; the Israelis recovered in 3-4 days;

3. In 1967 Arab airpower was eliminated at the outset; Israeli air, unchallenged, completed the demoralization of the Arab ground forces;

4. In 1973 Israeli air never had a completely free hand;

5. In 1967 Arab top leadership was abysmal;

6. In 1973 top leadership was competent.

Looked at in this way, the anomaly is quite understandable and reconcilable. But this, in turn, leads to another question: Why had the Israelis, already so far ahead of the Egyptians in combat effectiveness, been able to pull further ahead? There are several reasons:

1. The Arabs focused on correcting 1967 faults, and on perfecting set-piece plans; they were locked into an effort to excel over the 1967 Israelis;

2. Meanwhile, the Israelis were making unremitting efforts to improve performance at all levels and in all respects: training, schooling, mobilization plans and procedures, etc.;

3. There was a substantially higher Israeli research and development capability, and apparently more intensive effort;

4. There was sound, objective Israeli professional military analysis of historical experience and current capabilities;

5. There was and is an Arab cultural tendency to allow emotion and wishful thinking to influence planning, evaluation, and operational leadership.

I have been criticized for this last generalization. Nevertheless, the Arab cultural tendencies toward wishful thinking, exaggeration, and the substitution of words for action are discussed at some length by anthropologist Dr. Raphael Patai in his book *The Arab Mind*.[33] Noteworthy is

[33] New York, 1976; see particularly Chapter IV.

Dr. Patai's quote from a Palestinian Arab: "Our hearts do the job of our brains. We exaggerate both in love and hate. We are emotional rather than coldly analytical. Honor is exaggerated at the expense of real need. We would *like* to see certain things and we think they *are*."[34] Interestingly, in 1975, an Egyptian general spoke to me of this Arab cultural tendency in almost identical words.

Finally, there was one other phenomenon which kept appearing in the data, with remarkable regularity and consistency. And it probably relates to point number 5, above, about Arab cultural tendencies.

Figure 9-18 shows that in all five of the campaigns surveyed in this study, the Israeli CEV *increased during the war*. The average Israeli CEVs from the first engagements we analyzed are invariably less than the average for the later engagements. This suggests that during these campaigns the Arab combat effectiveness declined perceptibly, and regularly, apparently a morale reaction to defeat, after the brave, wishful thinking claims of victories could no longer be believed by the claimant. (The alternative possibility of a steadily increasing Israeli effectiveness in a brief war is less reasonable from the standpoint of military judgment.) Note that in the first part of the 1973 War the Israeli CEV did *not* decline as a result of a series of defeats.

Figure 9-18
EFFECTS OF DEFEAT ON ARABS

	Israeli CEV	Average CEV
1967 War		
Sinai Front		
First 24 Hours	1.71	
24-72 Hours	1.78	1.75
West Bank Front		
First 24 Hours	1.52	
24-48 Hours	1.54	1.54
Golan Front		
First 12 Hours	2.48	
12-30 Hours	2.88	2.63
1973 War		
Suez-Sinai Front		
First 3 Days	1.90	
5th to 18th Day	1.03	1.98
Golan Front		
First 24 Hours	2.13	
5th to 16th Day	2.64	2.54

[34] *Ibid.*, p. 52.

From all of this we derived several conclusions relative to the objectives of this study, and with considerable significance in the light of current Middle East realities.

1. The Israeli CEV superiority over Arabs did *not* decline between 1967 and 1973; if anything, it increased slightly;

2. There are no reasons to anticipate a decline in the 1973 Israeli CEV superiority over the Arabs (about 100 percent) in the proximate future.

3. New political and military stability is reflected in the Syrian performance in 1973, approaching Egyptian performance and effectiveness, which seems to be an Arab standard.

4. The Israeli CEV superiority over Arabs had not been as great as that of Germans over Russians during most of World War II.

5. The Arab military threat to Israel's existence is not grave in the foreseeable future—until or unless there is true Arab unity, when numbers and determination *could* overcome the Israeli CEV superiority, just as these factors overcame the superior German CEV for Russians in World War II.

There was also a major methodological conclusion. The value of the QJM was reaffirmed as a unique tool for combat experience analysis, as a coherent, comprehensive theory of combat, and as a valid simulation of modern combat with modern weapons.

Israeli reactions to this analysis are ambivalent. Their military men are pleased by the recognition of their superb military performance which emerges so clearly from the analysis. On the other hand, they and Israeli policymakers are unhappy that the report could be interpreted as indicating that American military assistance to Israel is not needed as urgently as the Israelis insist. It is beyond the scope of this book to deal with these issues.

Egyptian reactions have also been interesting. Those Egyptians with whom I had earlier discussed the results of the analyses of relative Israeli and Egyptian CEVs were upset by the fact that my analyses have upgraded the Israeli CEV from an original estimate of 25-50 percent to nearly 100 percent. Their operations research analysts, who have studied the QJMA intensely, have taken the methodology represented by Figure 9-1, which I discussed in some detail with them in Cairo in 1975, and applied it to their own classified data on the October War. They apparently were chagrined that even with their own data they had to agree with my initial assumption that the Israelis did indeed have a clear-cut combat effectiveness superiority. But according to their calculations—I am told—it was a superiority of less than 50 percent. I do not know whether they have seen, or have reacted to, the "Comparative Analysis" study, since we had no authority to discuss it with them.

10

The Model
and Operations
Research

The reactions of professional operations research analysts to the QJM have ranged from intense interest to amused condescension. However, expressions of interest, encouragement, and support from OR specialists have been rare. The most common reaction has been to seek to explain why such a historical approach is scientifically invalid. In this chapter, with all of the objectivity I can muster, I will try to present—and respond to—the most important of the several objections and criticisms the QJM has encountered from OR analysts and theoreticians, and also to acknowledge the occasional instances of OR support which have been forthcoming.

At this point I should make clear my realization that the work of most military OR analysts is related to weapons systems and the operation of the physical laws of nature in the context of sophisticated modern military technology. To the extent that their work is rigorously scientific—and most of it is—they have every right to be impatient with the dabbling of unqualified non-scientists in their technical field of expertise, or with any suggestion such as one that the precise effects of the law of gravity might possibly be affected by historical evidence that there was a worm in the apple that struck Sir Francis Newton on the head.

Thus, what appears in these pages should not be constructed as being critical either of the valid, essential importance of operations research as a discipline of the utmost significance to America's security, or of the intelligence or ability of the typical OR analyst of military data. As a group, OR analysts share with lawyers my admiration as professional communities made up of people who are for the most part intelligent, analytical, and objective. And they are probably less parochial than others of the two professional communities with which I am associated: historians and soldiers. Nonetheless, as human beings, they are parochial to some extent.

But, as most OR analysts know, and some are more willing to admit this than others, their scientific techniques and experience, so reliable in dealing with the physical laws of nature, have questionable relevance to human behavior. Few OR analysts have had historical training, or have developed historical perspective. In fact, as a group they tend to share the impatience of an American technological folk-hero, Henry Ford, who once dismissed history as "bunk." Nevertheless, to the extent scientific evidence is available and relevant, when it comes to the behavioral laws of nature, history has been demonstrated by evidence that even OR analysts must respect, to be mankind's most reliable guide.[35]

IS HISTORY RELEVANT?

Scientists and OR specialists are understandably impressed by the magnitude of the changes over the past represented by modern developments in weapons and related technology. They observe these changes without the benefit of trained historical perspective, and it seems clear to them that these new things have completely invalidated war of the past—even the recent past.

Many of these people—who do not represent all of the American Defense Research Community, but who probably constitute a majority of it—are convinced by their experience that any simulation or representation of combat based upon historical experience is simply not relevant to modern war. To them the only possible way to plan scientifically for the future is to take the results of tests and evaluation of modern weapons and equipment, and around this to build up theoretical mathematical models based upon a combination of game theory and educated forecasting of future trends. From the past they will accept only those mathematical formulations and theories that have been developed by scientists and scholars of like mind, ideas not contaminated by inputs from backward looking historians or (in the standard stereotype) conservative military men trying to refight the last war.

There is a dichotomy in the thinking of such people because, as highly intelligent human beings, they are aware of the need for some kind of data from the real world as input for the forward-looking models they develop. For instance, they must somehow or other be able to project forward the effectiveness of their new weapons on the basis of comparison with existing information about the past performance of the outmoded weapons. And so, while scorning history, they are anxious for "experiential data." This selected "experiential data," of course, provides them with a tenuous link to the "real world," without in any way changing their contempt for history as such. Many do not recognize, and in fact reject, any

[35] T.N. Dupuy and Janice B. Fain, "The Laws Governing Combat," *National Defense,* Nov.-Dec., 1975.

thought that their experiential data is merely a highly selective slice of history, and that history is in reality a seamless web.

Nor do many of them see—without historical perspective—that the tremendous changes in weaponry and equipment which they observe today are (with the possible exception of nuclear weapons) hardly any more startling than other technological and weapons developments since the dawn of the Industrial Revolution. (For instance, as noted in Chapter 1, in the last century there has not been a single change in weapons technology with as great a statistically measurable impact on war as the transition from smoothbore infantry musket to rifled small arms in the 1840s and 1850s.) The reason for this is that the principal weapon of war is, and always has been, man himself. Thus the nature of warfare has changed only in its details (sometimes dramatically, but always relatively slowly) as man adapts himself and his thinking to new weapons and technology.

In our time there could be no more striking demonstration of this truism than the 1973 October War.

In fact, it has been the experience of the October War, and the ability of the QJM to reproduce it—even though, as the general said, "no existing models" could do so—that has led to increasingly respectful attention to the QJM in the Defense Research Community. But, nonetheless, the arguments and objections continue.

One reason for this is the human reaction of many members of a group of highly specialized professionals who resent intrusions into their area of expertise by investigators who have no credentials in the Operations Research field, no matter what their credentials may be elsewhere. These mathematically oriented, scientifically trained scholars and specialists tend to be scornful of the trial-and-error, rough-approximation-and-refinement approach of people whose professional background is in the imprecise fields of history and military operations.

These specialists resent, also, any suggestions that their carefully developed mathematical models of combat—most of them based upon the theories of the patron saint of military OR analysts, Frederick William Lanchester—are not inherently more valid than a historically derived model, whose inputs are based upon outdated, and irrelevant, past experience. In fact, some are even affronted by the suggestion that such a backward-looking model, questionably adapted to modern weapons, can compete in projecting the future with models designed *ab initio* to represent the effects of modern weapons and equipment.

HOW RELIABLE ARE OUR CURRENT MODELS?

There are three facts, however, which are overlooked in this quite human reaction.

First is the fact that, as demonstrated in 1973 by two military operations research analysts, the real-world validity of the weapons representations of the various OR mathematical models is no more realistic than that of the OLI representation of the QJM. Furthermore, the wide range of values which emerge from different OR approaches to weapons representations demonstrate clearly that there is no scientific precision whatsoever in at least a majority of these models.[36]

Second, the serious lack of precision and reliability of modern military models was revealed to all the world by a member of the OR community —Dr. J.A. Stockfish, of the highly respected Rand Corporation—in a study report which appeared in early 1975, entitled *Models, Data and War: A Critique of the Study of Conventional Forces*. A quote from the summary of that report will show how dubious is the claim of some OR analysts to scientific precision in their work; when they deal with the performance of men in combat:

"The outputs or assertions of [current campaign] models are of questionable worth because of inadequate empirical work, which should consist of both operational testing . . . and empirical study of past wars. . . . Without increased and definitive operational testing and empirical studies, the use of detailed models to treat larger force aggregations is probably of limited value in the analysis of conventional wars. Overall, we are left with faulty concepts, such as the firepower indexes, as empirical inputs for aggregative models, and an abundance of unverified—or only partially verified—detailed models.

"This condition results from an imbalance between empirical and theoretical endeavor in DoD analysis and study. The image of scientific activity—an image that depicts theories and models as being independently tested by experiment or appeal to experience, with the empirical work in turn casting up new insight that contributes to theoretical advance—does not seem to prevail in the military establishment. One aspect of this situation is that the unverified findings of modeling conducted by one organization can be taken as fact by another organization and used as inputs for the latter's model. Another aspect is that a number or a set of numbers constituting *data* can be admixtures of subtle concepts, subjective evaluations, and limited but hard evidence based on actual physical testing. The particular testing, however, may have been undertaken for purposes remote from the use that another study makes of the data."[37]

Third, "the proof of the pudding is in the eating." The QJM model can reproduce or represent the results of modern war with modern weapons; it has done so for the 1973 October War, even though no other models in use in the Department of Defense or its services could do so.

CRITICISMS OF THE QJM

Nevertheless, it is useful to examine the principal objections which OR analysts have expressed regarding the QJM, since it has been asserted

[36] See MORS Proceedings, Summer, 1973.

[37] J.A. Stockfish, *Models, Data and War: A Critique of the Study of Conventional Forces* (Santa Monica, 1975), pp. vi, vii.

that the good results of the QJM with historical combat are explicable in terms of "manipulated" data. This assertion implies that the good results of the QJM have no relevance to any forward-looking analysis.

Let's look at this question of manipulating numbers. There are perhaps three different ways this could be done. First, the weapons or other variable values could be selected arbitrarily to fit the circumstances of an engagement. Another, really a variant of the first kind of manipulation, would be to use the values, tables, and formulae so painfully developed over the years, but if the results didn't seem to fit preconceived notions, then change some numbers to make them fit, on the argument that every situation is unique, and that reasonable "judgment" must be applied. Third, if—after going through the QJM and Result formulae—the comparison is not what we want, we might change one of the two truly judgmental inputs to the Result formula: the assessed mission accomplishment, or the distance-advanced figure by measuring on another part of the map.

Who would be the wiser if HERO were arbitrarily to select data to fit pre-conceived results? Possibly this is the way "judgment" is exercised in the Quantified Judgment Model.

It should be clear from the preceding chapters that the word "Judgment" in the title of the method and the model refer to the original values and relationships selected at the outset of the developmental process. When we had, in our painstaking trial-and-error, iterative—even curve-fitting—process achieved a correlation of about 90 percent between theoretical outcomes and actual outcomes with our 60-Engagement Developmental Data Base, we codified the tables, formulae, and procedures. These were published in a monograph, entitled, "The Quantified Judgment Method of Analysis of Historical Combat Data," and it is those codified procedures, tables, and formulae that we have used consistently ever since. We have on some occasions refined and improved the methodology, and made some adjustments in tabular values and in formulae. But all such modifications have been applied to all previous analyses, to be sure of their validity, before being adopted. There is no selection of values by whim, thus disposing of the first manipulatory possibility.

As to the second, it is certainly true that some engagements do not fit into the standard patterns we have evolved with the methodology. For instance, the terrain of the western Sinai is neither flat desert nor open rolling terrain. So, for this situation we take a value that is the mean of the tabular values between which it fits. And there are other instances where the analyst must use his judgment in applying the rules. But using judgment in this manner does not permit him to ignore the rules; he simply adjusts the rules (without changing them in the slightest) to whatever degree may be necessary, to fit a unique or special situation to the methodology. Again, there can be no capricious assigning of values, simply because the standard values don't fit; adjustments must be logical in relation to the rules.

Finally, my colleagues and I would be the first to admit that there have been a number of times when we have gone through the calculation process, either by hand or with the programs in our calculator-computer, and gotten results that were not satisfactory. At that point Step 9, Analysis, of the QJMA procedure is applicable. This is how it is stated in the Monograph:[38]

"a. Is comparison consistent with relevant historical experience?
"b. Plot P_f/P_e and $R_f - R_e$ results, and compare to "Normal Battle Line" (may be done by calculation instead of plotting).
"c. If a and b appear seriously inconsistent, review data and narrative for hint of discrepancy."

In taking a hard look at the data, or at the Result Formula, under such circumstances, we sometimes discover things not previously noted. For instance, there may have been surprise involved that becomes evident only on more careful scrutiny of the narrative. Or this close scrutiny may reveal that there was a battalion, or some guns that were not included that should have been—or that were included but were actually not present—and so forth. A review of the outcome analysis may suggest that a more appropriate mission accomplishment assessment would be 6 rather than 7. (A change of 1 in the mission accomplishment assessment is the equivalent of .2 in the Combat Power Ratio; a value that is not insignificant, but also that is not a major change.)

Whatever changes the analyst may make as a result of following the procedure of Step 9, *he cannot make any change that cannot be fully substantiated and justified from the historical record.* And that record is there—wherever HERO found it in its documented data base compilation—for the review and scrutiny of anyone else who wishes to check on either the data or the process.

So, HERO pleads guilty to manipulating the numbers in its QJM analyses. After all, the whole process is one of quantified manipulation of historical data. But our manipulations are always rigorously substantiable from the historical record and in strict accordance with recorded rules and procedures. After all, someone may try to check up on us someday, and it would be very easy to do so!

Next there is the question of the curve-fitting process which led to the tables of variable values and the formulae from which the QJM variables are obtained. The mathematicians' argument is that if we have more than 60 variables, and only 60 engagements, it is a relatively simple process to get variable values that will fit the 60 engagements. This, however,

---

[38] And in Figure 4-2 of this book; see also Appendix, A, p. 205.

raises serious questions as to the validity and reliability of the variable values thus obtained.

This argument can be adequately dealt with in both theoretical and practical terms.

As to theory, the problem is in part one of semantics. The combat variables listed in the QJM Monograph are quantified values to represent conditions or circumstances that change from engagement to engagement. These include number of men, numbers and types of weapons, the comparative mobility characteristics of the opposing forces, the nature of the terrain, the nature of the weather, and so forth. While these are things that vary from battle to battle, and thus are combat variables, for any given battle there are hard, fixed, constant values. Thus they are not mathematical variables, and are not susceptible to any curve-fitting modification.

Actually, of the 70-odd combat variables which can be represented in QJMA, there are fewer than 20 which are variables affecting the QJM formula mathematically. Thus, the theoretical argument simply does not apply.

But even if it did, once again "the proof of the pudding is in the eating." These variables, developed for and with the 60-Engagement World War II Developmental Data Base, were found to be fully applicable to the 21-Engagement World War II Validation Data Base, and have also provided completely consistent results for the 1967 and 1973 Arab-Israeli Wars. In the light of the startling nature of the engagement outcomes of these latter wars, a coincidence is simply impossible in practical terms.

Some OR analysts have suggested that HERO has taken partial results of its QJM analyses, then put these back into the equations as inputs to get final results. This makes the whole process "statistically invalid." It is possible to see how someone who was not intimately familiar with the method might have drawn such an inference. The different calculations for our initial analysis of the October 6-7 battles on the Sinai Front in the October War (Figure 9-1) could be interpreted as suggesting this. So, too, might the comparative figures for the four 1941-1943 Soviet-German battles, or for the early engagements of the October and Six-Day War, in which comparisons are shown between calculations with and without the three hypotheses.

In fact, however, each set of calculations is completely self-contained, and is related to the data. There are *no* new inputs from intermediate calculations in these examples, or in any other applications of the Quantified Judgment Model.

It has also been suggested, by people who have been exposed to Figures 9-1 and 9-2, and others that are similar, that we have made the QJM fit the October War data by postulating values for surprise and combat effectiveness. This inference, again understandable on the part of those who are not familiar with the method and model, is readily corrected.

For those October War battles for which the record indicates that surprise was present, we calculated the effects of surprise by using the same procedure for modified values for mobility and vulnerability that had been developed and tested for World War II data. As has been discussed above in Chapter 9 we found that these values for surprise—for reasons that may relate to war technology, or may relate to faulty handling of dispersion in the model—may actually have been too low by about 30 percent. But the values were close enough to prove the influence of surprise on the outcome in such calculations as that in Figure 5-3. The more refined, and we believe more accurate, values for surprise in 1973 could be ascertained only after we had analyzed enough engagements to see a pattern.

As to the combat effectiveness value, it is true that in our first examples of October War analysis we arbitrarily assigned a tentative combat effectiveness value, simply because we knew that it was closer to reality than no combat effectiveness value. Again, our initial calculations, using this arbitrary value, revealed just that, and no more: an Israeli CEV of 1.5, or 1.25, was closer to the correct value (later determined to be nearly 2.0) than no CEV differential, or a value of 1.

But, we only had to plot these few engagements on a graph to be able to see that the actual CEVs for most of the battles were larger than 1.25 or 1.5. And, with the larger data base, and with the benefit of prior analysis of comparable battles in the Soviet-German War, we were able to arrive at quite specific CEVs for each engagement and these CEVs bore a remarkably consistent relationship to each other.

So, no arbitrary or postulated values for surprise or for combat effectiveness are used in the QJM, except as a preliminary test procedure. Once we have enough data, we can calculate the correct values by adherence to fixed, consistently applied procedures and rules.

Finally there is an argument which is most difficult to deal with: HERO has proved the method is historically valid, and can faithfully represent real-world engagements of World War II and the Arab-Israeli Wars, but that provides no basis for confidence in the QJM's ability to predict the future.

It is difficult to deal with that argument because it is fundamentally a truism. There is no known methodology, no *conceivable* methodology, that can accurately predict future events. This of course applies to *all* models used for predictive purposes.

But the QJM has one tremendous advantage over all other known models of combat, historical or otherwise. It is the only known model that reliably represents real-life combat over the course of history, particularly very recent history. Thus it is the only model that provides a basis for confidence that it can extrapolate realistically to the future, permitting reliable probes within ranges of future possibilities.

THE QJM AND LANCHESTER'S EQUATIONS

Interestingly, there is reason to believe that, despite their totally different approaches to combat analysis, the QJM and the famous Lanchester Equations are fundamentally compatible with each other.

First, let's look at a layman's explanation of the relatively simple, but mathematically sophisticated, Lanchester Equations.

In essence, the Lanchester Equations show the loss rates of two opposing sides under two general conditions of combat: (a) when one or both of the sides have only a general knowledge of the location of the other (as in a meeting engagement, or as in the case of an attacker against defenders concealed behind prepared or fortified defenses); and (b) when one or both sides have accurate information of the location of the other (as, for instance, a defender in most prepared and fortified defense situations, or two forces opposing each other on a broad, flat desert).

These two conditions of combat were expressed by the late Frederick William Lanchester in 1914 in two sets of differential equations, which are shown in Figure 10-1 in their very simplest formulation. The Linear Equation (or "Law") shows the rate of change of each force with respect to time (in other words, the effect of casualty attrition), as a constant times the product of the two opposing forces. The Square Law shows the rate of change as a constant times the strength of the opposing side—the side that has the advantage of observation. (A stands for Attacker, D for Defender.)

Figure 10-1.
THE LANCHESTER EQUATIONS IN BRIEF

Linear Law:	$dA/dt=kDA$ $dD/dt=k'AD$	Opposing sides know only general locations of targets
Square Law:	$dA/dt=KD$ $dD/dt=K'A$	Opposing sides know precise locations of targets
General Formulation	$dD/dt=CAD^\gamma$ $dA/dt=C'DA^\gamma$	Linear Law, $\gamma=1$; Square Law, $\gamma=0$)

Some years ago Dr. Daniel Willard did a study to test the validity of the Lanchester Equations[39] against the best military historical data base then available, a massive book called the *Kriegslexicon*, by an Austrian

---

[39] Dr. Daniel A. Willard, *Lanchester as a Force in History: An Analysis of Land Battles of the Years 1618-1905* (McLean, Virginia, 1962).

historian named Gaston Bodart.[40] This is a compilation of data of some 1,500 battles stretching from the Thirty Years War, in the early 17th Century, through the Russo-Japanese War, in the early 20th Century; it has never been translated into English. Willard decided to use this data to test his thesis that every battle is made up of a number of small combats, some of which involve Lanchester's Square Law, and some the Linear Law. Furthermore, in a data base like Bodart's, there would be such a cross-section of battles that there would be some in which the Square Law predominated, and some in which the Linear Law predominated. So Willard made a general formulation of the Linear and Square Laws, as shown in Figure 10-1, in which we have the Linear Law when Gamma equals 1, and the Square Law when it equals 0. He postulated that (if his reasoning was correct) by consolidating the data for Bodart's 1,500 engagements, he should end up with a mixture of Square Law and Linear Law results, so that Gamma would be somewhere between 1 and 0. Hopefully the value of Gamma might be close to the middle, some nice simple value like 0.5.

When Willard consolidated the Bodart force strength data in his computer program, he got a result between $-.27$ and $-.87$, clustering around $-.5$.

This led him to the conclusion that either the Lanchester Equations do not apply to historical combat, or the casualty-producing power of a force increases as its size decreases; or in other words, a force grows stronger as it incurs casualties. This alternative did not impress him with its logic, and so he decided that the Lanchester Equations could not be supported by historical data.

More recently Dr. Janice Fain decided to make another attempt to relate the Lanchester Equations to historical data. She reasoned that Willard's unsatisfactory results might have been due to his data. In the first place, the Bodart data did not include any modern combat, and covered a wide range of tactics and combat circumstances. Second, the Bodart data was not necessarily reliable or verifiable from other sources. She decided to use modern war data, and also to use the most reliable data she could find—HERO's 60-Engagement Data Base of World War II combat in Italy. She also made some relatively minor refinements in Dr. Willard's mathematical methodology, but used fundamentally the same approach.[41]

Dr. Fain's results were just as disappointing as Dr. Willard's and remarkably similar. Her results were between $-.59$ and $-.41$, also clustering around $-.5$. The conclusions could only be identical to Willard's.

Then Dr. Fain remembered what I had been saying for several years about the fact that force ratios are meaningless unless they represent

---

[40] Bodart, Gaston, *Militär-historisches Kriegs-Lexicon (1618-1905)*, Vienna, 1908.

[41] Janice B. Fain, *The Lanchester Equations and Historical Warfare: An Analysis of Sixty World War II Land Engagements* (Arlington, Virginia, 1975).

interaction with the variables of combat. So, she went through her exercise again, but instead of using either the numerical values or the firepower values of the opposing forces to arrive at the force ratio, she took as force ratios the Combat Power Potential ratios (P/P) HERO had calculated with the QJM, in which all discernible variables of combat were considered.

As the result of this second effort, Dr. Fain got a Gamma value of +.47, right in the area that she and Willard had been seeking from the outset. This leads to the conclusion that the Lanchester Equations provide reliable casualty rates only when combat power values for opposing forces reflect the variables of combat, as formulated in HERO's QJM.

What Dr. Fain had done, of course, was to apply the Lanchester Equations to the kind of simple conflict relationships for which Lanchester had originally designed them, since the QJM ratio of P/P is, in effect, an *overall* summation of the relative combat power of the opposing forces, reflecting all of the identifiable combat variables influencing a given engagement.

This does not necessarily prove the validity either of the Lanchester Equations or of the QJMA. But it does show an interesting convergence between these two very different approaches to a representation of combat, one theoretical and one empirical. Above all, it demonstrates the significance of considering the variables of combat when attempting to analyze anything like a force ratio.

11

The Model and History

We have seen how the QJM has proved its ability to represent historical combat in World War II and the Arab-Israeli Wars of 1967 and 1973. It has also been tested briefly on battles in a few other wars. In another historical adaptation, the methodology has also provided a basis for analysis of trends in relative combat effectiveness over 50 years of this century. These historical uses of the QJM will be briefly discussed below.

QJM Analyses of Historical Battles

THE BATTLE OF AUSTERLITZ, DECEMBER 2, 1805

The reader can find his own reference source for the events and data of this and the other historical battles discussed in this chapter. My own favorite source is *The Battle of Austerlitz*, by Trevor N. Dupuy (New York, Macmillan, 1968). The discussion here will be limited to the data, and its adaptation to a methodology originally designed for World War II forces.

The principal statistics are:

| | Strengths | | | | | | |
Opponents	Infantry	Cavalry	Artillery	Total	Guns	Casu- alties	Distance Advanced
French	43,000	22,500	9,300	75,000	225	7,000	7.5 km
Allies	62,500	14,250	12,250	89,000	265	27,000	−7.5 km

The following were the principal assumptions necessary to make this data fit the QJM:

1. Artillery pieces and small arms of both sides are considered to be equivalent in quality. The OLIs (based on Figure 2-5) were:

Infantry musket:	2.2
Cavalry carbine:	1.5
Cavalry saber:	1.0
Combined cavalryman value:	2.5
Gribeauval 12-pder cannon:	47.0

2. Napoleon's leadership, which presumably would be a factor between 1.3 and 1.6 (if we accept the statement by Wellington or Blücher—or both—that his presence on the battlefield was "worth 40,000 men"), will be entered initially into the QJM formula as 1, and recalculated subsequently from a comparison of P/P and R − R.

3. Although the quality of troops on both sides was good, the French troops were undoubtedly slightly more effective than the allies; however no CEV factor will be used initially, but will be considered in subsequent analysis.

4. Although the French were initially on the defensive, they soon turned to the offensive; so no posture factor will be used.

5. Terrain was "rolling, mixed."

6. Weather was cold, wintry, sunny.

7. The mobility formula will use the cavalry combat value (strength × OLI factor) for W_i; and will substitute horses for trucks, with no multiplying coefficient, allowing one horse per cavalryman, and 100 horses per gun (allowing for supply train and artillery draft animals); since the French seized the initiative early in the battle, M_a will be calculated for them.

8. Depth of the French Army will be .75×2.5 kms. (average depth of an army of 100,000); the allied army's depth will be .89×2.5 kms.

9. In the casualty effectiveness formula, the casualty coefficient in the second term will be changed from 100 to 10, to allow for the difference between continuous multi-day engagements of modern conflict, and the typical one-day, high-loss battle of pre-20th-Century warfare.

10. The terrain effects on tanks will be applied to cavalry.

11. Vulnerability will not be considered in pre-20th-Century warfare.

12. Assessed mission accomplishment for the two sides: French = 9; Allies = 2.

Based upon the above assumptions, and using the relationship of formulae (6) through (13)—pp. 36-37—or the form on p. 186 of Appendix A, the calculations are as follows:

French			*Allies*	
S =				
W_n=43,200×2.2×.9	= 85,536		62,500×2.2×.9	=123,750
W_g=225×47×.9	= 9,518		265×47×.9	= 11,210
W_i=22,500×2.5×.8	= 45,000		14,250×2.5×.8	= 28,500
	S_{fr} =140,054			S_{al} =163,460
	S_{fr}/S_{al} = .8568			S_{al}/S_{fr} =1.1671

$$M_{fr}=\sqrt{\frac{(75,000+(22,500+22,500)+22,500\times2.5)/75,000}{(89,000+(14,250+26,500)+14,250\times2.5)/89,000}}=1.1246$$

$$m_{fr}=1.1246-(1-.8)(.1246)=1.0997$$

$P_{fr}=140,054\times1.0997=154,017$ $\qquad$ $P_{al}=163,460\times1=163,460$

$P_{fr}/P_{al}=0.94$ $\qquad\qquad$ $P_{al}/P_{fr}=1.06$

In other words, on the record, and assuming no difference in either the quality of forces or leadership on the opposing sides, and no surprise by either side, the battle was a toss-up (a battle outcome is indeterminate if P/P is between 0.90 and 1.10).

The Result Formulae—(14)—(16), pp. 48 and 49, or the form on p. 186 of Appendix A, however, permit further analysis:

$$E_{sp\text{-}fr}=\sqrt{[1.167\times(4\times7.5+2.5\times.75)]/(3\times2.5\times.89)}=2.3610$$

$$E_{cas\text{-}fr}=\sqrt{.8568\times27,000/7000}-\sqrt{70,000/75,000}\quad=0.8518$$

$$R_{fr}=9+2.3610+0.8518=12.2128$$

$$E_{sp\text{-}al}=\sqrt{[.8568\times(4\times-7.5+2.5\times.89)]/(3\times2.5\times.75)}=-2.0567$$

$$E_{cas\text{-}al}=\sqrt{(1.1671\times7000/27,000}-\sqrt{270,000/89,000}\quad=-1.1907$$

$$R_{al}=2-2.0567-1.1907=1.2474$$

Outcome$=12.2128+1.2474=13.4602$; effective P/P$=3.69$

If we accept the Wellington-Blücher assessment of Napoleon's presence on the battlefield as worth 40,000 men, we must recognize that it was based upon their experience against him in 1813, 1814, and 1815, after they and his other enemies had learned from him how to fight Napoleonic war. It would seem reasonable, therefore, to assume that his superiority over his enemies would have been worth at least half as much again—say 60,000 men—in 1805. If 60,000 troops are added to the French strength, the value of P_f increases to 292,457, with a new P_f/P_{al} of 1.79, instead of 0.94; an increase by a factor of 1.90, attributable to Napoleon's leadership.

Also contributing to the French victory was the factor of surprise, and its effect upon the allies, when the French attack unexpectedly ripped into their center. Using the World War II value for the effect of substantial surprise, M_{fr} is multiplied by $\sqrt{3}$. (There is no vulnerability effect, due to Assumption 11, above.) This results in a new m_{fr} of 1.7583, an increase by a factor of 1.5989.

Finally, there is no question that French troops were substantially superior in quality to the allies. A factor of 1.2 (comparable to German superiority in the World Wars) seems reasonable.

An analysis of the effects of these factors of surprise, leadership, and troop quality follows:

Calculated P_{fr}/P_{al} =0.94
Effective P_{fr}/P_{al} =3.69
Value of French superiority   =3.93 (3.69/0.94)
Napoleon's leadership   =1.90
French troop quality   =1.20
Surprise   =1.60

The product of $1.90 \times 1.20 \times 1.60$ is 3.65, very near the calculated value of French superiority (3.93).

Others may not agree with these assessments. This is a game anyone can play.

THE BATTLE OF WATERLOO, JUNE 18, 1815

For this battle I have used primarily *The Military Life of Napoleon, Emperor of the French,* by Trevor Nevitt Dupuy (New York, Franklin Watts, 1969). Also used as references are the West Point *Atlas of the Napoleonic Wars,* edited by Vincent J. Esposito and John R. Elting (New York, Praeger, 1964), and *The Campaigns of Napoleon,* by David Chandler (New York, Macmillan, 1966).

Based upon these sources, the principal statistics are:

Opponents	Infantry	Cavalry	Artillery[42]	Totals	Guns	Casualties	Distance Advanced
French	50,200	15,200	6,600	72,000	246	32,000	−6.0 km
English	55,600	8,600	3,800	68,000	160	—	—
Prussians	59,200	6,800	5,000	71,000	180	—	—
Allies	114,800	15,400	8,800	139,000	340	22,000	+6.0 km

The assumptions are the same as for Austerlitz, with the following exceptions:

1. The weather was sunshiny, but the ground was very wet; use a weather factor between "dry, sunshine, temperate" and "wet, light temperate":

2. Mission accomplishment—Allies = 8; French = 2.

The calculations are as follows:

	French		*Allied*	
S =				
$W_n = 50,200 \times 2.2 \times .9$	= 99,396	$114,800 \times 2.2 \times .9$	=227,304
$W_g = 246 \times 47 \times .9$	= 10,406	$340 \times 47 \times .9$	= 14,382
$W_i = 15,200 \times 2.5 \times .8 \times .85$	= 25,840	$15,400 \times 2.5 \times .8 \times .85$	= 26,180
	S_{fr} =135,642		S_{al} =267,866
	S_{fr}/S_{al} =0.5054		S_{fr}/S_{al} =1.9748

[42] Artillerymen's small arms may be included in W_n, if desired; it makes no real difference.

$$M_{fr}=\sqrt{\frac{[72,000+(15,200+24,600)+15,200\times2.5]/72,000}{[114,000+(15,400+34,000)+15,400\times2.5]/114,800}}=1.0877$$

$$m_{fr}=1.0855-(1-.8\times.9)(.0877)=1.0631$$

$$P_{fr}=135,642\times1.0631=144,201 \qquad P_{al}=267,866\times1=267,866$$
$$P_{fr}/P_{al}=0.54 \qquad\qquad P_{al}/P_{fr}=1.86$$

In other words, on the record, and assuming no difference in either the quality of forces or the leadership, and no surprise was accomplished by either side, the battle should have been a clear-cut Allied success.

The Result Formula provides the following answers:

$$E_{sp\text{-}fr}=\sqrt{[1.9748\times(4\times-6+2.5\times.75)]/(3\times2.5\times1.148)}=-2.2565$$

$$E_{cas\text{-}fr}=\sqrt{.5064\times22,000/32,000}-\sqrt{320,000/72,000}\quad=-1.5182$$

$$R_{fr}=2-2.2565-1.5182=-1.7747$$

$$E_{sp\text{-}al}=\sqrt{[.5064\times(4\times6=2.5\times1.148)]/(3\times2.5\times.72)}\quad=\ \ 1.5874$$

$$E_{cas\text{-}al}=\sqrt{1.9748\times32,000/22,000}-\sqrt{220,000/114,800}\quad=\ \ 1.3105$$

$$R_{al}=8+1.5874+0.3105=9.8979$$

$$\text{Outcome}=9.8979+1.7747=11.6726;\ \text{effect}\ P_{al}/P_f=3.33$$

In other words, the Allied victory was greater in magnitude than the raw data would lead us to expect. But was it? Let's see what happens if we assume that the Prussian attack on the right flank of the French Army was complete surprise (which, indeed, it was), and if we also assume that the French Army troops were of higher quality than the Allies, and that Napoleon was worth the 40,000 men his two opponents are supposed to have said he was. The effect of surprise will tend to move the two P/Ps closer together; the quality of French troops and Napoleon's leadership will tend to hold them apart. The calculations are summarized below.

First calculate the effect of surprise upon the relative mobility of the opponents. M_{fr} is divided by $\sqrt{5}$. The new m_{fr} is .6302. The value of French mobility has been decreased by a factor of 1.69; this is the effect of surprise.

For Napoleon's leadership we should calculate the effect of 40,000 troops, added to his entire army of 120,000. This would mean an army of 160,000, or a factor of 1.33.

Now for a summary of the calculations:

Calculated P_{al}/P_{fr}	=1.86	
Effective P_{al}/P_{fr}	=3.33	
Value of Allies superiority	=1.79	(3.33/1.86)
Napoleon's leadership (1.33)	=0.75	(reciprocal)
French troop quality (1.2)	=0.83	(reciprocal)
Surprise effect	=1.69	

The product of $.75 \times .83 \times 1.69$ is 1.05; this is not very close to the actual value of Allied superiority (1.79). If, however, we take the approach used for engagements 23 and 37 on P. 136, and apply a factor of 0.67 for a broken unit—as the French army was by nightfall—we get a calculated value of Allied superiority of 1.57, which is quite close.

THE BATTLE OF ANTIETAM, SEPTEMBER 17, 1862

I have taken the data for this battle from *The Compact History of the Civil War,* by R. Ernest Dupuy and Trevor N. Dupuy (New York, Hawthorn, 1960) and from Thomas L. Livermore's *Numbers and Losses of the Civil War* (reprint, Bloomington: University of Indiana, 1957).

The principal statistics are:

Opponents	Infantry	Cavalry	Artillery	Totals	Guns	Casu-alties	Distance Advanced
Union	59,300	10,700	10,000	80,000	240	12,410	1.0
Confederate	33,600	5,900	5,500	45,000	135	13,724	—1.0

The assumptions for Austerlitz apply here, except for those obviously inapplicable, and the following:

1. Lee's unquestionably superior leadership will be initially entered into the QJM formula as 1.0, and will be recalculated from a comparison of P/P and $R-R$.

2. For reasons shown on page 157, the quality of the forces is considered to be identical.

3. Terrain was "rolling, mixed."

4. Weather was sunshine, temperate.

5. Depth of the Union Army will be $3.0 \times .8$; depth of the Confederate Army will be $3.0 \times .45$.

6. Mission accomplishment for the Confederates is 6.0, for the Union troops is 4.0.

7. Artillery small arms have been included in W_n.

8. The Confederate army will have the terrain and posture benefits of hasty defense.

	Union			*Confederate*	
$S =$			$S =$		
$W_n = 69,300 \times 4.1 \times .9$	$= 255,717$		$39,100 \times 4.1 \times .9$	$= 144,279$
$W_g = 240 \times 38 \times .9$	$= 8,208$		$135 \times 38 \times .9$	$= 4,617$
$W_i = 10,700 \times 5.0 \times .8$	$= 42,800$		$5,900 \times 5.0 \times .8$	$= 23,600$

$$S_u = 306,725 \qquad S_c = 172,496$$
$$S_u/S_c = 1.7782 \qquad S_c/S_u = 0.5624$$

$$M_u = \sqrt{\frac{(80,000 + (10,700 + 24,000) + 10,700 \times 5)/80,000}{(45,000 + (5,900 + 13,500) + 5,900 \times 5)/45,000}} = 1.0050$$

$$m_u = 1.0050 - (.2 \times .005) = 1.0040$$

$$P_u = 269,825 \times 1.004 \times 1.1 = 297,994 \qquad P_c = 152,201 \times 1.3 \times 1.3 = 257,220$$
$$P_u/P_c = 1.16 \qquad P_c/P_u = 0.86$$

In other words, on the record, and assuming no difference in the leadership on the opposing sides, the Union troops should have won a narrow but unquestionable victory.

The Result Formula provides the following relevant information:

$$E_{sp\text{-}u} = \sqrt{[.5624\times(4\times0+3.0\times.8)]/(3\times3.0\times.45)} \quad =0.5782$$

$$E_{cas\text{-}u} = \sqrt{(1.7782\times12,410/13,724} - \sqrt{12,410/80,000} =0.0206$$

$$R_u=4.0+.5782+.0206=4.5988$$

$$E_{sp\text{-}u} = \sqrt{[1.7782\times(4\times0+3.0\times.45)]/3\times3.0\times.8)} \quad =1.5765$$

$$E_{cas\text{-}u} = \sqrt{.5624\times13,724/12,410} - \sqrt{137,240/45,000} = .7898=0.9566$$

$$R_c=6+1.5765-.9566=6.6199$$

$$\text{Outcome}=4.5988-6.6199=-2.0211; \text{ effective } P_c/P_u=1.40$$

Although the calculated P/P indicates that there should have been a Union success, in fact, there was a Confederate success. There was no surprise; there was no difference in the quality of troops. The only significant difference was in the quality of leadership. The QJM gives us a basis for calculating this.

Calculated P_c/P_u	=0.86
Effective P_c/P_u (PR/PR)	=1.40
Value of Confederate superiority	=1.63

That factor of Confederate superiority, of course, was the margin of General Lee's leadership superiority over General McClellan; a substantial but reasonable value.

THE BATTLE OF GETTYSBURG, JULY 1-3, 1863

The sources for this battle are the same as for Antietam.
The principal statistics are:

Opponents	Infantry	Cavalry	Artillery	Totals	Guns	Casualties per day	Distance Advanced per day
Union	64,100	11,800	12,389	88,289	264	7,683	0
Confederate	54,400	10,100	10,500	75,000	225	9,354	0

The assumptions for Antietam apply here, except as follows:

1. Depth of the Union Army—$3.0\times.883$; depth of the Confederate Army—$3.0\times.75$.
2. Mission accomplishment: Union—7.0; Confederate—3.0.
3. The Union army, on the defensive, gets the terrain and posture benefits of hasty defense.

Union			*Confederate*	

$S =$

$W_n = 76,489 \times 4.1 \times .9 \quad = 282,244$ $64,900 \times 4.1 \times .9 \quad = 239,481$

$W_g = 264 \times 38 \times .9 \quad = \quad 9,029$ $225 \times 38 \times .9 \quad = \quad 7,695$

$W_i = 11,800 \times 4 \times .8 \quad = \quad 47,200$ $10,000 \times 5 \times .8 \quad = \quad 40,400$

$$S_u = 338,473 \qquad\qquad S_c = 287,576$$
$$S_u/S_c = 1.1770 \qquad\qquad S_c/S_u = 0.8496$$

$$M_c = \sqrt{\frac{(75,000 + (10,100 + 22,500) + 10,000 \times 5)/75,000}{(88,289 + (11,800 + 26,400) + 11,800 \times 5)/88,289}} = 1.0020$$

$$m_c = 1.0020 - (.2 \times .002) = 1.0016$$

$P_u = 338,473 \times 1.3 \times 1.3 = 572,019$ $P_c = 287,576 \times 1.1 \times 1.0016 = 316,840$

$\qquad P_u/P_c = 1.81$ $P_c/P_u = 0.55$

In other words, on the record, General Lee and his army did not have a chance to defeat the Union Army, unless Lee's leadership could almost double the capability of his army.

The Result Formula gives the answers:

$$E_{sp\text{-}c} = \sqrt{[.8496 \times (4 \times 0 + 3.1 \times .883)\,]/(3 \times 3.0 \times .75)} \qquad = \quad .5774$$

$$E_{cas\text{-}u} = \sqrt{1.1770 \times 7,683/9,354} - \sqrt{76,830/88,289} = .9832 - .9329 \ = \quad .0503$$

$$R_u = 7 + .5774 + .0503 = 7.6277$$

$$E_{sp\text{-}c} = \sqrt{[1.770 \times (4 \times 0 + 3 \times .75)]/(3 \times 3 \times .883)} \qquad = \quad .5773$$

$$E_{cas\text{-}c} = \sqrt{.8496 \times 9,354/7,683} - \sqrt{93,540/75,000} = 1.0170 - 1.1168 = -.0998$$

$$R_c = 3 + .5773 - .0998 = 3.4775$$

$$\text{Outcome} = 7.6227 - 3.4775 = 4.1502; \text{ effective } P_u/P_c = 1.83$$

This suggests that the effect of General Lee's leadership on the outcome of the Battle of Gettysburg was negligible; this is consistent with his statement to Longstreet on the evening of July 3: "It's all my fault."[43]

THE SOMME OFFENSIVE, MARCH 21-APRIL 4, 1918

This is a quite general and highly aggregated representation of a vast and complex operation. I offer no apologies for this; the purpose was to see if the method could give a reasonable representation of an important World War I battle; clearly it does. Only three secondary sources were consulted in compiling the aggregated, and to a large extent estimated, data that is presented below.[44]

The first time I went through this exercise I assumed that the QJM

[43] Douglas Southall Freeman, *Lee's Lieutenants*, (New York, 1944, 3 vols.), v. 3, p. 166.

[44] Trevor N. Dupuy and Julia Crick, *The Military History of World War I; 1918: The German Offensive* (New York: Franklin Watts, 1967). Gerard L. McEntee, *Military History of the World War* (New York: Scribner's, 1937). T.J. Stamps and V.J. Esposito (eds.), *The West Point Atlas of American Wars* (New York: Praeger, 1959).

could represent the entire 15-day battle. It soon became evident that, merely on the basis upon which the QJM was developed, this was not possible. There was too great a change in forces and situations during the battle, particularly on the Allied side, as reinforcements were rushed to close the gap which the Germans had torn in the British lines. In reviewing the sources, it became obvious that the first major phase of the German offensive ended about March 26, as the Germans, after capturing Peronne, were forced to relax their efforts due to exhaustion and lack of supplies. This, also, was the day that major Allied reinforcements, sent by the new Allied Generalissimo, General Foch, began to reach the front in major numbers.

So, we have two distinct battles within the offensive: the Peronne Phase, March 21-26, and the Montdidier Phase, March 27-April 4. We shall analyze each in turn.

The aggregated statistics for the Peronne Phase are:

	Germans	Allies
Forces engaged	600,000	250,000
Machine guns	10,000	4,000
Mortars	3,532	1,400
Artillery tubes	6,473	2,500
Tanks	120	100
Aircraft	820	1,000
Casualties	70,000 (11,672/day)	120,000 (20,000/day)
Distance advanced (km)	30	—30

In general the use of procedures, tables, and formulae were as for World War II, modified by the following assumptions:

1. OLI values for weapons of both sides are considered to be identical, and are as follows:

Infantry rifles	1.2 (US Springfield was 1.4)
Machine guns	14.0
Mortars	200.0
Artillery (average)	1,600.0 (French '75 was 1,546)
Tanks	150.0
Aircraft	140.0

2. Allied posture for the Peronne Phase was fortified defense.
3. Data is not readily available for a precise mobility calculation; the mobility of both sides was essentially identical.
4. Terrain: flat, mixed; weather: wet, light, temperate; season: spring, temperate; no air superiority for either side.
5. The Germans had the advantage of slight surprise in their initial assault; the effects of this will be calculated after the direct comparison of forces.
6. Depth of both armies is maximum: 12 km.
7. Mission Factor, Peronne Phase: German 7, Allies 3.

The calculations are as follows:

| *Germans* | *Allies* |

S =

$$W_s = 600,000 \times 1.2 \times .9 \quad = \quad 648,000$$
$$W_{mg} = 10,000 \times 14 \times .9 \quad = \quad 126,000$$
$$W_{hw} = 3,532 \times 200 \times .9 \quad = \quad 635,760$$
$$W_g = 6,473 \times 1,600 \times 1 \quad = 10,356,800$$
$$W_i = 120 \times 150 \times .9 \times .7 \quad = \quad 11,340$$
$$W_y = 820 \times 140 \times 1 \times .5 \times .9 = \quad 51,660$$
$$S_g = 11,829,560$$

$$250,000 \times 1.2 \times .9 \quad = \quad 270,000$$
$$4,000 \times 14 \times .9 \quad = \quad 50,400$$
$$1,400 \times 200 \times .9 \quad = \quad 252,000$$
$$2,500 \times 1,600 \times 1 \quad = 4,000,000$$
$$100 \times 160 \times .9 \times .7 \quad = \quad 9,450$$
$$1,000 \times 140 \times 1 \times .5 \times .9 = \quad 63,000$$
$$S_{al} = 4,644,850$$

$$S_g/S_{al} = 2.5468 \qquad\qquad S_{al}/S_g = 0.3926$$
$$m_g = m_{al} = 1$$

$$V_g = 600,000 \times 1/1 \times .6266 = 375,970; \qquad v_g = 1 - 375,970/$$
$$11,829,560 = .9682$$

$$V_{al} = 250,000 \times .5/1.2 \times 1.5959 = 166,240; \qquad v_{al} = 1 - 166,240/$$
$$4,644,850 = .9642$$

$$P_g = 11,829,560 \times 1 \times .9682 = 11,453,379$$
$$P_{al} = 4,644,850 \times 1.6 \times 1.2 \times .9642 = 8,598,844$$
$$P_g/P_{al} = 1.33 \qquad\qquad P_{al}/P_g = 0.75$$

The effects of slight surprise are as follows:
Mobility: $M = \sqrt{1.3} = 1.1402$; $m = 1.1402 - (1, -.8 \times .9)(.1402) = 1.1010$

The effects on vulnerability are:
$$V_g = 338,373; \quad v_g = .9714 \qquad\qquad V_{al} = 1.2 \times 166,240 = 199,488$$
$$v_{al} = .9571$$

From this we can recalculate:
$$P_g' = 12,651,848 \qquad\qquad P_{al}' = 8,535,525$$
$$P_g'/P_{al}' = 1.48 \qquad\qquad P_{al}'/P_g' = .67$$

The Result Formula calculations are:

$$E_{sp\text{-}g} = \sqrt{(.3926 \times 1.6 \times (4 \times 5 + 12))/(3 \times 12)} = .7472$$

$$E_{cas\text{-}g} = (.9571)^2 \left(\sqrt{2.5468 \times 20,000/11,667} - \sqrt{1,166,700/600,000} \right)$$

$$= .9160(2.0895 - 1.3945) = .6367$$

$$R_g = 7 + .7472 + .6367 = 8.3839$$

$$E_{sp\text{-}al} = \sqrt{[2.5468 \times 1/1.6 \times (4 \times -5 + 12)]/(3 \times 12)} = -.5947$$

$$E_{cas\text{-}al} = (.9714)^2 \left(\sqrt{.3926 \times 11,667/20,000} - \sqrt{2,000,000/250,000} \right)$$

$$= .9436(.4786 - 2.8284) = -2.2173$$

$$R_{al} = 3 - .5947 - 2.2173 = 0.1880$$

Outcome $= 8.3839 - 0.1880 = 8.1959$; effect $P_g/P_{al} = 2.64$

Calculated P_g/P_{al} (with Surprise) $= 1.48$
Effective $P_g/P_{al} = 2.64$
Value of German Superiority $= 1.78 \quad (2.64/1.48)$

This 78 percent German superiority over the British in the spring of 1918 seems high, even though the Germans used their very best shock troops and British morale was low. However, that there was a German combat effectiveness superiority over the Western Allies has already been clearly demonstrated; the amount in this example may be a reflection of the many approximations and aggregations that went into the data. It will be interesting to check this value against that which emerges from the Montdidier Phase calculations.

The statistics for the Montdidier Phase are as follows:

	Germans	Allies
Forces engaged	600,000	500,000
Machine guns	10,000	8,500
Mortars	3,500	2,900
Artillery tubes	5,500	5,300
Tanks	100	150
Aircraft	700	1,400
Casualties	130,000 (14,444/day)	120,000 (13,333/day)
Distance advanced	12 km	−12 km (1.3/day)

The only important differences in the assumptions for the Peronne Phase are:

1. The Allied posture was mixed hasty defense and prepared defense.
2. The Missions Factors were: Germans 4; Allies 6.

The calculations are as follows:

$$
\begin{array}{lll}
& \textit{Germans} & \textit{Allies} \\
S = & & \\
W_s = 600,000 \times 1.2 \times .9 & = 648,000 & 500,000 \times 1.2 \times .9 = 540,000 \\
W_{mg} = 10,000 \times 14 \times .9 & = 126,000 & 8,500 \times 14 \times .9 = 107,100 \\
W_{hw} = 3,500 \times 200 \times .9 & = 630,000 & 2,900 \times 200 \times .9 = 522,000 \\
W_g = 5,500 \times 1,600 \times 1 & = 8,800,000 & 5,400 \times 1,600 \times 1 = 8,640,000 \\
W_i = 100 \times 150 \times .9 \times .2 & = 9,450 & 150 \times 150 \times .9 \times .7 = 14,175 \\
W_y = 700 \times 140 \times .5 \times .9 & = 44,100 & 1,400 \times 140 \times .5 \times .9 = 88,200 \\
& S_g = 10,257,550 & S_{al} = 9,911,475 \\
& S_g/S_{al} = 1.0349 & S_{al}/S_g = 0.9663
\end{array}
$$

$$m_g = m_{al} = 1$$

$$V_g = 600,000 \times 1/1 \times .9830 = 589,803; \quad v_g = 1 - 589,803/10,267,550 = 0.9425$$

$$V_{al} = 500,000 \times .65/1.2 \times 1.0173 = 275,519; \quad v_{al} = 1 - 275,519/9,911,475 = 0.9722$$

$$P_g = 10,257,550 \times .9425 = 9,667,741$$

$$P_{al} = 9,911,475 \times 1.2 \times 1.4 \times .9722 = 16,188,372$$

$$P_g/P_{al} = 0.5972 \qquad P_{al}/P_g = 1.6745$$

These figures say that the Allies should have won a clear-cut success. Let's see what the Result Formula tells us:

$$E_{sp\text{-}g} = \sqrt{(.9663 \times 1.4 \times (4 \times 1.3 + 12))/(3 \times 12)} \qquad\qquad = 0.8040$$

$$E_{cas\text{-}g} = (.9722)^2 \ (\sqrt{1.0349 \times 13,333/14,444} - \sqrt{1,444,400/600,000})$$

$$= .9452(.9774 - 1.5515) \qquad\qquad\qquad = - .5742$$

$$R_g = 4 + .8040 - .5742 = 4.2298$$

$$E_{sp\text{-}al} = \sqrt{[1.0349 \times 1/1.4 (4 \times -113 + 12)]/(3 \times 12)} \qquad = 0.3845$$

$$E_{cas\text{-}al} = (.9425)^2 \ (\sqrt{.9663 \times 14,444/13,333} - \sqrt{1,333,300/500,000})$$

$$= .883(1.0231 - 1.6330) \qquad\qquad\qquad = -0.5417$$

$$R_{al} = 6 + .3845 - .5417 = 5.8428$$

$$\text{Outcome} = 5.8428 - 4.2298 = 1.613; \text{ effective } P_{al}/P_g = 1.32$$

Calculated $P_{al}/P_g = 1.67$
Effective $P_{al}/P_g = 1.32$
Value of German Superiority$=1.27$

This 27 percent German superiority over the British and French is more consistent with other World War I calculations than is the 79 percent CEV calculated for the Peronne Phase. If, however, we assume the 1.27 figure is approximately correct, and if we give the German shock troops a 1.2 CEV superiority factor over average German troops, and if we give the Germans a 1.1 superiority factor in morale, then we would have a 1.67 German superiority factor for the Peronne Phase (1.27 × 1.2 × 1.1). This is very close to the 1.78 figure, in light of the approximations and aggregations used in these calculations.

The QJM thus does a good job of representing this major World War I battle. Admittedly, hindsight helps.

Trends in National Combat Effectiveness

COMPARING NATIONAL COMBAT PERFORMANCE

HERO's "Quick Win" and Arab-Israeli "Comparative Analysis" studies (mentioned in Chapter 9) provide a basis for some very interesting comparisons of historical combat effectiveness from 1918 through 1973.

In the "Quick Win" study we applied the QJM to highly aggregated (and sometimes approximate) data for the following campaigns:

Quick Wins
The British Megiddo Campaign, 1918
German Invasion of the Low Countries and France, 1940
Japanese Invasion of Malaya, 1941-1942
Soviet Invasion of Manchuria, August 1945
Third Arab-Israeli War, 1967

Almost Quick Wins
German Invasion of Russia (Operation "Barbarossa"), 1941
Allied Breakout from Normandy (Operation "Cobra"), 1944
North Korean Invasion of South Korea, 1950

Stalemates
Sinai Desert Front, 1915-1917
Winter and Gustav Lines, Italy, 1943-1944
Korea, 1951-1953

From these QJM analyses we were able to arrive at the CEVs shown at the top of Figure 11-1.

Figure 11-1.
SOME HISTORICAL COMBAT EFFECTIVENESS COMPARISONS

World War I
  Palestine (1917-18)
British	1.98					
Turks	1.00					

World War II
Germans	1.64	(1.26)	(1.57)			
Western Allies	1.30	(1.00)				
Russians	1.04		(1.00)			
Japanese	1.00					

Six Day War (1967)
Israelis	3.50	(1.54)	(1.75)	(2.63)		
Jordanians	2.27	(1.00)			(1.71)	(1.14)
Egyptians	2.00		(1.00)		(1.50)	(1.00)
Syrians	1.33			(1.00)	(1.00) (1.00)	
Palestinians	1.00					

October War (1973)
Israelis	3.43	(1.88)	(1.98)	(2.54)		
Jordanians	1.82	(1.00)			(1.35)	(1.05)
Egyptians	1.73		(1.00)		(1.28)	(1.00)
Syrians	1.35			(1.00)	(1.00) (1.00)	
Iraqis	1.00					

Our "Comparative Analysis" study permitted us to arrive at comparable campaign figures for the 1973 October War, and to check the aggregated campaign analyses against average values derived from detailed analysis of the separate engagements; the results from the two studies are also consolidated in Figure 11-1.

CONCLUSIONS

From a study of these figures several interesting things emerge:
1. Based upon the Battles of Gaza and Megiddo, the CEV of the British with respect to the Turks in 1917-1918 was very close to that of the

Israelis over the Arabs in 1967 and 1973. There are interesting similarities in the cultural backgrounds of the sets of opponents in these examples, more than 50 years apart.

2. The CEV of the Germans with respect to the Western Allies is almost identical to that calculated in HERO's World War II data base. As we have seen elsewhere, the relative CEV of Germans and Western Allies in World War I was almost identical to that of World War II; this ties the British-Turk comparison at least to some extent to the World War II relationships.

3. The CEV of the Germans with respect to the Russians in the Quick Win study is not so high as in earlier HERO analyses. We should remember, however, that the Quick Win analysis was based upon aggregated data, and the Russian CEV is strongly influenced by their overwhelming victory in Manchuria in 1945, against a weak and already defeated Japanese Army.

4. For that reason, incidentally, the Japanese value shown is perhaps lower than it would be if it were based on data for most of World War II; however, the results of their victory over the British in Malaya are at least to some degree offsetting.

These various considerations have led me to postulate that the CEVs of the two World Wars could be linked with those of the Arab-Israeli Wars. This can be done on the basis of two debatable, but not totally unreasonable, hypotheses:

a. Except where extraordinary and exceptional efforts to improve military posture are evident (as in Russia between the World Wars, and in Syria, between the 1967 and 1973 Wars), relative national force effectiveness comparisons change only slowly in brief historical periods (say, half a century); and

b. Modern Israel is (in a kind of historical switch) the cultural, technological, social heir of Western society, particularly the US, Britain, and France; thus its CEVs can be related to those of Western nations of the past 50 years (as seems to be suggested by the British-Turk, and Israeli-Arab comparisons).

Based upon these hypotheses, the national CEVs in Figure 11-1 can be related to each other, and normalized on the Palestinian CEV (1967 value). This is shown in Figure 11-2.

The numbers in Figure 11-2 are plotted graphically in Figure 11-3.

There is one important word of caution needed here. We know that Russia made an intensive effort to improve itself militarily between the two World Wars, and that that improvement continued during World War II. Thus it would be a serious mistake to assume that current Soviet CEVs are as low as shown in Figures 11-2 and 11-3. We must assume that the Soviet CEV is at least close to that of the Western allies (with West Germany probably about the same).

Figure 11-2.
TENTATIVE NATIONAL FORCE EFFECTIVENESS COMPARISONS
1918-1973

Germans (1940-44)	4.42	1.26	1.57							
Western Allies (1918-44)	3.50	1.00	—	1.30	—	1.98				
Israelis (1967-73)	3.50	—	—	—	—	—	1.88	1.98	2.54	3.43
Russians (1941-45)	2.80	—	1.00	—	1.04					
Japanese (1941-45)	2.69	—	—	1.00	1.00					
Jordanians (1967-73)	1.86	—	—	—	—	—	1.00			
Turks (1918)	1.77	—	—	—	—	1.00				
Egyptians (1967-73)	1.77	—	—	—	—	—	—	1.00		
Syrians (1967-73)	1.38	—	—	—	—	—	—	—	1.00	
Iraqis (1973)	1.02	—	—	—	—	—	—	—	—	1.00
Palestinians (1967)	1.00									

Figure 11-3.
GRAPHICAL REPRESENTATION; TENTATIVE
NATIONAL FORCE EFFECTIVENESS COMPARISONS;
1918-1973

	0	1.0	2.0	3.0	4.0	5.0
Germans					————	
W. Allies				————		
Israelis				————		
Russians			——— ? - - ? - - ?			
Japanese				———		
Jordanians		———				
Turks		———				
Egyptians		———				
Syrians		——				
Iraqis		—				
Palestinians		——				

Assumptions
1. Israelis, 1967-1973, comparable to Western Allies, 1918-45
2. W. Allies constant, 1918-45

CEV (Normalized to Palestinians, 1967)

12

The Model, Fun, and Games

Playing at War

As far as I am concerned, the most important book ever written by H.G. Wells was entitled: *Little Wars*.[45] It was written about the turn of the last century, describing Mr. Wells' favorite (or at least second favorite) form of recreation: playing with toy soldiers. I am no less impressed today than I was a half century ago at the many photographs in the book, showing Mr. Wells and his middle-aged companions on hands and knees, in white flannel trousers and dark blazers, playing with their soldiers both on typical English countryhouse lawns, and in specially fitted-out wargame rooms.

They were very serious about it, and their modern successors—some of whom play with model soldiers, and some of whom play with cardboard markers on specially designed map boards—are equally serious. Nor is this a modern phenomenon, ushered in by Mr. Wells and his cronies; its origins go back to the inventors of chess, wei-chi, and I-go. And, interestingly, there has always been a tendency for some wargamers-for-entertainment to adapt their work to the grim issues of real-world peace and war. This, in fact, was the origin of the 19th Century *kriegspiel* of the Prussian-Germany Army, which played an important part in German military planning and decision-making as recently as World War II.

Thus the idea of adapting the QJM to entertainment has honored precedents, though the transition in the past has usually been in the other direction. In fact, the QJM has a splendid potential as a source of recreation and entertainment. Three possibilities spring immediately to mind, and will be demonstrated in the following pages. Imaginative readers will undoubtedly find other adaptations. (And if they do, I hope they will write to me about them.)

First, with this book and any standard military history book about any war or wars in history, it is possible to recreate historical battles; two imaginative opponents can play a historical campaign, to see if they can plan and direct operations better than historical generals. Second, it is possible to forecast the outcomes of hypothetical future wars and battles,

[45] H.G. Wells, *Little Wars* (New York: Macmillan, 1970, Reprint).

by linking the QJM methodology to the data that is to be found, for instance, in such books as *The Almanac of World Military Power*.[46] Again, two people can engage in friendly competition in such projections of future wars.

Finally, it is possible for a person interested in military affairs to experiment—or play, depending on how seriously he becomes involved—with different kinds of imaginary armies or force structures with modern men and weapons, with hypothetical forces for the future, or imaginary forces of the past. Readers who are serious about such matters may want to compete with the author of this book in his next planned endeavor: applying the QJM to past, present, and future naval and aerial warfare.

Recreating the Past—Waterloo

This recreation of the Waterloo Campaign makes no pretenses of offering insights into the operations, or the generalship of the three principal commanders: Napoleon, Wellington, and Blücher. It does, however, give us an opportunity to compare results with those of the historical summary of the previous chapters. The student who is very familiar with the campaign might disagree with the assumptions listed below, or the commentaries that follow. In that case, he is invited to improve on the game as set out here.

The following is an overall campaign comparison of the opposing forces, based generally on the sources cited in the previous chapter.

	Infantry	*Cavalry*	*Artillery*	*Personnel*	*Guns*
French	91,500	22,100	9,100	122,700	366
Eng.-Allies	90,000	14,000	6,000	110,000	222
Prussian	97,500	11,200	8,300	117,000	296
Allies Total	187,500	25,200	14,300	227,000	518

Now let's make a few assumptions that enable us to develop some of the factors we shall need to apply:

1. Weapons values are as for the Battles of Austerlitz and Waterloo in the previous chapter.

2. As calculated in the previous chapter, Napoleon's presence on the battlefield was worth a factor of about 1.33.

3. French troops had demonstrated a consistent superiority over the Prussians, even when Napoleon was not on the battlefield. They had proven slightly inferior to the English in Spain, but Wellington's hodgepodge army in Belgium in June 1815 was far below British standards, and this was Napoleon's best army since Friedland. A French CEV of 1.2 will be used against both British and Prussians.

[46] T.N. Dupuy, John A.C. Andrews, and Grace P. Hayes, *The Almanac of World Military Power*, 3d edition (New York: R.R. Bowker, 1974).

4. Appendix A includes a table of movement rates, including those for pre-World War II movements. There is also a table of general casualty rates, and sample casualty rates for Napoleonic War battles.

5. When taking deliberate defensive positions such as the British at Quatre Bras and Waterloo, or the Prussians at Wavre, a hasty defense posture factor of 1.3 will be used; at Ligny, the Prussians in less deliberate defensive posture in the open will be given a posture factor of 1.15.

6. Unless there is some special reason to the contrary, the terrain will be considered to be "rolling, mixed."

7. The weather will be considered to be "dry, sunshine, temperate," except on the afternoon of June 17, when it was "wet, heavy, temperate," and the morning of June 18, when it was "wet, light, temperate," and the afternoon of June 18, when its value is as shown in the previous chapter.

8. Dispositions of forces at the outset will be as shown on Map 157 of the West Point Atlas (*A Military History and Atlas of the Napoleonic Wars*, edited by Brig. Gen. V.J. Esposito and Col. John R. Elting).

9. On June 16 all of the French Army could be committed; Wellington could commit only 36,000 at Quatre Bras; Blücher could commit only 84,000 at Ligny.

When I ran through the campaign it fell into exactly the same battles as were actually fought between June 16 and 18, 1815, but in slightly different time sequence, and with substantially different results. These results are summarized below.

In my recreation of the campaign, the Battle of Ligny turned out just about as it actually did. However at Quatre Bras, Ney (with D'Erlon's corps fully engaged) was able to defeat Wellington, and pursue him part way back to Mt. St. Jean before dark. As a result Napoleon was able to attack Wellington in the Waterloo position in mid-morning of the 17th (about 27 hours earlier than the actual battle) and would have won a decisive victory had it not been for the torrential rainstorm the afternoon of the 17th. Wellington was able to extract most of his beaten army and retreat toward Brussels. On the 18th Napoleon was able to converge most of his Army against the Prussians at Wavre while Ney with two corps pursued the defeated English. Again Napoleon's victory, while clear-cut, was not decisive, because Blücher began to withdraw as soon as he realized that a junction with Wellington was impossible.

Now you can try it; it's fun!

Hypothetical Campaign of the Future—Fulda

This hypothetical campaign analysis is slightly modified from a problem that was under consideration in the higher echelons of Pentagon planning not long ago. In the form in which the problem was presented to the author of this book, it did not require any detailed QJM analyses. On the other hand, the solution to the problem, as presented below, *should* have been tested with a series of QJM analyses. Some day I hope to have a chance to do the testing. Meanwhile, readers may wish to try their hands at it.

First, the Problem Scenario and Problem Requirements are set out, almost exactly as in an official letter to several American military historians. Then, with minor modifications, my original responses are presented.

PROBLEM SCENARIO

The time is 1976. A US corps has occupied positions along critical avenues of advance near the Fulda Gap with the mission of defending in depth a 75-kilometer-wide sector against penetration and loss of critical terrain and installations within the corps area. A Soviet combined arms army attacks the corps with a mission to destroy the US forces in its zone and to obtain an objective located some 100 kilometers inside the West German border (Frankfurt, for instance). Only conventional weapons are used by both sides.

The US forces in the sector consist of an armored cavalry regiment (54 M60 tanks), a mechanized division, consisting of six mechanized and five armored battalions (270 M60 tanks), an armored division, consisting of six armored and five mechanized battalions (324 M60 tanks), and corps artillery. The corps has a total of 648 M60 tanks at the start of the conflict. There are no US or Allied reinforcing units available. The covering force consists of the armored cavalry regiment (ACR) and some elements of the two divisions and corps artillery that are forward of the main battle area. Limited close air support will be available during the first few days of this conflict.

The attacking Soviet army consists of three motorized rifle divisions and two tank divisions (a total of 1,450 T-62 tanks at the start of conflict), and an army artillery brigade. A second echelon tank army consisting of three tank divisions (a total of 970 tanks), and another artillery brigade are available should the US sector be designated a main attacker sector. Soviet air will initially be allocated to penetration efforts and then will revert to army control.

The terrain is generally rolling, with some rugged and heavily forested areas, but is generally suitable for armored operations. There are three avenues of advance into the corps sector. The defense is characterized as prepared-hasty and is organized in depth in a series of battle positions. It incorporates the judicious use of terrain, selection of weapon sites, and employment of minefields. Approximately 30 kilometers of distance exists between the border and the main battle area. (Defensive action in front of the main battle area would be characterized as delay.)

Assume you are the US corps commander. You are concerned about how the various phases of the battle will be fought. These phases incorporate the covering force battle and the defense of your main battle area. You are particularly concerned about your anticipated loss of main battle tanks (destroyed and damaged) as a result of enemy action.

Your analysis should consider the following possibilities:

1. That the enemy may be able to achieve surprise.
2. The enemy may make his main effort in your sector, employing a combined arms army reinforced by a tank army.
3. The enemy may make a secondary attack in your sector, for the purpose of preventing you from redeploying forces into other corps areas; such an attack is likely to be made by a combined arms army only.
4. The enemy may undertake only a holding action in your sector, without initiating a general attack.

PROBLEM REQUIREMENTS

A. Assuming no surprise:
  1. How long (in hours) will the covering force battle last:
     a. If the main attack is in your sector?
     b. If the secondary attack is in your sector?
  2. How many tanks do you expect to lose during the covering force battle:
     a. If the main attack is in your sector?
     b. If the secondary effort is in your sector?
  3. How long (in days) will the main battle last:
     a. If the main effort is in your sector?
     b. If the secondary effort is in your sector?
  4. If you remain in defensive posture do you expect your losses in the main battle sustained during the first few days to be different from those sustained over a longer period of time?
  5. Estimate the average number of tanks you expect to lose during the initial assaults against your main battle position during the first five days (if the battle lasts that long):
     a. If the main effort is in your sector?
     b. If the secondary effort is in your sector?
     c. If there is a holding action in your sector?
  6. Estimate the average number of tanks you expect to lose every day after the fifth day, if the battle lasts more than five days:
     a. If the main effort is in your sector?
     b. If the secondary effort is in your sector?
     c. If there is a holding action in your sector?
B. Assuming that the enemy is able to achieve surprise:
  Identical requirements as without surprise.

ASSUMPTIONS

The problem as presented assumes that the responder has extensive information available as to the numbers and types of troops, weapons, and equipment available to the opposing sides. It also assumes that the responder has other background information needed for the essential decisions and calculations. Listed below are the key assumptions believed necessary for response to the requirements as stated:

1. Figure 12-1 shows a presumed Table of Organization for the US forces, including OLI values for weapons;

2. Figure 12-2 presents a similar Table of Organization for the Soviet forces which can be deployed in the corps sector;

3. Both sides provide approximately proportional air support to their ground forces; thus these air support efforts cancel each other out in terms of influencing the outcomes;

4. The ground forces of both sides have equal combat effectiveness—no bonus for superior training, leadership, morale, etc., will be allocated;

5. No replacements are expected by either side during the course of the operations;

6. Rates of advance, based upon Appendix A are as follows:
   a. Soviet Combined Arms Army against light-to-moderate resistance as offered by US Covering Force: 20 km per day;
   b. Soviet advance in the main battle area will be calculated from Part Two, Section III (Rules for Advance Rates) in Appendix A.

7. Casualty rates are as "normal," Appendix A, except that greater intensity may be assigned in main effort sectors.

8. Weapons effects values are based upon application of the OLI Methodology to weapons characteristics to be found in unclassified sources.

9. QJM factors for moderate surprise as developed from World War II data, and amplified and applied successfully to October War data, will be used in analyses of potential surprise situation.

SECONDARY ATTACK, WITHOUT SURPRISE

Figure 12-3 is a daily listing of troops, personnel casualties, medium tanks, and losses for both sides, on a day-by-day basis for the first ten days of the campaign in the situation of Secondary Attack, without surprise. Also included is the daily advance and cumulative advance for the Soviet Combined Arms Army. It is assumed that the Soviet army will advance to contact on a broad front with one motorized rifle regiment, supported by tanks, as a covering force for each of the two or three divisions in the first echelon, and that the resistance of the American covering force is such as to limit the initial Soviet rate of advance to the main battle position to 20 km per day. The American covering force is assumed to incur 2 percent personnel casualties per day during the two-day covering force engagement; the Soviet ratio is 1 percent.

Figure 12-1
WEAPONS INVENTORY LIST–US CORPS

	Armd Div	Mech Div	ACR	Corps Troops	Corps Totals	OLI/ Item	Corps OLI Total	Cov Force Total	Cov Force OLI Total
Personnel	20,200	20,200	2,000	10,100	52,500	–	–	5,200	–
Rifles	16,400	16,400	1,650	8,200	42,650	.35	14,928	4,300	1,505
Pistols	3,800	3,800	350	1,900	9,850	.02	197	900	18
Machine Guns, lt	3,634	3,548	600	300	8,082	.82	6,627	1,000	820
Machine Guns, cal .30	670	732	–	50	1,452	1.04	1,510	75	78
Mortars, 81mm	54	66	–	10	130	50	6,500	8	400
Mortars, 4.2"	65	60	–	30	155	90	13,950	8	720
APC, 113	732	642	–	–	1,374	27	37,098	60	1,620
APC, 114	106	148	10	30	294	75	22,050	5	375
Flame Throwers	54	66	–	20	140	1.0	140	4	4
Grenade Launcher, 40mm	1,069	972	–	60	2,101	8.0	16,808	80	640
LAW	1,000	900	100	400	2,400	18	43,200	75	1,350
RR 90mm	121	143	–	–	264	79	20,856	28	2,212
RR 106mm	48	60	–	–	108	133	14,364	8	1,064
ATGM TOW	30	36	–	–	66	176	11,616	6	1,056
How, SP, 105mm	18	18	–	54	90	160	14,400	18	2,880
How, SP, 155mm	54	54	–	36	144	235	33,840	18	4,230
Gun, SP, 155mm	–	–	–	54	54	303	16,362	–	–
Gun, SP, 175mm	–	–	–	54	54	356	19,224	–	–
How, SP, 8"	12	12	–	24	48	212	10,176	–	–
SSM, Honest John	4	4	–	8	8	107	856	–	–
SSM, Pershing	–	–	–	8	8	300	2,400	–	–
AAMG, cal .50	450	500	35	600	1,585	1.7	2,695	96	163
Light AAG, Vulcan	24	24	–	24	72	86	6,192	6	516
Med SAM, Chaparral	24	24	–	24	72	158	11,376	6	948
SAM Hawk	–	–	–	24	24	300	7,200	–	–
ARV	27	27	54	–	108	81	41,148	54	20,574
Tank, Med M60	324	270	54	–	648	796	515,808	54	42,984
Helicopter	98	106	3	150	357	88	31,416	6	528
Trucks	3,780	4,050	690	1,000	9,520	APC	–	786	–
Armd Spt Veh (incl)	1,100	1,100	100	200	2,500		–	200	–
OLI Totals							925,100		84,685

172

The battle for the main battle position thus begins late on the second day or early on the third day. The QJM analysis shows that the Soviets have a slight preponderance of force, but the balance is so close that the outcome is unpredictable. It is assumed that after three days of inconclusive combat (with .6 percent daily casualties for Americans and .8 percent for Soviets) the Soviets will revert to a holding action, with .2 percent daily personnel casualties for both sides.

SECONDARY ATTACK, WITH SURPRISE

Figure 12-4 is a daily listing of strengths, losses, and movement for this Secondary Attack situation, with Soviet surprise. Based upon analyses of Middle East war data, the force superiority provided to the attacking combined arms army is sufficient to warrant the assumption that the covering force battle will last only one day, with 3 percent casualties for the Americans, 1 percent for the Soviets.

The battle for the main battle position is assumed to begin late on the first day, and (on the basis of Middle East war data) it is assumed that the disruption following surprise lasts for three days. During this time the US force suffers personnel casualties at the rate of 1.2 percent per day. The Soviets incur casualties at the rate of .8 percent per day. After the effects of surprise wear off, US casualties fall back to .6 percent per day; the Soviet rate remains unchanged.

The QJM analysis for this three-day engagement was performed to reflect conditions of surprise. At the end of this engagement the Soviets' combat power advantage increases to about 1.1, thus permitting a slow but steady advance in subsequent days. During the period of surprise the assumptions regarding rate of advance permit an advance of 6 km per day. During the subsequent engagement this rate is presumed to decline to 2 km per day.

MAIN ATTACK WITHOUT SURPRISE

Figure 12-5 is a daily listing of strengths, losses, and advances during a presumed main attack, without surprise. It assumes a 3 percent daily casualty rate for the US covering force, a 2 percent rate for the Soviets, with the Soviets advancing 30 kilometers the first day.

The battle for the main position begins at the end of the first day or beginning of the second. During that battle both forces incur casualties at the rate of .9 percent per day. The combat power ratio provides for a level of resistance providing for a 13 km per day advance by the Soviet forces. At this rate the Soviets reach their objective during the 7th day, bringing the operation to a conclusion.

Figure 12-2
WEAPONS INVENTORY LIST—SOVIET FORCES

	Tank Div	Mot Rifle	Comb Arms Army Troops	Comb Arms Army	OLI/ Item	OLI C A Army	Tank Army Troops	Army Group Troops	Army Group Totals	Army Group OLI Totals
Personnel	8,415	10,485	10,000	58,285	–	–	5,000	7,500	96,030	–
Rifle	6,415	8,951	8,500	48,183	.32	15,302	4,250	6,500	78,178	25,017
Pistols	2,000	1,534	1,500	10,102	.03	302	750	6,000	17,852	536
MG, lt	720	1,160	600	5,600	.66	3,696	356	600	8,780	5,795
MG, hvy	240	360	280	1,840	.89	1,638	140	280	2,980	2,652
Mortar 82mm		54		162	50	8,100			162	8,100
Mortar 120mm	54	54	20	290	68	19,720	10	20	482	32,776
BTR-50	157	300	20	1,234	70	86,380	10	20	1,735	121,450
Flame Thrower	20	20	20	120	1	120	10	20	210	210
RPG-7	220	400	100	1,740	31	53,940	50	100	2,550	79,050
Sagger, AT 3	32	40	20	204	70	14,280	10	20	330	22,400
RR 82mm	12	20		84	41	3,444			120	4,920
RR 107mm	12	10		54	101	5,454			90	9,090
SPG-9	34	30	24	182	77	14,014	24	24	332	25,564
Gun, AT, 85mm		16	36	84	192	16,128		36	120	23,040
Gun, AT, 100mm	12	8	36	84	205	17,220		36	156	31,980
MRL, 122mm, BM-21	12	12	12	72	559	40,248	12		120	67,080

Gun How 122mm	36	54	36	270	227	61,290	36	—	414	93,978
Gun 130mm	—	—	36	36	317	11,412	36	12	84	26,628
Gun How 152mm	—	12	36	72	236	16,992	36	—	108	25,488
Gun 180mm	—	—	24	24	329	7,896	24	12	60	19,740
Frog	9	9	9	54	69	3,726	9	9	99	6,831
Scud	—	—	—	—	86			9	9	774
ZSU-23-4	64	64	64	384	179	68,376	32	64	672	120,288
AA-S-60	16	12	12	80	168	13,440	6	12	146	24,528
SA 7	50	81	80	423	34	14,382	40	80	693	21,862
SA 6	12	6	12	54	266	14,364	6	12	108	28,728
BRDM-1	10	120	20	400	11	4,400	10	20	460	5,060
BRDM-2	12	16	90	162	237	38,394	10	50	258	61,146
BMP	14	14	10	80	328	26,240	5	10	137	44,936
BMP-Sagger	12	14	10	76	207	15,732	5	10	127	26,289
Tank PT76	30	—	20	80	160	12,800	20	20	210	33,600
Tank JS-III	—	—	60	60	308	16,960	60	60	180	44,520
Tank T-62	323	188	240	1,450	767	1,112,115	10	—	2,420	1,856,140
Helicopter	2	2	20	30	68	2,040	10	20	66	4,488
Trucks	1,300	1,300	1,500	8,000	—	—	750	1,200	13,850	—
Armd Spt Veh	400	250	200	1,750	—	—	150	150	3,250	—
OLI Totals						1,740,697				2,904,684

Figure 12-3
SECONDARY ATTACK SITUATION
I. WITHOUT SURPRISE

	US Forces					Soviet Forces					Advance	
	Personnel		M 60 Tanks			Personnel		T-62 Tanks				
Days	Strength	Losses	Strength	Losses	Returns	Strength	Losses	Strength	Losses	Returns	Per Day	Cum
1	52,500	104	648	5	—	58,285	104	1,450	9	—	20	—
2	52,396	104	643	6	1	58,180	104	1,441	9	1	10	30
3	52,292	314	638	21	2	58,076	465	1,433	62	2	1	31
4	51,978	314	619	21	2	57,611	465	1,373	62	8	1	32
5	51,664	314	600	21	3	57,146	465	1,319	62	14	0	33
6	51,350	103	582	6	4	56,681	113	1,271	14	19	0	33
7	51,247	103	580	7	6	56,568	113	1,276	14	20	0	33
8	51,144	103	579	6	7	56,455	113	1,282	14	21	0	33
9	51,041	103	580	7	5	56,342	113	1,289	14	16	0	33
10	50,938	103	578	6	3	56,229	113	1,291	14	12	0	33
	50,835	—	575			56,116	—	1,289				
Total Losses		1,665			} 73		2,168			} 161		

Figure 12-4
SECONDARY ATTACK SITUATION
II. WITH SURPRISE

	US Forces					Soviet Forces					Advance	
	Personnel		M 60 Tanks			Personnel		T-62 Tanks				
Days	Strength	Losses	Strength	Losses	Returns	Strength	Losses	Strength	Losses	Returns	Per Day	Cum
1	52,500	156	648	9	—	58,285	105	1,450	17	—	30	30
2	52,344	629	639	42	2	58,180	465	1,433	62	2	6	36
3	51,715	629	599	42	2	57,715	465	1,373	62	8	6	42
4	51,086	629	559	42	6	57,250	465	1,319	62	14	6	48
5	50,457	303	523	17	7	56,785	465	1,271	55	19	2	50
6	50,154	303	513	17	9	56,320	465	1,235	55	24	2	52
7	49,851	303	505	17	9	55,855	465	1,204	55	29	2	54
8	49,549	303	497	17	8	55,390	465	1,178	55	28	2	56
9	49,245	303	488	17	6	54,925	465	1,151	55	28	2	58
10	48,942	303	477	17	5	54,460	465	1,124	55	27	2	60
	48,639	—	465			53,995	—	1,096				
Total Losses		3,861			} 183		4,290			} 354		

176

MAIN ATTACK WITH SURPRISE

In the event of main attack with surprise, the Soviet force preponderance is such that the covering force is presumed driven back to the main battle position by the middle of the first day. For that first half day it is assumed that the US covering force suffers casualties at a 6 percent rate, the Soviets at a 2 percent rate. Figure 12-6 presents a daily listing of strengths, losses, and advances during this operation.

The battle for the main battle position is presumed to begin at mid-day of the first day. US casualties are incurred at the rate of 1.8 percent per day for three days after the initiation of this engagement, with half the daily rate being lost during the afternoon of the first day. The Soviets incur casualties during this period at the rate of .9 percent per day, and also lose half the daily rate on the afternoon of the first day.

During the period of surprise, including the afternoon of the first day, the Soviets are able to advance at a rate of 16 km per day. On the fifth day, the advance rate declines to 13.5 km per day, but this is enough for them to reach their objective by evening of the fifth day.

RESPONSE TO REQUIREMENTS

A. Assuming no surprise:
 1. How long (in hours) will the covering force battle last:
    a. If the main attack is in your sector?
    (answer) Less than 24 hours
    b. If the secondary attack is in your sector?
    (answer) Between 24 and 48 hours
 2. How many tanks do you expect to lose during the covering force battle:
    a. If the main attack is in your sector?
    (answer) Nine tanks
    b. If the secondary attack is in your sector?
    (answer) Five tanks
 3. How long (in days) will the main battle last:
    a. If the main effort is in your sector?
    (answer) Seven days
    b. If the secondary effort is in your sector?
    (answer) More than 30 days
 4. If you remain in defensive posture do you expect your losses in the main battle sustained during the first few days to be different from those sustained over a longer period of time?
    (answer) Yes, because the nature of the enemy attack will change, becoming either more or less intensive
 5. Estimate the average number of tanks you expect to lose during the initial assaults against your main battle position during the first five days (if the battle lasts that long):
    a. If the main effort is in your sector?
    (answer) 22 per day
    b. If the secondary effort is in your sector?
    (answer) 13 per day
    c. If there is a holding action in your sector?
    (answer) 7 per day

Figure 12-5
MAIN ATTACK SITUATION
I. WITHOUT SURPRISE

	US Forces					Soviet Forces					Advance	
	Personnel		M 60 Tanks			Personnel		T-62 Tanks				
Days	Strength	Losses	Strength	Losses	Returns	Strength	Losses	Strength	Losses	Returns	Per Day	Cum
1	52,500	156	648	9	—	96,030	210	2,420	32	—	30	—
2	52,344	471	639	31	1	95,820	864	2,388	115	3	13	43
3	51,875	471	609	31	4	94,956	864	2,276	115	13	13	56
4	51,414	471	582	31	7	94,092	864	2,174	115	22	13	69
5	50,933	471	558	31	9	93,228	864	2,081	115	32	13	82
6	50,462	471	536	31	12	92,364	864	1,998	115	38	13	95
7	49,991	471	517	31	15	91,500	864	1,921	115	47	13	108
	49,520	—	501		} 147	90,636	—	1,853		} 577		
Total Losses		2,980					5,394					

Figure 12-6
MAIN ATTACK SITUATION
II. WITH SURPRISE

	US Forces					Soviet Forces					Advance	
	Personnel		M 60 Tanks			Personnel		T-62 Tanks				
Days	Strength	Losses	Strength	Losses	Returns	Strength	Losses	Strength	Losses	Returns	Per Day	Cum
1	52,500	629	648	48	—	96,030	642	2,420	89	—	38	—
2	51,871	945	600	58	2	95,388	864	2,331	115	8	16	54
3	50,926	945	544	58	7	94,524	864	2,224	115	32	16	70
4	49,981	945	493	58	10	93,660	864	2,141	115	43	16	86
5	49,036	441	445	22	15	92,796	864	2,069	115	43	14	100
	48,595	—	438		} 210	91,932	—	1,997		} 423		
Total Losses		3,905					4,098					

6. Estimate the average number of tanks you expect to lose every day after the fifth day, if the battles lasts more than five days:
   a. If the main effort is in your sector?
      (answer) 31 per day for 6th and 7th days, when battle ends
   b. If the secondary effort is in your sector?
      (answer) 17 per day
   c. If there is a holding action in your sector?
      (answer) 7 per day

B. Assuming the enemy achieves surprise:
   1. How long (in hours) will the covering force battle last:
      a. If the main attack is in your sector?
         (answer) Less than 24 hours
      b. If the secondary attack is in your sector?
         (answer) Less than 24 hours
   2. How many tanks do you expect to lose during the covering force battle:
      a. If the main attack is in your sector?
         (answer) 9 tanks
      b. If the secondary attack is in your sector?
         (answer) 5 tanks
   3. How long (in days) will the main battle last:
      a. If the main effort is in your sector?
         (answer) 5 days
      b. If the secondary effort is in your sector?
         (answer) Between 10 and 20 days
   4. If you remain in defensive posture do you expect your losses in the main battle sustained during the first few days to be different from those sustained over a longer period of time?
      (answer) Yes (same as for A-4, above)
   5. Estimate the average number of tanks you expect to lose during the initial assaults against your main battle position during the first five days (if the battle lasts that long):
      a. If the main effort is in your sector?
         (answer) 42 per day
      b. If the secondary effort is in your sector?
         (answer) 27 per day
      c. If there is a holding action in your sector?
         (answer) 7 per day
   6. Estimate the average number of tanks you expect to lose every day after the fifth day, if the battle lasts more than five days:
      a. If the main effort is in your sector?
         (answer) Battle is over
      b. If the secondary effort is in your sector?
         (answer) 17 per day
      c. If there is a holding action in your sector?
         (answer) 7 per day

COMMENTARY

This exercise provided the author with an opportunity to offer the following comments (slightly edited) to the Pentagon planners:

This problem reveals the general inadequacy of data upon which to base such evaluations. It is evident from past HERO research that there is much raw information available in primary and reliable secondary source materials, but only a small effort has been allocated to the review, distillation, compilation, and organization of such information so that it can be useful to the analyst. (It is interesting to note that Soviet analyses of World War II data are literally voluminous.)

Such processed data as is available to HERO has provided a basis for assessment of casualties and tank losses, as well as advance rates, that are quite possibly low. On the other hand, the rates shown above are not inconsistent with those observable in the 1967 and 1973 Middle East Wars. What is missing, however, is an assessment of the extent to which a willingness to incur more casualties might cause faster rates of advance. There is some evidence that this would be consistent not only with past Soviet doctrine, but also with what we know about current doctrine. Without such information analysis, it is possible to use only the limited data that is available.

In this regard, it is assumed from what we know of current Soviet doctrine that they will (with or without surprise) endeavor to reach the main battle area in five or six hours. But while this may be doctrine, and might well be their objective in the situations herein analyzed, delaying action by a substantial number of tanks and antitank weapons will—in most cases—almost certainly dictate a slower advance rate, as is suggested above.

Without allocation of time and effort far beyond the scope of this exercise, it is impossible to test the effects o⁵ various configurations of Soviet force strengths and echelonments to the different avenues of approach. To do full justice to the methodology employed in this analysis, separate QJM assessments should be undertaken of the covering force engagements in each of these approach areas, and on a daily basis for each division sector of the main battle area—particularly for that area where the main Soviet breakthrough effort is likely to be made, which will probably be no wider than 18 kilometers of the 75-kilometer corps front.[47]

An Experiment—Air Mobility vs. Armor

How would an army, dependent primarily upon tanks for its mobility and firepower, fare against an army primarily dependent upon helicopters for air mobility? In large part the answer to such a question depends upon the nature of the terrain and the opportunities for movement available both to tanks and helicopters. But let's look at a situation where the opportunities appear to be similar for both sides.

[47] This 18 kilometers estimate is based upon HERO's study report entitled: *A Study of Breakthrough Operations*, 1976.

Rather, let's look at two situations. In one the armor-heavy force, on the defensive, will be given half the raw OLI value of the airmobile force. In the other situation the roles will be reversed. To provide some opportunity for maneuver, in each case the defender will be a corps of two divisions, with the attacker a corps of four divisions. We will equip each side with the kind of American weapons which we used in the previous hypothetical combat situations and both will have standard support units.

Carry on!

Is There a Future in Prediction?

Whether in earnest, or for recreation, no human being can possibly predict the future. The best we can do is to be satisfied that we can project current trends over the range of reasonable possibilities. For those who are interested in looking into the future of war, or in taking a second look at historical might-have-beens, the QJM has proven itself.

From its original base in World War II, the methodology readily is projected forward in time to represent with precision the operations of the 1967 and 1973 Middle East Wars.

With equal ease it can not only represent battles of the Napoleonic and Civil Wars, it can restructure those battles in reasonable alternative possibilities. It can reflect the generalship of a Napoleon; it can represent the élan and skill of the *Grande Armée*, and the professional competence of the Reichswehr and Wehrmacht. It can project a range of reasonable and realistic operational potentialities in a hypothetical war between NATO and the Warsaw Pact.

If only Lee had had it at Gettysburg! Future General Lees may profit from the example!

Epilogue

In discussing her book, *Stilwell and the American Experience in China,* Barbara Tuchman once likened it to an egg with two yolks. Possibly this book is an egg with three yolks: analytical quantification of military history; the vicissitudes of an ugly duckling simulation in the Defense Research Community; and a morsel for the wargames-for-entertainment enthusiast.

It is my hope that these three aspects of the book come into a reasonably sharp focus through a historically based methodology which is a serious approach to analysis of some fundamental aspects of modern military theory, and which is of legitimate interest to that substantial segment of modern American and British society which is fascinated by the drama of human conflict. I have the feeling that some of my professional colleagues in the two academic disciplines where my feet are now somewhat unsteadily planted—history and military operations research—will recognize the logical interrelationship of the first two aspects of the book—whether or not they agree with my treatment. But they are likely to be critical of the third, as unprofessional pandering to a popular audience and market.

Let me remind those who have such a reaction, however, that a substantial number of modern young historians were drawn to that profession through adolescent exposure to commercial, entertainment wargames. Let me also remind both historians and operations researchers that some of the most serious analyses of historical conflict are appearing in the periodicals of the wargames-for-entertainment community. Not least is the fact that at least one commercial manufacturer of such games has, as a result of the sophistication of its products, performed consulting and developmental services for the US armed forces.

So, I have no apologies for attempting to interest this audience—which includes a number of historians and operations research analysts with graying hair—in a book intended as a very serious contribution to modern military literature. And if I have been unable to achieve the single, sharp focus for which I have striven, then I trust the result, rather than an egg with three yolks, is more like the three interlocking rings of a well-known brewing firm.

Appendix A
The Quantified Judgment
Model and Method;
Rules and Procedures

PART ONE—Engagement Analysis by QJM

Introductory Note

The rules and procedures that follow are an elaboration of the summary procedures shown on Figure 4-2, p. 51. Each of the following steps is numbered (using Roman numerals) to be consistent with that figure.

I. *Compile Data*

A. QUANTITATIVE

1. A complete order of battle (OB) of each of the opposing forces is necessary. This OB should list all significant weapons for each unit cited. Figures 9-9 and 12-1 are examples.
2. It is assumed that all weapons assigned in T/O&Es, and/or known to be in a unit, are available for combat, even those carried by or operated by personnel in support roles.
3. A consolidated list of all of the weapons in the inventory of each force is thus necessary. Figures 8-2 and 8-3 are samples. This list, or a separate compilation, should provide space for entry of all characteristics needed for the OLI calculation in Step II. Figure 2-3 (with dispersion factor included) can be used as a guide.
4. An engagement data sheet should be prepared for each engagement. Figure A-1 is a useful form, with space for entry of all relevant information.

B. QUALITATIVE

It is desirable, although not absolutely necessary, to prepare a narrative, or outline, of the principal events in each campaign and each battle or

Figure A-1

Engagement No.:   Terrain:
Date: Weather:
Unit: Season:
Depth: Personnel losses:
Posture: Tank losses:

Personnel

Small Arms
Pistol, Makarov PM, 9mm
Rifle, AKM/AK-47, 7.62mm
M/G, SGM, 7.62mm
    DK, 12.7mm

Mortars
Medium, M-43, 82mm
    M-43, 120mm

Antitank
G.Msl. AT-3, Sagger
Gun, M-43, 57mm
    D-44, 85mm
    M-44, 100mm
Rcl. Gun, SPG-9, 73mm
    B-10, 82mm
    B-11, 107mm
Rocket, RPG-7, 82mm

Field Artillery
Mortar, M-53, 160mm
    M-53, 240mm
MRL, BM-21, 122mm
    M-13, 132mm
How, M-38/D-30, 122mm
Gun, D-74, 122mm
    M-46, 130mm
Gun/How, M-37, 152mm
    M-55, 180mm
Gun, Corps, M-31/37, 122mm

Missiles and Rockets, SS, Tactical
FROG-7

Air Defense
M/G, ZPU-4, 14.5mm
Gun, SS, M-39, 37mm
    S-60, 57mm
    KS-12, 85mm

Air Defense (cont.)
    KS-19, 100mm
    KS-30, 130mm
Auto Cannon, ZU-23, 23mm
    ZSU-23-4, 23mm
    ZSU-57-2, 57mm
SAM, SA-2/3, Guideline/Goa
    SA-6, Gainful
    SA-7 Grail

Tanks (including Assault Guns)
Battle:
    SU-100/JSU-152
    Heavy, JS-2/3, 122mm
    Medium, T-62, 115mm
        T-54/44, 100mm
        T-34, 85 mm
Recon:
    Light, PT-76, 76mm

Other Armored Vehicles
IFV,   Tracked, BMP, 73mm
                  BMP, 73mm/Sagger
       Wheeled, BRDM-2/Sagger
ARV, Wheeled, BRDM
                  BRDM-2
APC, Tracked, BTR-50
       Wheeled, BTR,60
                  BTR-152

Aircraft
Fighter-heavy attack, SU-7, Fitter, Sorties
Fighter-bomber, MiG-17, Fresco, Sorties
Helicopters

Vehicles
GP, trucks
     motorcycles
SP, SP Mounts

engagement. The following definitions of battles, engagements and campaigns may be useful:

A *battle* is a combat encounter between two hostile military forces, each having opposing aims or objectives (assigned or implicit) and each seeking to impose its will on the opponent by achieving its objective, while preventing the enemy from achieving his. A battle ends when one side or the other has clearly achieved its objective, or when one (sometimes both) has clearly failed to achieve its objective. Modern battles between large forces can last many days.

An *engagement,* more or less synonymous with battle, usually designates a combat encounter between forces smaller than an army, and may not last as long as a "battle." Thus during a battle between two armies there are a number of engagements involving subordinate units. A modern division engagement rarely lasts more than two or three days.

A *campaign* usually comprises several battles, usually lasts longer than a battle, and stretches out over greater distance. A campaign is concluded when a strategic objective is achieved, or when a lull or stalemate occurs in combat operations.

II.   *Calculate OLI Values—*
"Proving Ground"
Weapons Effectiveness

A.   CATEGORIZE WEAPONS

1.   For purposes of calculating Operational Lethality Indexes (OLIs), or "proving ground" values, weapons are divided into two major employment categories:

  a. *Non-mobile weapons,* which have no inherent mobility capability, and are either fixed (in stationary emplacements), carried, towed, or mounted on platforms (as self-propelled artillery);

  b. *Mobile fighting machines (MFM),* in which firepower and inherent mobility are combined—usually with some kind of protection—to permit and facilitate direct engagement of the enemy in a primary combat role (as opposed to the support role of self-propelled artillery, for instance). MFMs such as tanks, armored cars, and aircraft usually have one primary weapon and may also have one or more secondary weapons.

2.   Separate calculation forms are recommended for the non-mobile weapons and for the mobile fighting machines of each side. The same form suggested for Step IA(3) may be used, or separate calculation sheets can be prepared. Figures A-2 and A-3 are examples of such forms.

Figure A-2
OLI CALCULATION SHEET
Soviet Non-Mobile Weapons

Identification Code	Weapon Designation or Description	Caliber mm	RF	PTS	RIE	Range	Effect Factor	MV		Caliber Factor	Di	A	R	GE	MCE	MBE	SME	AE	RN	OLI MV	Final
09-1-9	Pistol, Makarov, auto pistol, PM	9	350	1	0.7	—	—	315	$.1\sqrt{9}$	1.00	.7	.8								0.03	0.03
09-1-91	Machine Pistol Stechin, APS	9	1400	1	0.7	—	—	340	$.1\sqrt{9}$	1.00	.7	.7								0.12	0.12
09-1-47	Rifle, AKM/AK47/AMD	7.62	1280	1	0.8	2,250	2.50	710	$.1\sqrt{7.62}$	1.37	.8	.8							0.41	0.22	0.32
09-2-33	Machine Gun RPK/MG	7.62	2600	1	0.8	2,250	2.50	745	$.1\sqrt{7.62}$	1.44	.8	.8	.8						0.83	0.48	0.66
	PKM/PHJ	7.62	2600	1	0.8	3,700	2.92	855	$.1\sqrt{7.62}$	1.65	.8	.8	.8						1.16	0.55	0.86
	hvy M38/46	12.7	2280	2	1	2,000	2.41	840	$.1\sqrt{12.7}$	2.09	.8	.8	.8						1.76	1.52	1.64
09-3-37	Mortar, M 1937	82	168	760	1	3,040	2.74	210	$.1\sqrt{82}$	1.33	.6	.95							50	24	50
09-5-3	Sagger, AT-3, Manpack	120	95	1900	1	3,000	2.73	120	$.1\sqrt{82}$	1.00	.6	.7						2	104	35	70
09-5-76	Gun, AT 76mm 215-3	76.2	148	640	1	11,961	4.46	950	$.1\sqrt{76.2}$	5.80	.9	.9							91	119	119
09-6-21	MRL, BM21 (MTD)	122	120	1975	1	20,000	5.47	450	$.1\sqrt{122}$	3.48	.6	.8					418	1.05	683	434	559
09-6-30	How D30/M34	122	120	1975	1	15,000	4.87	690	$.1\sqrt{122}$	5.33	.9	.9							234	256	256

Figure A-3
OLI CALCULATION SHEET
Soviet Mobile Fighting Machines

Identification Code	Designation	CC Speed km/hr	Range km	Wgt. tons	Composite OLIs	MOF	RA	Prelim. Product	T/4	$\sqrt{T}$	PF	Raw OLI	RFE	FCE	ASE	CL	APC	AM	Wht OLI	Refined OLI
09-0-54	Tank, T-54	33	400	36	343.2	1.15	1.6	631	36/4	$\sqrt{36}$	54	685	.92	.9	.68			1.05		405
09-0-55	Tank, T-55	33	500	36	341.4	1.15	1.79	703	36/4	$\sqrt{36}$	54	758	.92	.9	.87			1.05		573
09-0-62	Tank, T-62	33	450	37.6	488.5	1.15	1.70	955	37.6/4	$\sqrt{37.6}$	58	1013	.91	.9	.88			1.05		767
09-0-76	Tank, Recon PT-76	44	200	14	119.7	1.33	1.29	205	14/4	$\sqrt{14}$	13	218	.96	.9	.77			1.1		160
09-8-3	ICV, BMP w/Sagger	50	500	13.6	176.9	1.41	1.79	446	13.6/4	$\sqrt{13.6}$	13	459	.93	.9	.49			1.1		207
09-8-1	ARV, BRDM-1	53	500	5.6	4.2	1.46	1.79	11	5.6/4	$\sqrt{5.6}$	3	14	.99	.9	.9			1.1		11
09-8-2	ARV, BRDM-2 w/Sagger	53	750	7	184	1.46	2.19	588	7/4	$\sqrt{7}$	5	593	.99	.9	.44			1.1		230
09-0-100	Assault Gun, ASU, 100	37	305	31.6	340	1.22	1.40	581	31.6/8	$\sqrt{31.6}$	22	603	.8	.9	.9			1.1		439
09-4-152	APC, BTR 152	43	780	9	26.4	1.31	2.23	77	9/8	$\sqrt{9}$	3	80	—	—	—			—		79
09-09-17	Aircraft MiG-17	1163	1205	6.3	54.4	4.76	2.78	720	6.3/8	$\sqrt{6.3}$	2	722	—	—	—			—		810
09-09-23	Aircraft, MiG-23	2966	960	15	91.2	4.96	2.48	1122	15/8	$\sqrt{15}$	7	1127	—	—	—			—		1296

189

3. Note that OLIs of weapons mounted on mobile fighting machines must be calculated before OLIs of MFMs can be determined.

4. For the purpose of calculating the effects of weapons in the QJM, weapons are divided into six mission categories:

    a. *Infantry Weapons,* those which are involved directly or indirectly in the land battle in the traditional foot combat role of the infantry; these include small arms, machine guns, various kinds of heavy weapons (other than AT weapons), and armored personnel carriers (other than infantry fighting vehicles —IFV—which are classified as armor);

    b. *Armor* includes those mobile fighting machines which have a direct ground combat operational role (as opposed to a support or antitank or air defense role); armor includes tanks, armored reconnaissance vehicles (ARV, usually synonymous with light tank), armored cars, assault guns, and tank destroyers;

    c. *Antitank Weapons* (other than those mounted on armored vehicles) are those whose primary function is to engage hostile armored forces; these may be self-propelled; however, heavily armored tank destroyers (TDs) are classified as armored vehicles;

    d. *Artillery* includes those weapons (guns, missiles, and rockets) whose function is to provide land-based firepower support to infantry and armored units;

    e. *Air-Defense Weapons* are those land-based weapons whose primary function is to engage hostile air forces;

    f. *Air Support* includes each sorty of those aerial mobile fighting machines (fixed wing aircraft or helicopters) with the mission of providing fire support to, or engaging ground targets in the immediate vicinity of, ground combat units. QJM calculations do not *directly* include air-based firepower employed in an interdiction or air-superiority role. Unlike the other five categories (where all potentially available weapons are included), air support firepower is included directly in QJM calculations only for those combat aircraft sorties which were actually engaged in the close support role in historical engagements, or which are specifically scheduled for such employment in discrete hypothetical engagements.

B. NON-MOBILE WEAPONS

The first seven general factors, listed below, must be considered in calculating the lethality of all weapons. Five other factors are relevant to specific kinds of weapons.

1. *Rate of Fire (RF)*. This is the practical sustained rate of fire for a weapon on a per-hour basis. Logistical constraints are not considered at this point.
   a. Rule of thumb for a crew-served automatic weapon: RF=4× cyclic rate per minute.
   b. Rule of thumb for a hand or shoulder automatic weapon: RF= 2×cyclic rate per minute.
   c. Rule of thumb for an aircraft-mounted automatic weapon: RF= 2×cyclic rate per minute.
   d. For most other weapons, the graph of Figure A-4 shows the normal rate of fire for most non-automatic weapons by caliber.
   e. Mortar rate of fire is 1.2× that shown in Figure A-4.

2. *Number of Potential Targets per Strike (PTS)*. Individual weapons and light machine guns are usually limited to one target per strike. Machine guns with a caliber of 10-15 cms are assumed capable of hitting two targets per strike. Pre-high-explosive artillery (i.e., 19th Century and earlier) could hit up to 25 targets per strike; see Figure 2-3 for guidance). High-explosive weapons hit one man per square meter within the lethal area of burst. Figure A-5 is a graph which shows the PTS for standard weapons of most calibers.

3. *Relative Incapacitating Effect (RIE)*. This shows the likelihood that a single strike will be incapacitating. For weapons more powerful than small arms and light machine guns, the effect is always 1. See Figure 2-3 for guidance for RIE of small weapons.

4. *Range Factor (RN)*. The effective range is assumed to be 90 percent of the theoretical maximum range, if no other information is available. The minimum effective range of any weapon is the average reach of a man, assumed (with the weapon) to be at least 1 meter. The value RN can be calculated on the basis of either a weapon's effective range or its muzzle velocity (MV), both should be calculated whenever the data permits.
   a. Using effective range:
      $RN=1+\sqrt{.001\times\text{Effective Range (in meters)}}$
   b. Using muzzle velocity (MV): $RN=.007\times MV$ (in meters/sec) $\times.1\times\sqrt{\text{caliber (mm)}}$
   c. The minimum RN factor, whether calculated on basis of range or MV, is 1.0.
   d. Use the MV calculation result whenever it is higher than the range calculation result except for mortars and missiles.
   e. When the range calculation result is higher than the MV calculation result, RN should be the average of the two.
   f. For mortars and missiles, take the higher of the two values, not the average.

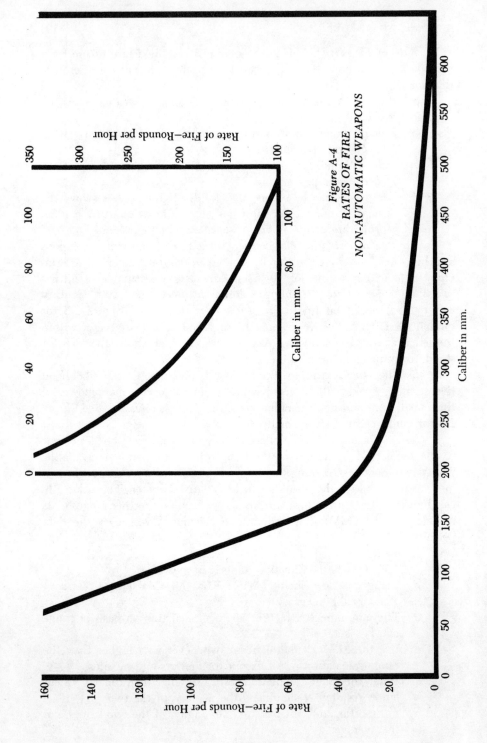

Figure A-4
RATES OF FIRE
NON-AUTOMATIC WEAPONS

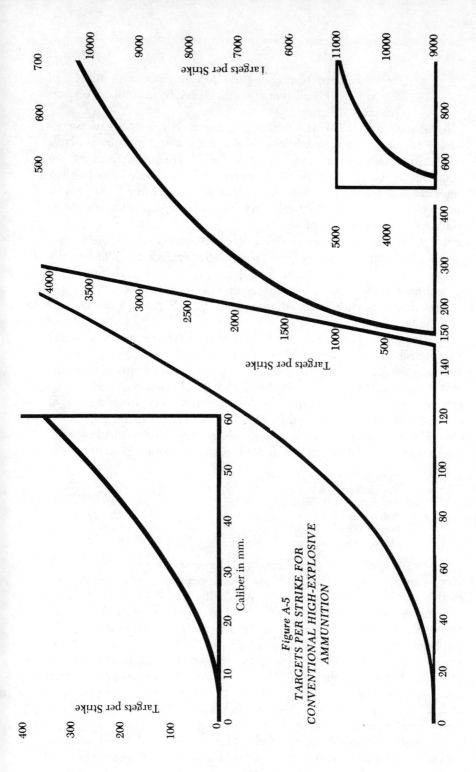

Figure A-5
TARGETS PER STRIKE FOR
CONVENTIONAL HIGH-EXPLOSIVE
AMMUNITION

193

    g. For air-dropped bombs; use the MV formula, with an MV of 250, and a caliber value from the "Weight to Caliber" conversion chart (Figure A-6).

5. *Accuracy (A).* This is a judgmental factor. For weapons whose accuracy factors at mean battlefield ranges are not included in available official manuals or other data, A is estimated. Guidance for such estimations will be found in Figure 2-3. In general a high muzzle velocity guarantees high accuracy; automatic weapons, mortars, and free-flight missiles or rockets tend to be relatively inaccurate; weapons with electronic guidance tend to have high accuracy.

6. *Reliability (RL).* This is also a judgmental factor. Hand-held, non-mechanical weapons are assumed (with slight exaggeration) to be fully reliable. Weapons subject to misfires, jamming, or to a high proportion of malfunctions or duds, are relatively unreliable. Where official or other sources do not provide information on reliability, Figure 2-3 can be used as a guide.

7. *Dispersion Factor (Di).* The dispersion factor converts a weapon's Theoretical Lethality Index (TLI) value—derived for basic weapons by applying the six previous rules to the weapon's characteristics—to a currently relevant Operational Lethality Index (OLI) showing the "proving ground" value of the weapon under contemporary circumstances of combat. The OLI is calculated by dividing the TLI by the average number of square meters per man in contemporary combat deployments. These dispersion values are as follows for major historical periods:

Ancient armies	1
Napoleonic Wars	20
American Civil War	25
World War I	250
World War II	3,000
Mid-1970s (conventional weapons)	4,000

8. *Self-propelled Artillery Factor (SME).* A self-propelled (SP) artillery weapon is a standard artillery piece, permanently mounted on a mobile platform with cross-country capability, usually with light armor side protection, and sometimes with light overhead armor. Although the terms are sometimes used interchangeably, an SP artillery piece should not be confused with a heavily armored assault gun, or with a tank destroyer, both of which are classified as armored weapons in the category of mobile fighting machines (MFM; see below). For SP artillery there is a self-propelled mobility effect (SME), an enhancement of the static or towed gun value of the weapons by a factor of 1.05. If there is overhead cover the SME factor is 1.10.

9. *Missile Guidance Effect (GE).* This is calculated for missiles or rockets with special electronic guidance. This factor is 2.0 where guidance

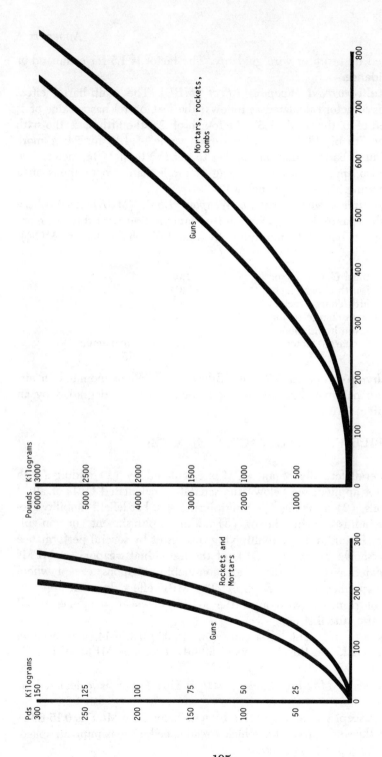

Figure A-6
AVERAGE RELATIONSHIP OF
AMMUNITION WEIGHTS TO CALIBER

195

is provided by beam or wire guidance. The factor is 1.5 for command or radar guidance.

10. *Multi-barreled Weapons Effect (MBE).* The multi-barrel effect (MBE) is a factor calculated as follows: the first barrel has a value of 1, the second of .5, the third of .33, the fourth of .25, the fifth of .2, the sixth of .19, the 7th of .18, etc. to a maximum value of 4.18 for 24 or more barrels. These barrel values are added to get the total MBE factor. The MBE is also applied to any grouping of more than two weapons on a mobile fighting machine (see below).

11. *Multiple Charge Artillery Weapons Effect (MCE).* An artillery piece with separate-loading or semi-fixed ammunition with three or more charges has its basic OLI multiplied by a multiple-charge factor (MCE), as follows:

third charge factor	1.05
fourth charge factor	+.04
fifth charge factor	+.03
sixth charge factor	+.02
seventh and more charge factors	+.01, or a maximum factor of 1.15.

12. *Aircraft Mounted Weapons Effect (AE).* When mounted on aircraft, weapons have their normal land operation OLIs degraded by an aircraft effect (AE) of 0.25.

C. MOBILE FIGHTING MACHINES (MFMs)

The overall lethality of an MFM is calculated by (1) adding (with MBE factor applied; see below) the separately calculated OLIs of all of its weapons, (2) applying (by multiplication) a battlefield mobility factor and a radius of action factor, (3) adding a punishment (or non-vulnerability) factor, and (4) multiplying this result by several performance factors as shown below. The OLIs of the individual weapons on MFMs are calculated as though they were non-mobile weapons, except where otherwise specified rules may apply. The MBE effect does not apply to the first or principal weapon of the MFM; however, it applies to all weapons after the first one.

For instance: If a tank has a main gun of 300 OLI, a 14.7mm machine gun of 3.0 OLI, and three rockets of 20 OLI each, the MFM OLI = 337 $(300 + 20 + 0.5 \times 20 + .33 \times 20 + .25 \times 3)$.

1. *Battlefield Mobility Effect (MOF).* This factor is calculated as follows:

   a. Except where indicated otherwise below, the MOF is 0.15 times the square root of a vehicle's road speed, or maximum air speed, in kilometers per hour;

b. For an aircraft, the optimum speed for close support is 500 km/hr. For an increment of speed above 500 kmh and less than 1,500 kmh, multiply the increment by 0.1; for an additional increment above 1,500 kmh, multiply the additional increment by 0.01. Thus for an aircraft with a maximum air speed of 2,900 kmh, the OLI calculation speed value is 604 (500+100 +4).

2. *Radius of Action Factor (RA)*. The RA factor is .08 times the square root of the radius of action, or range, of the machine in kilometers.

3. *Punishment Factor (PF)*.

a. The ability of an MFM (tank, ARV, or armored car) to withstand punishment is calculated as follows (with Weight in metric tons): $PF = Weight/4 \times \sqrt{2 \times Weight}$

b. For an aircraft, assault gun, or tank destroyer, the PF is half of the value for a tank of identical weight.

c. This is an additive (not multiplicative) factor; see paragraph 4(a) below.

4. *Armored Vehicles*. The following special rules apply to tanks, ARVs, armored cars, assault guns (but not self-propelled artillery), and tank destroyers.

a. A "raw" OLI is calculated by (1) adding the individual OLIs of all weapons of the MFM (with MBE effect considered), then (2) multiplying this sum by the MOF and RA factors, and then (3) adding the PF value to this product.

b. *Rapidity of Fire Effect (RFE)*. This is a multiplicative factor, representing the speed with which the MFM main armament can be fired and reloaded, as related to the sustained hourly rate of fire of that weapon. The value is measured on the curve in Figure 2-1 (p. 24)

c. *Fire Control Effect (FCE)*. This is a multiplicative, judgmental value, reflecting practical fire control effectiveness; for 1973 tanks the US M60A1 had a typical FCE of 0.9.

d. *Ammunition Supply Effect (ASE)*. This multiplicative factor is measured on the curve in Figure 2-2 (p. 25)which relates the amount of main armament ammunition the MFM can carry to its sustained hourly rate of fire.

e. *Wheel/Halftracks Effect (WHT)*. Armored vehicles which are not fully tracked are degraded as follows:

i. The WHT factor for wheeled vehicles is 0.9;

ii. The WHT factor for half-tracked vehicles is 0.95.

f. *Adverse Environmental Effects*. In bad weather or bad terrain, the calculated OLI of an armored vehicle cannot go below its minimum value as artillery, which is assumed to be 0.5 times the theoretical performance of its principal weapon in artillery configuration, under the existing environmental and operational conditions.

   g. *Amphibious Capability Effect (AME).* A factor of 1.1 is applied to a weapon with amphibious capability. For a snorkeling, or limited amphibious capability, a factor of 1.05 is applied.

5. *Armored Personnel Carriers (APCs).* The following rules are applicable:

   a. APCs are classified as infantry heavy weapons and as such are subject to environmental and operational factors affecting infantry weapons.

   b. The OLI is calculated as for assault guns and TDs, but without the first three performance characteristics (RFE, FCE, and ASE), unless the weapon is used essentially as a weapons platform.

   c. The weapons value for an APC includes permanently mounted weapons, plus the small arms for a full load of infantry. This does not require a deduction from the overall small arms total, but rather in effect means giving double value to all small arms carried into battle on APCs.

6. *Fixed Wing Aircraft.* The following rules are applicable:

   a. A "raw" OLI is calculated as for armored vehicles. (See, however, the special rule for aircraft MOF, paragraph II-c-1-b above.)

   b. *Ceiling Effect (CL).* For an aircraft with a maximum operational ceiling of 30,000 feet, CL=1. When the maximum ceiling is lower, CL is reduced below 1.0 by 0.02 for each 1,000 feet below 30,000 feet. When the maximum ceiling is higher, the CL is increased above 1.0 by .005 for each 1,000 additional feet of ceiling.

7. *Helicopters.* The OLI value for helicopters is included with the air support component, and calculated as for high-performance aircraft, except as follows. To reflect the greater vulnerability of the helicopter, the value w_{yh} is the mean between the normal aircraft OLI calculation and the composite OLI value for the helicopter's unmounted weapon or weapons, as per the following formula: $W_{yh}=[(W \times MOF \times RA+PF)+W]/2$. The ceiling effect for all helicopters is assumed to be 0.6.

D. SUMMATION: OLI FORMULAE

1. Non-mobile weapon OLI value (W) based on weapon characteristics:

$$W = (RF \times PTS \times RIE \times RN \times A \times RL \times SME \times GE \times$$

$$\uparrow$$
$$\text{or MV}$$

$$MCE \times MBS \times WHT \times AE)/Di$$

See list of symbols and abbreviations on p. xv for an explanation of items in this formula.

2. *Mobile Fighting Machine OLI Value* (W_{iy}), based on application of special characteristics of such weapons, as applied to W values for their component weapons:

$$W_{iy} = [(W \times MOF \times RA) + PF] \times RFE \times FCE \times ASE \times AME \times CL$$

See list of abbreviations and symbols pp. xv-xvi.

III. *Determine Variables*

A. GENERAL

The total list of variables considered in the QJM is found in Figure 3-1. Subsequent paragraphs show how these are currently reflected in the model. For explanation of symbols, see pp. xv-xvi.

B. TERRAIN EFFECTS

Table 1 tabulates the operational effects of terrain on general mobility and upon defensive posture, and the environmental effects upon the six categories of weapons.

C. WEATHER EFFECTS

Table 2 lists the operational effects of weather upon mobility and posture, and its environmental effects on four of the weapons categories.

D. SEASON EFFECTS

Table 3 presents values for the operational effect of season upon posture, for environmental effects upon three categories of weapons, and for a tentative estimation of the effect of season upon Score Effectiveness (see below).

E. AIR SUPERIORITY EFFECTS

Table 4 lists the operational effects of air superiority upon mobility and vulnerability, and the environmental effects upon three of the six weapons categories.

F. POSTURE

Table 5 lists the operational effects of combat posture.

G. MOBILITY

1. The value of the comparative mobility force characteristics (M) of the opposing sides is represented as follows for typical World War II forces:

$$M_a = \sqrt{[(N_a + 20J_a + W_{ia}) \times m_{ya}/N_a]/[(N_d + 20J_d + W_{id}) \times m_{yd}/N_d]}.$$

For the mid-1970s the constant factor modifying J is 12, for World War II it was 20.

2. The value of the operational factor for mobility (m) is:

$$m_a = M_a - (1 - r_m \times h_m)(M_a - 1).$$

3. For the defender, $m_d = 1$.

H. VULNERABILITY

1. The vulnerability characteristics (V) of the opposing sides are calculated by the following formula (shown below for the friendly side only):

$$V_f = N_f \times u_v / r_u \times \sqrt{S_e/S_f} \times v_y \times v_r$$

The value for v_y (effect of air superiority) is taken from Table 4. The value of v_r (shoreline vulnerability factor) is taken from Table 6.

2. The value of the operational factor for vulnerability (v) is shown below (for the friendly side only): $v_f = 1 - (V_f/S_f \times Di/3000)$.

3. The maximum value for the vulnerability factor (v) is 0.6. If the calculated value of V/S is greater than 0.3, the effective value of V/S is calculated as follows, in these circumstances only:

Effective $V/S = 0.3 + 0.1$(Calculated $V/S - 0.3$).

Thus, if V/S is calculated as 0.42, the effective value is 0.312 (0.3 + .012).

4. The values of V_e and v_e are calculated in identical fashion, with obvious transpositions.

I. SURPRISE

When the record indicates that effective tactical surprise has been achieved by one side or the other (usually, but not always, the attacker), the application of surprise factors is required. Before these are calculated or applied, however, the Model Formula output should be calculated. Then the surprise factors are calculated as follows:

1. The record is consulted to make a judgmental decision as to the degree of surprise achieved. Surprise can be *complete* (as, for example, that achieved by the Germans at the Ardennes in 1944, or that achieved by the Arabs in the October War, 1973), *substantial* (as that achieved by

the Germans in their invasion of Russia in 1941, or by the Israelis in their invasion of the Sinai in 1967), or *minor* (as that achieved by the Allies in their Normandy landing in 1944, or by the Pakistanis in their abortive attack upon India in 1971).

2. Based upon the category of surprise assessed, values for factors modifying the comparative mobility characteristics (M) and the vulnerability characteristics (V) of the two sides are determined from Table 9. After applying these modifying factors to the previously calculated values of M and V, new values are calculated for the model mobility factor (m) and the respective model vulnerability factors (v). The Power Potential (P) values for each side are then recalculated (Step V., below), and a new combat Power Ratio (P/P) determined (Step VI., below).

3. Effects of surprise appear to be greater in more recent wars than they were in World War II; it is not yet clear whether this is a phenomenon related to modern technology, or to the model. In any event, for wars since 1966, the calculated surprise effects should be multiplied by 1.33.

4. The disruptive effects of surprise continue to affect the surprised force for at least two days after the actual surprise is achieved on the battlefield. It is assumed that the effects of the first day's surprise are reduced by one-third on the second day, two-thirds on the third day, and that they have disappeared by the fourth day. Thus, if the calculated effect of surprise in a World War II battle was 2.24, then the effect of post-surprise disruption on the second day is 1.83; on the third day it is 1.41. These figures are achieved by the following calculations:

First day effect of surprise: 2.24, or a difference of 1.24

                        from no surprise (1.00)

Second day effect: $1+2/3\times1.24=1.83$

Third day effect: $1+1/3\times1.24=1.41$

If the same calculated effect for surprise is found for an October War engagement, the results would be slightly different:

First day effect of surprise: $2.24\times1.33=2.98$, or a difference

                        of 1.98 from no surprise (1.00)

Second day effect: $1+2/3\times1.98=2.32$

Third day effect: $1+1/3\times1.98=1.66$

J. COMBAT EFFECTIVENESS

1. Only when the record provides clear evidence that a degradation factor is appropriate for leadership (le), training, and/or experience (t), morale (o), or logistical capability (b), should a judgmental factor be entered in the QJM formula for these intangible variables. If factors do seem appropriate, guidance on how these may be assessed is provided by Table 7, showing Morale Factors.

2. Otherwise, Combat Effectiveness is calculated *after* the Model Formula and Result Formula operations have been completed and their respective outputs calculated (see below).

IV. *Calculate Force Strength*

A. FORCE STRENGTH (S)

The Force Strength (S) of each side is calculated by applying the appropriate environmental variables to the combined OLI values of the inventory of each category of weapons on each side in accordance with the following formula:

$$S=[(W_s+W_{mg}+W_{hw})\times r_n]+(W_{gi}\times r_n)+$$
$$[(W_g+W_{gy})\times(r_{wg}\times h_{wg}\times z_{wg}\times w_{yg})]+$$
$$(W_i\times r_{wi}\times h_{wi})+(W_y\times r_{wy}\times h_{wy}\times z_{yw}\times w_{yy})$$

B. ANTITANK WEAPONS (W_{gi})

The following considerations apply to antitank weapons:
1. Both environmental and operational factors are applied to AT weapons as to infantry weapons.
2. Full value for AT weapons (symbol: W_{gi}) is included in Force Strength (S) calculations only up to the total OLI value of hostile armored weapons (symbol: W_{ei}). Only half of any excess AT value, above hostile W_{ei}, is included in friendly W_{tgi}.

C. AIR DEFENSE WEAPONS (W_{gy})

There are two principal categories of air defense (AD or AA) weapons: (1) antiaircraft artillery (AAA), and (2) surface-to-air missiles (SAMs).
1. Both environmental and operational factors are applied as for artillery.
2. Full value for AD weapons (W_{gy}) is included in Force Strength (S) only up to the total OLI value of hostile close air support (W_{ey}: actual sorties in historical analyses; proportional share of available hostile aircraft in hypothetical simulations). Only half of any excess AD value above W_{ey} is included in the total friendly W_{tgy}.

D. LIMITS TO CONVERTIBILITY OF AIR FIREPOWER

Air Firepower (W_y) greater than the sum of all ground firepower is not fully effective,
1. When $W_y > W_s+W_{my}+W_{hw}+W_{gi}+W_g+W_{gy}+W_i$ only half value is given to the excess of W_y over the sum of ground weapons firepower.

2. The maximum allowable value for W_y is three times the sum of the ground weapons firepower.

V. *Calculate Combat Power*

A. COMBAT POWER FORMULA

The Combat Power, or Power Potential, of each side is then calculated by applying all relevant operational variables to the respective Force Strengths (S) of each side in accordance with the following formula:

$$P = S \times \text{operational variables}$$

$$S \times [M_a - (1 - r_m \times h_m)(M_a - 1)] \times le \times t \times o \times b \times u_s \times r_u \times h_u \times z_u \times v$$

$$\sqrt{\frac{(N_a + 20J_a + W_{ia}) \times m_{ya}/N_a}{(N_d + 20J_d + W_{id}) \times m_{yd}/N_d}} \qquad 1 - (N \times c \times \sqrt{S_e/S_f} \times v_y \times v_r)/S_f$$

$$u_v/r_u$$

$$(W_s + W_{mg} + W_{hw}) \times r_a + W_{gi}{}^{*} \times r_n + W_g + W_{gy}{}^{**} + (W_i \times r_{wi} \times h_{wi}) + W_y$$

$$\times r_{wg} \times h_{wg} \times z_{wg} \times w_{yg} \qquad \times r_{wy} \times h_{wy} \times z_{wy} \times w_{yy}.$$

* Up to total of W_{ei}; thereafter only half value.
** Up to total of W_{ey}; thereafter only half value.

B. SURPRISE CALCULATION

It will be noted from the discussion of Surprise (paragraph III-I above), that in engagements where the element of surprise was known to be present, this step is done twice: once without consideration of surprise, and once with the surprise factor applied.

C. SET-PIECE FACTOR

When there is a substantial combat effectiveness difference known or suspected between the opponents (CEV of 1.5 or more), a set-piece factor must be calculated whenever the force with lower combat effectiveness has an opportunity to make detailed, thoroughly planned and (often) rehearsed preparations for an operation. Examples of such preparations can be found in some Soviet set-piece attacks of World War II, and in the Arab set-piece attacks at the outset of the 1973 October War. Under such circumstances, it is assumed that the known (or estimated) relative combat effectiveness value (CEV) of the less combat effective, but carefully prepared, side is increased by one-third of the differential between the CEV and unity. In other words, when the German CEV value with respect to the Soviets was about 2.7 the set-piece factor was 1.57 (1+1/3×1.7).

VI. *Calculate Relative Combat Power*

This calculation is a simple ratio, P/P, of the two Combat Power values calculated in the previous step. If P_f/P_e is >1, then the friendly side should theoretically have been successful, on the basis of the input data compiled in Step 1. If $P_f/P_e<1$, then the enemy side should have been successful. A ratio in the range of 0.9 to 1.1 is considered to be "unpredictable."

When behavioral factors (such as surprise and set-piece preparations) are to be considered, two or more combat power ratios will have to be calculated. For instance, to determine the quantitative effects of surprise, the P/P should be calculated both with and without the surprise factors, and then one of these ratios is divided by the other.

The symbol P'/P' is usually used to indicate a combat power ratio in which behavioral factors (other than combat effectiveness) are considered. In other words, the P/P ratio calculated by means of the non-behavioral variable factors becomes P'/P' when it is multiplied by set-piece and/or surprise factors, whenever these are identified as present in an engagement.

VII. *Calculate Actual Outcome*

The actual outcome of an engagement is calculated in the following steps:

a. *Mission Accomplishment.* On the basis of evidence to be found in primary sources (of both sides, if possible), the extent to which each side in an engagement accomplished its assigned or perceived mission is assessed, in the terms shown in Table 8. A Mission Factor (MF) value is then determined for each side.

b. *Spatial Effectiveness.* The extent to which each side was able to gain or hold ground is assessed through the following formula (shown here only for the friendly side):
$E_{fsp} = \sqrt{[(S_e \times u_{se})/(S_f \times u_{sf})]} \times (4Q + D_e)/3D_f$. Q is a plus value for one side and a negative value for the other. Whenever $(4Q + D_e)$ has a negative value, the whole factor E_{fsp} is negative.

   i. If no other values are suggested from the data, the depths of the opposing forces are calculated with the benefit of the Maximum Depth Factor (for a force of 100,000 troops): [shown in Figure 2-5, and summarized below]

Ancient armies	.15 kms
Napoleonic Wars	2.5 kms
American Civil War	3.0 kms
World War I	12.0 kms
World War II	60.0 kms
Mid-1970s	67.0 kms

Thus, for World War II, a force of 100,000 (or larger) has a depth factor of 60; a force of 50,000 has a depth factor of 30.0; a force of 25,000 a depth factor of 15.0; etc. When a unit is a component of a larger unit (up to a corps in size) the depth of the smaller unit is the same as that of the larger unit.

ii. The same procedure is used to calculate E_{esp}, with obvious transpositions and substitutions.

c. *Casualty Effectiveness.* The casualty effectiveness of a force is calculated by the following formula (shown here only for enemy forces):

$$E_{cas} = v_f{}^2[\sqrt{(Cas_f \times u_{se}/S_f)/(Cas_e \times u_{sf}/S_e)} - \sqrt{100Cas_e/N_e}]$$

The same procedure is used to calculate E_{fcas}, with obvious transpositions and substitutions.

d. *Result Formula.* A Result Formula is calculated for each side. Mission accomplishment, spatial effectiveness and casualty effectiveness are combined in the following formula: $R = MF + E_{sp} + E_{cas}$.

e. *Result Comparison.* This is accomplished as follows:

$$\text{Outcome} = R_f - R_e.$$

A positive value represents a friendly success, a negative value an enemy success. A value between -0.5 and $+0.5$ is considered to be "inconclusive."

VIII. *Compare Theoretical and Actual Outcomes*

1. The following relationships are to be expected:

If $P_f/P_e > 1$, then $R_f - R_e$ should be positive;
If $P_f/P_e < 1$, then $R_f - R_e$ should be negative.

2. If the results of this comparison should prove seriously inconsistent, then the next step, Analysis, is critical.

IX. *Analysis*

1. In undertaking an analysis of the results of applying the two formulae to the data for any engagement, two things should always be borne in mind.

a. It is not possible to fit human behavior into precise and undeviating models; records are never either complete or totally accurate; human memories are fallible. Even if the method were perfect, there would still be anomalies in the results because of vagaries in human behavior; some of the anomalies can never be fully explained by even the most thorough analysis.

b. The methodology, which is to a large extent actuarial (in part because it reflects the performance of large numbers of human beings over substantial periods of time and in part because it is based on many historical examples) has provided remarkably consistent results for World War II and the Arab-Israeli Wars; thus *most* of the anomalies *should* be reconcilable through analysis.

2. Two major kinds of anomalies may be discerned in the results of Step VIII.

a. Inconsistencies in the P/P comparison with R—R, i.e., a theoretically predicted success (P/P>1) and an actually calculated failure (negative R—R), or vice-versa;

b. Even when there is consistency in success or failure, there may be significant discrepancies in the actual numerical values, i.e., a large P/P value for a theoretically predicted success is not easily reconcilable with a small R—R value which shows a very narrow success. The degree of consistency can be determined by plotting the P/P values and R—R values on a graph like that of Figure 5-1, and relating the plot to the Normal Battle Line; or may be compared numerically by calculating the Effective Power Ratio (PR/PR) by means of the following equation:

$$PR/PR = (R-R)/5 + 1.$$

PR/PR is the symbol used to show the *effective* P/P value derivable from the Result Comparison (R—R). If there is a difference of 1.0 or more between the P/P calculated in the QJM and the PR/PR shown by the Normal Battle Line (or converted from the Result Formula by the above equation) the reason for the difference should be sought.

3. In the event either of the anomalies above occurs, comparison should be made with historical battles or engagements which have any comparable characteristics, and particularly previous combat between the same two opponents that has already been analyzed by the QJMA. If similar anomalies have been discovered in other engagements, particularly between the same opponents, or opponents of the same national identities, it is likely that there is a discernible difference in combat effectiveness of the opposing units, or of the opposing national forces.

4. The data and combat narrative should be reviewed, to seek errors, to determine possible need for revision of factors, or to find inconsistency between data and narrative, on the one hand, and operational events (such as surprise) on the other, which could explain the anomalies. If so, it will be necessary to proceed to Step X.

5. If there are no serious anomalies, or after these have been corrected by the procedures of Step X., it is desirable (but not necessary if this does not contribute to the original objective of the analysis) to calculate the actual effects of weapons, of standard combat variables, of surprise and of relative combat effectiveness on the outcome. This can be done as follows:

    a. Calculate manpower ratio: N_f/N_e;

    b. Calculate Force Strength ratio: S_f/S_e;

    c. Calculate effects of non-behavioral operational variables in a power ratio: P_f/P_e;

    d. If set-piece or surprise considerations are involved, use revised m and v factors to calculate refined power ratio: P'_f/P'_e;

    e. Calculate outcome: $R_f - R_e$;

    f. Calculate PR/PR (effective P/P) by use of equation, paragraph IX-2-b, above;

    g. Determine Relative Combat Effectiveness (CEV)=5d/5f;

    h. Compare these ratios and values and draw conclusions.

For examples of this process, see Figure 9-10 (p. 129) and 9-12 (p. 131).

X. *Apply New or Revised Factors*

1. This step is performed only if there was an anomaly in the relationship of P/P and R−R in Steps VIII and IX.

2. Having performed 9(4), determine new factors (as for surprise, or to correct errors in first iteration). Then proceed to a second iteration beginning with Step IV (rarely) and/or Step V, continuing through Steps VI to IX as before.

XI. *Record Data*

1. This step follows Step IX., either on first or second (or subsequent) iterations.

2. At a minimum, the record of the analysis must relate the engagement (identified verbally and/or by number) to calculated P/P and R−R values. Additional data in the record will depend on the purpose of the analysis, but generally should include the effects of surprise (if any), and the calculated CEV or CEVs.

PART TWO—QJM Wargame Rules

I. Campaign Scenario Procedures

A. INITIAL REQUIREMENTS

1. Force inventory both sides, to include starting locations of all units (divisions, or smaller independent units), with the unit weapons and equipment translated into the OLI values and related inputs to QJM.
2. Terrain, to include such major terrain features as mountains, cities and towns, roads, rivers, and the entire area for each campaign categories in terms of the fourteen basic QJM terrain characteristics, or combinations thereof.
3. Defensive works, to include field fortifications, minefields, major antitank ditches, etc., located with considerable precision on the map.
4. Offensive plans in terms of:
   a. Overall force objectives:
      (i) geographic locations
         —immediate,
         —intermediate (one or more), and
         —final;
      (ii) time;
      (iii) force relationships with enemy and friendly forces;
   b. Similar objectives for all component elements, down to and including divisions;
   c. Planned axes of advance of FEBA and reserve units;
   d. Contingencies for commitment of reserves.
5. Defensive plans in terms of:
   a. Overall force objectives, related to:
      (i) geographic locations or defensive positions
         —mission at each location (in terms of defense or delay)
         —mission between each two locations (in terms of delay or withdrawal);
   b. Similar objectives for all component elements, down to and including divisions and smaller independent units;
   c. Planned axes of withdrawal;
   d. Contingencies for commitment of reserves.

B. ANTICIPATED SEQUENCE OF OPERATIONS, ATTACKING DIVISION

1. Movement to first hostile contact at rate indicated in rules for rate of advance.

2. Preliminary QJM analysis (if necessary) to determine if opposition is of sufficient significance to start an engagement, or whether advance continues under circumstances of negligible or slight opposition.

3. At first encountered hostile defense position, QJM analysis; from this the following will be determined:

    a. Outcome, on basis of P/P ratio:

        (i) If P/P favors defender, advance stops at FEBA thus established;

        (ii) If P/P favors attacker, advance continues at rate set in rules.

    b. Duration of engagement:

        (i) If P/P favors defender, engagement lasts two days, losses are calculated, and there is no further significant action (until or unless one side or the other is reinforced); loss rates are thereafter calculated daily at "holding" rate;

        (ii) If P/P favors attacker, engagement ends when:

        —attacker advances through depth of defensive position; defender breaks off and withdraws;

        —either defender or attacker receives reinforcements of 20 percent or more;

        —at the end of five days if none of above have occurred.

In that case there is no further significant action until one side or the other is reinforced; loss rates are thereafter calculated at "holding" rate.

    c. Distance advanced during engagement.

    d. Total personnel losses during engagement.

    e. Total armor loss during engagement.

    f. Total artillery loss during engagement.

4. If defender is successful, or if attacker does not gain objective within five days, an inactive "holding" situation exists until one side or the other initiates a new engagement by an attack.

5. If attacker is successful, he moves to contact on next defensive position at the rate prescribed for movement against Moderate, Slight, or Negligible Resistance, dependent on the following:

    a. If defender adopts "delay" posture, attacker's rate is against Moderate or Slight Resistance, with attacker's P/P arbitrarily doubled during period of movement only.

    b. If defender elects withdrawal, his rate and that of attacker are those for movement against Negligible Resistance.

6. Exhaustion and recovery rates will be calculated for the period between engagements, to arrive at an ex (exhaustion) factor for each side for the subsequent engagement.

7. At the next encountered hostile defensive position, a new QJM analysis will be performed, as for Step B(3), above.

8. This procedure will continue until:
   a. Attacker reaches final objective.
   b. Attacker is stopped at an intermediate objective by a successful defense, or inability to take objective in a five-day battle (situation in Step B(4), above).

C. ANTICIPATED SEQUENCE OF OPERATIONS, ATTACKING CORPS OR ARMY

1. All committed or first echelon divisions advance to first hostile contacts simultaneously. All supporting and reserve units also advance simultaneously at rates indicated for their axes of advance.
2. Engagement outcomes and advance and attrition rates are calculated separately for each component division of the attacking force.
3. Reserve units (divisions or major fractions thereof treated as independent units) may be committed by attacker or defender in a front-line division sector or between sectors.
   a. If between divisions, then new sector boundaries will be established, and new QJM calculations will be based on these new sectors.
   b. If in the sector of a committed division, then the new QJM calculations may be for the two forces (original, plus reserve) in the previously established sector, or may be for two divisions separately.
4. At the close of each day the locations of each attacking and defending unit (division or major fraction) will be plotted, whether these are involved in engagements or are between engagements.
5. The corps or army is assumed to have achieved its objective when half of its component divisions have reached their terrain objectives, and no major defending reserves are immediately available to reverse the trend.
6. For army group or theater forces, QJM calculations can be by corps or division, following the above procedures.

II. Rules For Defensive Strength and Depth

Method: Depends upon size of force with respect to front, number of days in position, and availability of engineer support.

A. GENERAL CONSIDERATIONS

1. The maximum effective depth of a prepared or fortified defensive position cannot exceed $0.3 \times$ the depth component of the dispersion factor in meters; the maximum effective depth of a hasty defense position is $0.5 \times$ that of prepared or fortified defense.

2. For calculation of overall preparation strength, when non-organic engineers are assigned to assist troops in position preparation, one engineer is assumed to be the equivalent of ten non-engineer troops.

3. The depth of a subordinate command in an integrated defensive position will be that of the major unit (usually division).

B. HASTY DEFENSE

1. This condition exists when criteria for prepared defense have not been met.

2. Depth of a hasty defense position begins at $0.5 \times .00001N \times$ depth component of dispersion factor in meters, and increases proportionally in ten days to a maximum of one-half of maximum effective depth (see A(1), above).

C. PREPARED DEFENSE

1. This condition exists:
   a. When front to be covered is less than one meter per man, and unit has been in position five days; depth of the position is then half of the maximum possible effective depth; after unit has been in position ten days, the depth equals the maximum possible effective depth.
   b. When front to be covered is greater than one meter per man, and less than two meters per man, and unit has been in position ten days; depth of the position is then half of the maximum possible effective depth; after unit has been in position twenty days, the depth equals the maximum possible effective depth.

2. When front to be covered is greater than two meters per man, prepared defense is not possible without additional (non-organic) engineer strength, to reach an effective preparation strength of more than one man per two meters per front.

D. FORTIFIED DEFENSE

1. Three times the preparation time required to achieve a prepared defense capability will provide a fortified defense.

2. Under certain time circumstances part of a defensive position can be fortified and part prepared.

E. EXAMPLES OF APPLICATION

1. A World War II division of 15,000 men, holding a defensive sector of 12 km, has been in position for 7 days:
   a. Relationship of front to force strength—12/15, or less than 1/1;

    b.   Defensive posture: Prepared defense;

    c.   Defensive depth: .5×.3×60=9 km.

2.   A 1977 US division in Europe, holding a defensive position of 14 km, has been in position for 10 days:

    a.   Relationship of front to force strength: 14/15, or less than 1/1;

    b.   Defensive posture: Prepared defense;

    c.   Defensive depth: 1×.3×67=20.1 km.

3.   A 1977 US division in Europe, holding a defensive position of 14 km, has been in position for 16 days:

    a.   Relationship of front to force strength: 14/15, or less than 1/1;

    b.   Defensive posture: Fortified defense, half of depth; prepared defense, remainder of depth;

    c.   Defensive depth: .5×.3×.67=10.05 km, fortified; 10.05 km, prepared.

4.   A World War II division of 15,000 men, in a defensive sector of 18 km for 8 days:

    a.   Relationship of front to force strength: 18/15, more than 1/1, less than 2/1;

    b.   Defensive posture: Hasty defense;

    c.   Initial depth: .5×60×.15=4.5 km; maximum hasty defense depth, 9 km; difference, 4.5 km; daily increase in effective depth: .45 km; after 8 days depth is 8.1 km.

5.   A 1977 US division of 15,000 men, in a defensive sector of 18 km for 8 days, with support of an engineer battalion of 600 men:

    a.   Engineer preparation strength equivalent: 6,000 troops;

    b.   Relationship of front to force strength: 18/21, less than 1/1;

    c.   Defensive posture: Prepared defense;

    d.   Defensive depth: .5×.3×.67=10.5 km.

6.   A 1977 independent mechanized infantry brigade of 4,000 troops as a covering force in a defensive sector of 30 km; in position 7 days:

    a.   Relationship of front to force strength: 30/4, more than 2/1;

    b.   Defensive posture: Hasty defense;

    c.   Initial depth: .5×67×.04=1.34; maximum hasty defense depth; 10.5 km; difference, 9.16 km; daily increase in effective depth: .92 km; in 7 days depth is 7.78 km.

7.   A 1977 mechanized infantry brigade of 4,000 troops, part of a division of 15,000 troops, in main defensive position for 4 days; brigade sector is 5 km; division sector is 13 km:

    a.   Relationship of front to force strength: 13/15, less than 1/1;

    b.   Defensive posture: Hasty defense;

    c.   Initial depth: .5×67×.15=5.03 km; maximum hasty defense depth 10.5 km; difference 5.02 km; daily increase in effective depth: .5 km; after 4 days, depth=7.03.

8.   A 1977 mechanized infantry brigade of 4,000 troops, part of a

division of 15,000 troops in main defensive position for 6 days; brigade sector is 5 km; division sector is 13 km:
   a. Relationship of front to force strength: 13/15, less than 1/1;
   b. Defensive posture: Prepared defense;
   c. Depth: .5×.3×67=10.05 km.

III. *Rules for Advance Rates**

Method: Standard rate times relevant factors

STANDARD (UNMODIFIED) ADVANCE RATES

	Armored Division	Mechzd. Division	Rates in km/day Infantry Division or Force	Horse Cavalry Division or Force
Against Intense Resistance (P/P: 1.0–1.10)				
Hasty defense/delay	4.0	4.0	4.0	3.0
Prepared defense	2.0	2.0	2.0	1.6
Fortified defense	1.0	1.0	1.0	0.6
Against Strong/Intense Resistance (P/P: 1-11–1.25)				
Hasty defense/delay	5.0	4.5	4.5	3.5
Prepared defense	2.25	2.25	2.25	1.5
Fortified defense	1.85	1.85	1.85	0.7
Against Strong Defense (P/P: 1.26–1.45)				
Hasty defense/delay	6.0	5.0	5.0	4.0
Prepared defense	2.5	2.5	2.5	2.0
Fortified defense	1.5	1.5	1.5	0.8
Against Moderate/Strong Resistance (P/P: 1.46–1.75)				
Hasty defense	9.0	7.5	6.5	6.0
Prepared defense	4.0	3.5	3.0	2.5
Fortified defense	2.0	2.0	1.75	0.9
Against Moderate Resistance (P/P: 1.76–2.25)				
Hasty defense/delay	12.0	10.0	8.0	8.0
Prepared defense	6.0	5.0	4.0	3.0
Fortified defense	3.0	2.5	2.0	1.0
Against Slight/Moderate Resistance (P/P: 2.26–3.0)				
Hasty defense/delay	16.0	13.0	10.0	12.0
Prepared defense	8.0	7.0	5.0	6.0
Fortified defense	4.0	3.0	2.5	2.0

	Armored Division	Mechzd. Division	Rates in km/day Infantry Division or Force	Horse Cavalry Division or Force
Against Slight Resistance				
(P/P: 3.01–4.25)				
Hasty defense/delay	20.0	16.0	12.0	15.0
Prepared defense	10.0	8.0	6.0	7.0
Fortified defense	5.0	4.0	3.0	4.0
Against Negligible/Slight Resistance°°				
(P/P: 4.26–6.00)				
Hasty defense/delay	40.0	30.0	18.0	28.0
Prepared defense	20.0	16.0	10.0	14.0
Fortified defense	10.0	8.0	6.0	7.0
Against Negligible Resistance				
(P/P: 6.00 plus)				
Hasty defense/delay	60.0	48.0	24.0	40.0
Prepared/fortified defense	30.0	24.0	12.0	12.0

° Based on HERO studies: ORALFORE, Barrier Effectiveness, and Combat Data Subscription Service.

°° For armored and mechanized infantry divisions, these rates can be sustained for 10 days only; for next 30 days standard rates for armored and mechanized infantry forces cannot exceed half these rates.

GENERAL TERRAIN FACTORS

	Infantry (Combined Arms) Force	Cavalry or Armored Force
1 Rugged, heavily wooded	0.4	0.2
2 Rugged, mixed	0.5	0.4
3 Rugged, bare	0.6	0.5
4 Rolling, heavily wooded	0.6	0.6
5 Rolling, mixed	0.8	0.8
6 Rolling, bare	1.0	1.0
7 Flat, heavily wooded	0.7	0.7
8 Flat, mixed	0.9	0.9
9 Flat, bare, hard	1.05	1.0
10 Flat, desert	0.95	1.0
11 Desert, sandy, dunes	0.3	0.6
12 Swamp, jungled	0.3	0.2
13 Swamp, mixed or open	0.4	0.3
14 Urban	0.7	0.7

ROAD QUALITY FACTORS

Road Quality:	Good roads	1.0
	Mediocre roads	0.8
	Poor roads	0.6
Road Density:	European standard	1.0
	Moderate density	0.8
	Sparse	0.6

OBSTACLE FACTORS

	width (meters)	20	50	100	500	
River or stream:	Fordable	0.9	0.85	0.8	0.7	
	Unfordable	0.85	0.8	0.7	0.5	
Minefields:°	Density/km of front,	10	20	50	100	500
	to 10 km depth	.9	.8	.7	.6	.5

°Included in fortified defense rates

OTHER OBSTACLES

Day/Night—When using increments of time less than 24 hours and distinctions can be made between night and day, night advance rate will be one-half daytime advance rate.

EXAMPLES OF APPLICATION

1. Assault crossing of an unfordable, strongly defended river 500 meters wide by an infantry division with P/P preponderance of 1.45, in rolling, heavily wooded terrain:

    a. Standard rate (against strong resistance): 1.5 km/day;
    b. General terrain factor: 0.6;
    c. Road quality factor: 1.0 (but not really relevant);
    d. Obstacle factor: 0.5;
    e. Rate of advance: $1.5 \times .6 \times 1 \times .5 = 0.45$ km/day.

This means that the assault crossing is unsuccessful, since a minimum rate of .5 km/day is necessary to get across an unfordable river 500 meters wide.

2. An armored force advancing in Western Europe against slight resistance (P/P=4.25) offering hasty defense, with roads and fields only slightly mined, terrain rolling, heavily wooded:

    a. Standard rate (against slight resistance): 20 km/day;
    b. General terrain factor: 0.6;
    c. Road quality factor: 1.0;
    d. Obstacle factor: 0.9;
    e. Rate of Advance: $20 \times .6 \times 1 \times .9 = 10.8$ km/day.

3. A mechanized infantry division operating in rugged, heavily wooded terrain in the Balkans (poor roads, moderate density) against an enemy capable of offering moderate resistance (P/P=2.25) in prepared defenses, with moderately dense minefields in front of the position (average 20-30 mines per km front):

a. Standard rate (against moderate resistance): 5.0 km/day;
b. General terrain factor: 0.4;
c. Road quality factor: 0.6×0.8=0.48;
d. Obstacle factor: 0.8;
e. Rate of advance: 5×.4×.48×.8=0.77 km/day.

MAIN EFFORT FACTOR

This factor is applicable to no more than one-third of a force of division size (approximately 10,000 men or more) or larger.

a. Main effort sector: 1.2;
b. Other sectors: 1.0.

IV. *Rules For Casualty Rates*

A. BEFORE 1900

Standard Rate. For average army of 50,000 men in a one-day battle as shown in Figure A-7. These are battlefield losses; defeated army may lose more in pursuit.
For Smaller Force. Percentage on graph is increased by a factor of 0.1 for every 5,000-man decrease below 50,000 men.
For Larger Force. Percentage on graph is decreased by a factor of 0.05 for every 25,000-man increment above 50,000 men, up to a maximum decrease of 0.3, or a minimum factor of 0.7 applied to percent found on graph.

FOR MULTI-DAY BATTLE

1.   Factor on Figure A-7, modified as appropriate for size of force, is increased by a factor of 0.5 per day, to a maximum increase of 1.0, or 100 percent.
2.   Prior to 1900 three days is the maximum battle duration.

NON-BATTLE CASUALTIES

Under normal circumstances, in temperate climates, non-battle losses are:
a. 16 April-15 Oct., inc.; 0.1 percent per day
b. 16 Oct.-15 April, inc.; 0.2 percent per day
Under normal circumstances, in non-temperate climates, non-battle losses are 0.2 percent per day.

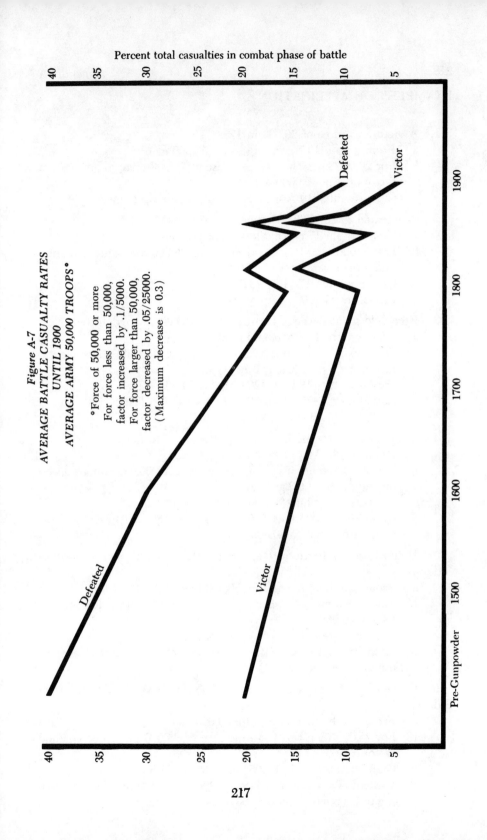

Figure A-7
AVERAGE BATTLE CASUALTY RATES
UNTIL 1900
AVERAGE ARMY 50,000 TROOPS*

*Force of 50,000 or more
For force less than 50,000,
factor increased by .1/5000.
For force larger than 50,000,
factor decreased by .05/25000.
(Maximum decrease is 0.3)

Percent total casualties in combat phase of battle

Defeated

Victor

Defeated

Victor

Pre-Gunpowder   1500   1600   1700   1800   1900

EXAMPLES OF APPLICATION

1. A victorious force of 20,000 in 1750:
    a. From graph: 10.7 percent loss for 50,000 men;
    b. For 20,000 men, this is a decrease of 30,000 men; augmentation factor of .1 per 5,000 men=0.6;
    c. Casualty rate=10.7×1.6=17.12, or a loss of 3,424 men.

2. A defeated force of 30,000 men in 1800:
    a. From graph: 17 percent loss for 50,000 men;
    b. For 30,000 men this is a decrease of 20,000 men; augmentation factor of .1 per 5,000 men=0.4;
    c. Casualty rate=17×1.4=23.8;
    d. Casualties=7,140.

3. French losses at Battle of Leipzig, 1814; 180,000 men, defeated:
    a. From graph: 19.8 percent for 50,000 men;
    b. For 180,000 men this is an increase of 130,000; decremental factor of .05 per 25,000=0.26;
    c. Casualty rate=19.8 (1−.26)=19.8×.74=14.65;
    d. Casualties=.1465×180,000×(1+1)=52,740 (Historical estimates are 45,000 to 55,000).

4. Allied losses at Leipzig, 1814; 300,000 men, victorious:
    a. From graph: 14.8 percent for 50,000 men;
    b. For 300,000 men this is an increase of 250,000; maximum decremental factor of 0.3 applies;
    c. Casualty rate=14.8 (1−.3)=14.8×.7=10.36;
    d. Casualties=.1036×300,000×(1+1)=62,160 (Historical estimates are 50,000 to 60,000).

5. Union losses at Battle of Gettysburg, 1863; 87,312 men, victorious; 3 days:
    a. From graph: 15 percent for 50,000 men;
    b. For 87,000 men, this is an increase of 37,000 men; decremental factor is 0.08;
    c. Casualty rate=15 (1−.08)=15×.92=13.8;
    d. Casualties=.138×87,312×(1+1)=24,098 (Actual loss, according to Livermore, was 23,049).

6. Confederate losses at Battle of Gettysburg, 1863; 75,054, defeated; 3 days:
    a. From graph: 18.5 percent for 50,000 men;
    b. For 75,000 men this is an increase of 25,000 men; decremental factor is 0.05;
    c. Casualty rate: 18.5 (1−.05)=18.5×.95=17.58;
    d. Casualties=.1758×75,054×(1+1=26,389 (Actual loss, according to Livermore, was 28,063).

B. 1900 TO PRESENT

Method: Standard rate times relevant factors

SPECIAL HISTORICAL RATES

1. For period 1900-1945, Russian and Japanese rates are double those calculated below.
2. For period 1914-1918, rates as calculated below must be doubled; for Russian, Turkish, and Balkan forces they must be quadrupled.
3. For 1950-1953 rates as calculated below will apply for UN forces (other than ROK); for ROK, North Koreans, and Chinese rates are doubled.

STANDARD (UNMODIFIED) CASUALTY RATES (PERCENT DAY)

Attack	2.8
Defense	1.5

STRENGTH/SIZE FACTOR

Less than 5,000 men	2.0
5,000-10,000	1.5
10,000-20,000	1.0
20,000-30,000	0.9
30,000-50,000	0.8
50,000-100,000	0.7
More than 100,000	0.6

MISSION FACTOR

	Normal Combat	Main Effort Zone°
Attack	1.0	1.5
Defense	1.0	1.2
Delay	0.7	0.9
Withdrawal	0.5	0.7
Holding	0.3	—

OPPOSITION FACTOR

P/P	Factor
Above 3.00	0.7
3.00-2.00	0.8
2.00-1.00	0.9
1.00-0.67	1.00
0.66-0.51	1.1
0.50-0.41	1.2
0.40-0.31	1.3
0.30-0.21	1.4
0.20-0.15	1.5
Below 0.15	1.6

°Is dictated by attacking side; can involve no more than one-third of a force of division size or larger; can be sustained by attacker for 48 hours only without rest; can be regained after 48-hour rest.

DAY/NIGHT

When using increments of time less than 24 hours, and distinctions can be made between night and day, night attrition rates will be one-half daytime attrition rates.

NON-BATTLE CASUALTIES

Same as pre-1900 period; see above.

EXAMPLES OF APPLICATION

1. An infantry division of 15,000 men with a P_a/P_d of 1.55 making a main effort attack, at the outset of an offensive:
   a. Standard rate=2.8 percent/day;
   b. Strength/size factor=1.0;
   c. Mission factor=1.5;
   d. Opposition factor=0.9;
   e. Casualty rate=2.8×1.5×.9=3.78 percent/day, or .0378.

2. Defending force—elements of a division (8,000 men) defensive posture—in same situation:
   a. Standard rate=1.5 percent/day;
   b. Strength/size factor=1.5;
   c. Mission factor=1.2;
   d. Opposition factor (P/P of .65)=1.2;
   e. Casualty rate=1.5×1.5×1.2×1.2=3.24 percent/day, or .0324.

3. Defending force—independent regiment of 3,000 men in delay posture—in same situation:
   a. Standard rate=1.5 percent/day;
   b. Strength/size factor=2.0;
   c. Mission factor=0.9;
   d. Opposition factor (P/P of .65)=1.2;
   e. Casualty rate=1.5×2.0×.9×1.2=3.24 percent/day, or .0324.

4. Example no. 1, above, in third day of combat:
   a. Standard rate=2.8 percent/day;
   b. Strength/size factor=1.0;
   c. Mission factor=1.0;
   d. Opposition factor=0.9;
   e. Casualty rate=2.8×.9=2.52 percent/day, or .0252.

5. Example no. 2, above, in third day of combat for both sides:
   a. Standard rate=1.5 percent/day;
   b. Strength/size factor=1.5.
   c. Mission factor=1.0;
   d. Opposition factor=0.9;
   e. Casualty rate=1.5×1.5×.9=2.03 percent/day, or .0203.

6. Example no. 3, above, in third day of combat for attacker, but defender is fresh:
- a. Standard rate=1.5 percent/day;
- b. Strength/size factor=2.0;
- c. Mission factor=0.7;
- d. Opposition factor=1.2;
- e. Casualty rate=$1.5 \times 2.0 \times .7 \times 1.2 = 2.52$ percent/day, or 0.252.

ARMORED LOSS RATES

STANDARD RATE (PERCENT/DAY)

$5.4 \times$ personnel rates/day.

MISSION FACTOR

Normal Combat: 1.0

Main Effort Zone*: 2.0

STRENGTH/SIZE FACTOR

Less than 100 tanks	1.5
100-300 tanks	1.0
300-600 tanks	0.9
more than 600 tanks	0.8

RECOVERY RATES

1. Of attacker's losses, 50 percent are recoverable over a five-day period, one-fifth per day.
2. Of defender's losses, 50 percent are recoverable over a five-day period, one-fifth per day.

EXAMPLES OF APPLICATION

- a. See Figures 12-3 and 12-4, p. 176.
- b. Armored Division of 300 tanks is in a main effort, major attack; its personnel loss rate the first two days is 1.76; drops to 1.22 for next two days, and rises back to 1.76 for next two days:

---

* Is dictated by attacking side; can involve no more than one-third of a force of a division size or larger; can be sustained by attacker for 48 hours only without rest; can be regained again after 48-hour rest.

(1) Tank loss rate 1st two days=1.76×5.4×2.0=19.01 percent;
(2) Tank loss rate next two days=1.22×5.4=6.59 percent;
(3) Tank loss rate next two days=1.76×5.4×2=19.01 percent;
(4) Results of loss and recovery rates over 6 days:

Day	No.	Loss	Recovered	Total
1	300	57	0	252
2	243	46	6	203
3	203	13	11	201
4	201	13	13	201
5	201	38	15	178
6	178	34	17	161

ARTILLERY LOSS RATES

STANDARD RATES

1. 0.20×personnel rates per day for towed weapons.
2. 0.50×personnel rates per day for S/P weapons.

RECOVERY RATES

1. 50 percent of loss is permanent; 50 percent is recoverable in two days, half per day.

EXAMPLES OF APPLICATION

1. Force has 560 towed weapons, 320 self-propelled weapons; its personnel loss rate is 2.00 percent/day:
   a. Towed weapon loss rate: 2.00×.2=0.40 percent/day, or .004;
   b. Self-propelled weapon loss rate: 2.00×.5=1.00 percent/day, or 1.01;
   c. Results of loss and recovery rates over 6 days:

Day	Towed Weapons				SP Weapons			
	No.	Loss	Recovered	Total	No.	Loss	Recovered	Total
1	560	2	0	558	320	3	0	317
2	558	2	1	557	317	3	1	315
3	557	1	1	557	315	3	2	314
4	557	2	0	555	314	3	1	312
5	555	1	1	555	312	3	2	311
6	555	2	0	553	311	3	2	310

OTHER WEAPONS AND EQUIPMENT

STANDARD RATES

Same rate as for personnel.

EXAMPLE OF APPLICATION

A force with 6,000 trucks has a personnel casualty rate of 1.15 percent. Truck losses: $1,000 \times .0115 = 12$ trucks.

V. *Rules For Exhaustion Rates, 20th Century*°

1. The exhaustion factor (ex) of a fresh unit is 1.0; this is the maximum ex value.

2. At the conclusion of an engagement, a new ex factor will be calculated for each side.

3. A unit in normal offensive or defensive combat has its ex factor reduced by .05 for each consecutive day of combat; the ex factor cannot be less than 0.5.

4. An attacking unit opposed by delaying tactics has its ex factor reduced by 0.05 per day.

5. A defending unit in delay posture neither loses nor gains in its ex factor.

6. A withdrawing unit, not seriously engaged, has its ex factor augmented at the rate of 0.05 per day.

7. An advancing unit in pursuit, and not seriously delayed, neither loses nor gains in its ex factor.

8. For a unit in reserve, or in non-active posture, an exhaustion factor of less than 1.0 is augmented at the rate of .1 per day.

9. When a unit in combat, or recently in combat, is reinforced by a unit at least half of its size (in numbers of men), it adopts the ex factor of the reinforcing unit or—if the ex factor of the reinforcing unit is the same or lower than that of the reinforced—both adopt an ex factor 0.1 higher than that of the reinforced unit at the time of reinforcement, save that an ex factor cannot be greater than 1.0.

10. When a unit in combat, or recently in combat, is reinforced by a unit less than half its size, but not less than one quarter its size, augmentations or modifications of ex factors will be 0.5 times those provided for

---

° Approximate reflection of preliminary QJM assessment of effects of casualty and fatigue, WWII engagements. These rates are for division or smaller size; for corps and larger units exhaustion rates are calculated for component divisions and smaller separate units.

in paragraph 9, above. When the reinforcing unit is less than one-quarter the size of the reinforced unit, but not less than one-tenth its size, augmentations or modifications of ex factors will be 0.25 times those provided for in paragraph 9, above.

EXAMPLES OF APPLICATION

1. A division in continuous offensive combat for five days stays in the line in inactive posture for two days, then resumes the offensive:
    a.   Combat exhaustion effect: $1-(5\times.05)=0.75$;
    b.   Recuperation effect: $75+(2\times.1)=0.95$.
2. A division in defensive posture for fifteen days is ordered to undertake a counterattack:
    a.   Combat exhaustion effect: $1-(15\times.05)=0.25$; this is below the minimum ex factor, which therefore applies: 0.5;
    b.   Recuperation effect: None; ex factor is 0.5.
3. A division in offensive posture for three days is reinforced by two fresh brigades:
    a.   Combat exhaustion effect: $1-(3\times.05)=0.85$;
    b.   Reinforcement effect: Augmentation from 0.85 to 1.0.
4. A division in offensive posture for three days is reinforced by one fresh brigade:
    a.   Combat exhaustion effect: $1-(3\times.05)=0.85$;
    b.   Reinforcement effect: $0.5\times$augmentation from 0.85 to $1=0.93$.

VI.   Rules For Air Support in Hourly Increments

The allocation of air power in the QJM will usually consider only close support sorties; unless other information is available, it will be assumed that the interdiction and anti-air efforts of the opposing sides will approximately cancel each other out.

Allocation of close air support (CAS) under the QJM-OLI concept presumes that the total value of air support for a given day is applied for the whole day. When considering periods of less than 24 hours, it will be assumed that the air support will be given during the hours of daylight only. For any period which includes at least one hour of daylight, and for which air support sorties are considered, the number of sorties will be multiplied by 24, divided by the number of hours in the period to get the number of sortie equivalents in the period. (Thus, for a six-hour period, the multiplier is 4.0; for an eight-hour period it is 3.0.) For example, if a total of 50 sorties are available in a division's sector during the period from 0600 to 1200 hours, and 15 sorties are available during the period from 1200 to 1800 hours, the calculation would be as follows:

Round 1 begins at 0400 hours, and lasts till 1200 hours (eight hours);
Round 2 begins at 1200 hours and lasts until 2000 hours;
Round 3 begins at 2000 hours and lasts until 0400 hours the next
   morning.
Round 1: 50×3=150 sortie equivalents;
Round 2: 15×3=45 sortie equivalents;
Round 3: 0×3=0 sortie equivalents.

(Note, the total of 195 sortie equivalents, when divided by 3 is 65
sorties per day; the number we started with.)

OLI CALCULATION SHEET

Identification Code	Weapon Designation or Description	Caliber mm	RF	PTS	RIE	Range Effect	Range Factor
09-1-9	Pistol, Makarov, auto pistol, PM	9	350	1	0.7	—	—
09-1-91	Machine Pistol Stechin, APS	9	1400	1	0.7	—	—
09-1-47	Rifle, AKM/AK47/AMD	7.62	1280	1	0.8	2,250	2.50
09-2-33	Machine Gun, RPK/MG	7.62	2600	1	0.8	2,250	2.50
09-2-35	PKM/PHJ	7.62	2600	1	.8	3,700	2.92
09-2-38	hvy M38/46	12.7	2280	2	1	2,000	2.41
09-3-37	Mortar, M 1937	82	168	760	1	3,040	2.74
09-5-3	Sagger, AT-3, Manpack	120	95	1900	1	3,000	2.73
09-5-76	Gun, AT 76mm 215-3	76.2	148	640	1	11,961	4.46
09-6-21	MRL, BM21(MTD)	122	120	1975	1	20,000	5.47
09-6-30	How D30/M34	122	120	1975	1	15,000	4.87

OLI CALCULATION SHEET

Identification Code	Designation	Speed km/hr	Range km	Weight tons	Composite OLIs	MOF	RA
09-0-54	Tank, T-54	33	400	36	343.2	1.15	1.6
09-0-55	Tank, T-55	33	500	36	341.4	1.15	1.79
09-0-62	Tank, T-62	33	450	37.6	488.5	1.15	1.70
09-0-76	Tank, Recon PT-76	44	200	14	119.7	1.33	1.29
09-8-3	ICV, BMP, w/Sagger	50	500	13.6	176.9	1.41	1.79
09-8-1	ARV, BRDM-1	53	500	5.6	4.2	1.46	1.79
09-8-2	ARV, BRDM-2 w/Sagger	53	750	7	184	1.46	2.19
09-0-100	Assault Gun, ASU, 100	37	305	31.6	340	1.22	1.40
09-4-152	APC, BTR 152	43	780	9	26.4	1.31	2.23
09-09-17	Aircraft, MiG-17	1163	1205	6.3	54.4	4.76	2.78
09-09-23	Aircraft, MiG-23	2966	960	15	91.2	4.96	2.48

Soviet Non-Mobile Weapons

MV	Muzzle Velocity Caliber	Factor	Di	A	R	GE	MCE	MBE	SME	AE	OLI RN	MV	Final
315	.1√9	1.00	.7	.8									0.03	0.03
340	.1√9	1.00	.7	.7									0.12	0.12
710	.1√7.62	1.37	.8	.8								0.41	0.22	0.32
745	.1√7.62	1.44	.8	.8								0.83	0.48	0.66
855	.1√7.62	1.65	.8	.8								1.16	0.55	0.86
840	.1√12.7	2.09	.8	.8								1.76	1.52	1.64
210	.1√82	1.33	.6	.95								50	24	50
120	.1√82	1.00	.6	.7	2							104	35	70
950	.1√76.2	5.80	.9	.9								91	119	119
450	.1√122	3.48	.6	.8				418	1.05			683	434	559
690	.1√122	5.33	.9	.9								234	256	256

Soviet Mobile Fighting Machines

Prelim. Product	T/4	√T	PF	Raw OLI	RFE	FCE	ASE	CL	APC	AM	WHT	Refined OLI
631	36/4	√36	54	685	.92	.9	.68			1.05		405
703	36/4	√36	54	758	.92	.9	.87			1.05		573
955	37.6/4	√37.6	58	1013	.91	.9	.88			1.05		767
205	14/4	√14	13	218	.96	.9	.77			1.1		160
446	13.6/4	√13.6	13	459	.93	.9	.49			1.1		207
11	5.6/4	√5.6	3	14	.99	.9	.9			1.1		11
588	7/4	√7	5	593	.99	.9	.44			1.1		230
581	31.6/8	√31.6	22	603	.9	.9	.9			—		439
77	9/8	√9	3	80	—	—	—			—		79
720	6.3/8	√6.3	2	722	—	—	—			—		810
1122	15/8	√15	7	1127	—	—	—			—		1296

TABLE 1.   TERRAIN FACTORS (r)

Terrain Characteristics	Mobility r_m	Defense Position[1] r_u	Infantry Weapons[2] r_n	Arty[3] r_{wg}	Air r_{wy}	Tanks r_{wt}
1. Rugged—Heavily Wooded	0.4	1.5	0.6	0.7	0.8	0.2
2. Rugged—Mixed (or extra rugged—bare)	0.5	1.55	0.7	0.8	0.9	0.4
3. Rugged—Bare	0.6	1.45	0.8	0.9	0.95	0.5
4. Rolling—Heavily Wooded	0.6	1.35	0.8	0.8	0.9	0.6
5. Rolling—Mixed	0.8	1.3	0.9	0.9	0.95	0.8
6. Rolling—Bare	1.0	1.2	1.0	1.0	1.0	1.0
7. Flat—Heavily Wooded	0.7	1.1	0.8	0.9	0.9	0.7
8. Flat—Mixed	0.9	1.2	0.9	1.0	0.95	0.9
9. Flat—Bare, hard	1.05	1.05	1.0	1.0	1.0	1.0
10. Flat Desert	0.95	1.18	1.0	1.0	1.0	1.0
11. Rolling Dunes	0.3	1.4	1.0	1.0	1.0	0.6
12. Swamp—jungled	0.3	1.4	0.6	0.8	0.8	0.2
13. Swamp—mixed or open	0.4	1.3	0.8	0.9	0.95	0.3
14. Urban	0.7	1.4	0.8	0.9	0.9	0.7

[1] For all defense postures; Attacker is always 1.0.

[2] Applied to small arms, machine guns and other infantry weapons; also to antitank weapons.

[3] Also applies to air defense weapons.

TABLE 2. WEATHER FACTORS (h)					
Weather Characteristics	*Mobility* h_m	*Attack* h_{ua}	*Artillery*° h_{wg}	*Air* h_{wy}	*Tanks* h_{wt}
1. Dry—Sunshine— Extreme Heat	0.9	1.0	1.0	1.0	0.9
2. Dry—Sunshine— Temperate	1.0	1.0	1.0	1.0	1.0
3. Dry—Sunshine— Extreme Cold	0.9	0.9	0.9	1.0	0.9
4. Dry—Overcast— Extreme Heat	1.0	1.0	1.0	0.7	1.0
5. Dry—Overcast— Temperate	1.0	1.0	1.0	0.7	1.0
6. Dry—Overcast— Extreme Cold	0.9	0.9	0.9	0.7	0.8
7. Wet—Light— Extreme Heat	0.9	0.9	0.9	0.5	0.7
8. Wet—Light— Temperate	0.8	0.9	1.0	0.5	0.7
9. Wet—Light— Extreme Cold	0.8	0.9	1.0	0.5	0.7
10. Wet—Heavy— Extreme Heat	0.5	0.6	0.9	0.2	0.6
11. Wet—Heavy— Temperate	0.6	0.7	0.9	0.2	0.5
12. Wet—Heavy— Extreme Cold	0.5	0.6	0.8	0.2	0.5

° Also applies to AD weapons.

TABLE 3. SEASON FACTORS (z)

Seasonal Variations	Attack[1] z_u	Artillery[2] z_{wg}	Air z_{wy}
1. Winter—Jungle	1.1	0.9	0.7
2. Winter—Desert	1.0	1.0	1.0
3. Winter—Temperate	1.0	1.0	1.0
4. Spring—Jungle	1.1	0.9	0.7
5. Spring—Desert	1.0	1.0	1.0
6. Spring—Temperate	1.1	1.0	0.9
7. Summer—Jungle	1.1	0.9	0.7
8. Summer—Desert	1.0	1.0	1.0
9. Summer—Temperate	1.1	0.9	1.0
10. Fall—Jungle	1.1	0.9	0.7
11. Fall—Desert	1.0	1.0	1.0
12. Fall—Temperate	1.1	1.0	0.9

[1] Defender is always 1.0.
[2] Also applies to AD weapons.

TABLE 4. EFFECTS OF AIR SUPERIORITY (y)

	Mobility m_{yd}[1]	m_{yw}	Artillery[2] w_{yg}	Air w_{yy}	Vulnerability v_y
1. Air Superiority	1.1	1.0	1.1	1.1	0.9
2. Air Equality	1.0	1.0	1.0	1.0	1.0
3. Air Inferiority	0.9	1.0	0.9	0.8	1.1

[1] Subscript d for dry or flyable weather; w for wet weather when h_{wy} is .5 or lower.
[2] Also applies to AD weapons.

TABLE 5. POSTURE FACTORS (u)

	Force Strength u_s	Vulnerability u_v
1. Attack	1.0	1.0
2. Defense (hasty)	1.3	0.7
3. Defense (prepared)	1.5	0.6
4. Defense (fortified)	1.6	0.5
5. Withdrawal	1.15	0.85
6. Delay	1.2	0.65

TABLE 6.   *SHORELINE VULNERABILITY FACTORS*

Hostile Fire on Shoreline	Across Beach	Across Unfordable River	Across Major Fordable or Minor Unfordable River
Small Arms Fire (up to 1,000 meters from shore)	2.0	1.5	1.3
Light Artillery (up to 10,000 meters from shore)	1.6	1.3	1.1
Medium Artillery (up to 15,000 meters from shore)	1.3	1.1	1.0

TABLE 7.   *MORALE FACTORS*

Excellent morale	1.0
Good morale	0.9
Fair morale	0.8
Poor morale	0.7
Panic	0.2

TABLE 8.   *MISSION FACTORS*

	Range	Normal
Complete accomplishment of the mission, a weight of	7-10	8
Substantial, relatively satisfactory, accomplishment	5-7	6
Partial, less than satisfactory, accomplishment	3-5	4
Little achievement of the mission	1-3	2

TABLE 9.   *TACTICAL SURPRISE FACTORS (sur)*

	Surpriser's Inherent Mobility Characteristics (M_{sur})	Surpriser's Vulnerability (V_{sura})	Surprised's Vulnerability (V_{surd})
Complete Surprise	$\sqrt{5}$	.4	3
Substantial Surprise	$\sqrt{3}$	.6	2
Minor Surprise	$\sqrt{1.3}$	.9	1.2

Appendix B
HERO'S QJM Data Base

No.	Year & Date			Battle Designation	Force X Designation		Posture	Force Y Designation
D- 1	1943,	Sept	9-11	Port of Salerno	B	46 ID	A G	16 PzD
2			9-11	Amphitheater		56 ID	A	16 PzD
3			11	Sele-Calore Corridor	U	45 ID	A	16 PzD
4			12-14	Vietri I	B	46 ID	HD	HG PzD
5			12-15	Battipaglia		56 ID	HD	16 PzD
6			13-14	Tobacco Factory	U	45 ID	HD	16 & 29 PzD
7			17-18	Vietri II	B	46 ID	HD	HG PzD
8			17-18	Battipaglia II		56 ID	A	16 PzD
9			17-18	Eboli	U	45 ID	A	16 & 26 PzD
10		Oct	12-14	Grazzanise	B	7 AD	A	15 PzGrD
11			13	Capua		56 ID	A	HG PzD
12			13-14	Triflisco	U	3 ID	A	HG PzD
13			13-14	Monte Acero		45 ID	A	3 PzGr & 26 Pz
14			13-14	Caiazzo		34 ID	A	3 PzGrD
15			13-15	Castel Volturno	B	46 ID	A	15 PzGrD
16			15-17	Dragoni	U	34 ID	A	3 PzGrD
17			15-20	Canal I	B	46 ID	A	15 PzGrD
18			16-17	Monte Grande		50 ID	A	HG PzD
19			17-18	Canal II		7 ID	A	15 PzGrD
20			20-22	Francolise		7 ID	A	15 PzGrD
21		Nov	4-5	Santa Maria Oliveto	U	34 ID	A	3 PzGrD
22			5-7	Monte Camino I	B	56 ID	A	15 PzGrD
23			6-7	Monte Lungo	U	3 ID	A	3 PzGrD
24			6-7	Pozzilli		45 ID	A	3 PzGrD
25			8-12	Monte Camino II	B	56 ID	HD	15 PzGrD
26			8-10	Monte Rotondo	U	3 ID	A	3 PzGrD
27		Dec	1-2	Calabritto	B	46 ID	A	15 PzGrD
28			2-6	Monte Camino III		56 ID	A	15 PzGrD
29			2-3	Monte Maggiore	U	36 ID	A	15 PzGr & 29 PzD
30	1944,	Jan	25-26	Aprilia I	B	1 ID	A	3 PzGrD
31			27	The Factory		1 ID	HD	3 PzGrD
32			29-31	Campoleone		1 ID	A	3 PzGrD
33		Feb	3-5	Campoleone Counterattack		1 ID	HPD	CC Greizer
34			7-8	Carroceto		1 ID	HPD	3 PzGrD
35			7-9	Moletta River Defense	U	45 ID	HPD	65 ID
36			9	Aprilia II	B	1 ID	HPD	CC Greizer
37			11-12	Factory Counterattack	U	45 ID	A	715 LtID
38			16-19	Bowling Alley		45 ID	HPD	Four D
39			16-19	Moletta River II	B	56 ID	HPD	65 I & 4 ParaD
40			21-23	Fioccia	U	45 ID	PD	114 LtI
41		May	12-13	Santa Maria Infante		88 ID	A	94 & 71 ID
42			12-13	San Martino		85 ID	A	94 ID
43			14-15	Spigno		88 ID	A	94 & 71 ID
44			14-15	Castellonorato		85 ID	A	94 ID
45			16-18	Formia		85 ID	A	94 ID
46			17-19	Monte Grande		88 ID	A	94 ID
47			20-22	Itri-Fondi		88 ID	A	94 ID
48			22-24	Terracina		85 ID	A	94 ID
49			23-24	Moletta Offensive	B	5 ID	A	4 ParaD
50			23-24	Anzio-Albano Road		1 ID	A	65 ID
51			23-25	Anzio Breakout	U	1 AD	A	3 PzGr & 362 ID
52			23-25	Cisterna		3 ID	A	362 ID
53			25-27	Sezze		85 ID	A	29 PzD
54			26	Velletri		1 AD	A	362 ID
55			26-28	Campoleone Station		45 ID	A	65 ID
56			27-28	Villa Crocetta		34 ID	A	3 PzGrD
57			28-30	Ardea	B	5 ID	A	4 ParaD
58			29-Jun 1	Lanuvio	U	34 ID	A	3 PzGrD
59			29-31	Campoleone		1 AD & 45 ID	A	3 PzGr & 65 ID
60		June	3-4	Tarto-Tiber	B	1 & 5 ID	A	4 ParaD
501		Aug	23-25	Seine River	U	XX Corps	A	First Army
2		Sept	6-11	Moselle Metz		XX Corps	A	First Army
3			13	Metz		XX Corps	A	First Army

234

Posture	N_z	N_y	Air % Firepower				Set Piece		PR_z/PR_y	CEV_z	% cas/day°°		I_z	I_y	SE_z	SE_y
			S_z/S_y	W_{yz}	W_{yy}	P_z/P_y	Surp	P'_z/P'_y			x	y				
PD	12,917	4,250	1.83	0	22	0.73	1.50	1.10	0.87	0.79	3.51	0.94	7.4	2.3	1.02	3.85
PD	12,917	4,250	1.34	0	17	1.20	1.50	1.80	0.82	0.46	2.68	0.78	6.7	1.8	0.99	2.75
HD	12,447	8,390	1.55	0	3	0.75	1.17	0.88	0.70	0.80	1.92	0.71	6.0	2.6	1.12	2.45
A	12,917	15,000	0.90	2	5	1.51			1.57	1.04	2.11	1.49	6.2	5.7	1.78	2.30
A	11,230	14,730	2.42	52	8	7.43			1.44	0.19	3.50	1.40	6.9	6.0	1.61	2.86
A	12,691	14,733	1.61	20	7	3.75			1.69	0.45	1.53	2.14	5.6	6.3	1.96	2.51
A	18,912	13,300	1.24	3	2	2.40			1.87	0.78	0.67	1.48	4.7	5.6	1.59	1.74
Del	14,730	6,995	2.52	6	4	1.94			1.42	0.73	1.00	0.76	5.2	2.6	0.88	2.02
Del	15,576	6,702	2.51	15	4	1.68			1.14	0.68	1.22	0.83	5.4	2.9	0.96	2.44
PD	14,557	8,068	2.69	0	0	2.47			1.14	0.46	0.85	0.33	5.0	1.2	0.68	2.05
PD	16,857	8,000	3.10	1	0	2.41			0.32	0.13	2.49	1.18	6.6	2.7	1.08	3.94
PD	18,476	7,250	3.71	2	2	1.98			1.64	0.83	0.71	0.51	5.1	1.9	0.75	2.50
Del	21,265	6,435	2.63	0	11	1.76			1.06	0.60	0.29	1.01	1.1	3.3	1.26	1.22
Del	18,210	6,435	3.51	1	5	2.61			1.36	0.52	0.35	0.40	2.6	1.2	0.58	1.66
PD	17,765	8,158	3.69	3	0	2.92			1.21	0.41	1.13	0.25	5.3	1.0	0.51	2.94
Del	17,034	5,152	2.68	2	9	1.63			1.38	0.85	0.11	0.33	2.1	0.9	0.89	1.33
PD	17,500	8,138	2.96	1	1	1.29			1.17	0.90	0.42	0.57	3.0	2.1	0.93	1.73
PD	16,400	7,239	3.54	3	0	1.98			1.41	0.71	0.61	0.45	4.2	1.7	0.76	2.20
PD	14,600	8,138	2.26	0	0	1.37			1.25	0.91	0.43	0.28	2.6	1.1	0.75	1.60
PD	14,000	8,088	1.77	0	0	1.13			0.96	0.85	0.18	0.18	1.3	1.3	0.96	1.06
PD	16,870	6,321	3.84	6	10	2.43			1.18	0.49	1.17	1.64	5.5	5.1	1.28	3.28
FD	19,513	6,750	3.15	6	1	1.12			0.58	0.52	0.41	0.09	3.0	1.1	0.81	2.06
FD	16,600	6,566	3.02	13	7	1.08			0.56	0.52	1.05	1.32	5.5	4.6	1.34	2.82
FD	20,116	6,566	2.45	1	13	0.66			0.58	0.87	0.34	0.20	2.6	0.6	0.54	1.59
A	5,200	7,942	1.51	2	2	1.80			0.46	0.26	1.97	0.14	5.7	1.2	0.42	2.24
FD	16,350	7,942	2.68	4	4	0.96			0.49	0.51	0.33	0.25	1.9	1.0	0.66	1.36
FD	17,765	7,588	3.13	3	0	1.35			1.07	0.79	0.70	0.13	5.0	2.0	0.84	2.95
FD	20,744	3,288	4.18	5	0	1.39			1.10	0.79	0.67	1.05	5.0	3.9	1.25	3.27
FD	5,551	3,288	4.22	8	0	1.58			1.07	0.67	0.72	0.29	2.1	0.8	0.59	1.82
HD	19,350	6,750	3.26	0	3	1.91	1.42	2.71	1.32	6.49	2.94	0.74	7.1	2.5	0.81	4.60
A	17,976	15,317	1.59	3	6	3.19	1.17	3.73	2.14	0.59	0.32	0.46	2.3	3.0	0.73	1.10
PD	17,766	15,098	1.66	1	2	1.10			0.85	0.77	1.38	0.49	5.6	3.1	0.88	1.71
A	9,734	26,029	0.60	2	2	1.31			1.12	0.85	7.35	2.50	8.9	7.1	3.14	3.11
A	4,515	26,490	0.52	1	1	1.48			1.45	0.98	4.08	0.64	6.6	5.1	1.56	1.47
A	5,000	7,418	1.22	1	1	3.27			1.26	0.39	0.81	1.12	2.0	3.9	1.40	1.33
A	17,730	27,518	1.31	28	0	3.05			0.65	0.21	1.75	0.84	6.0	5.4	1.35	2.08
HPD	13,400	7,077	2.04	0	1	0.81			0.53	0.65	0.43	1.46	4.5	6.1	1.77	1.50
A	20,496	41,974	0.92	31	5	2.02			1.69	0.83	1.58	1.13	5.3	6.0	1.88	1.26
A	9,761	21,478	1.59	2	2	7.22	0.20	1.44	0.97	0.67	4.29	1.67	7.2	6.0	1.88	4.56
A	19,613	15,637	1.60	3	4	5.10			1.79	0.36	0.96	0.56	2.9	3.9	0.78	1.28
FD	18,702	9,250	1.93	15	0	1.08			1.53	1.42	1.48	5.18	5.7	8.1	3.09	2.33
FD	17,970	8,141	2.81	11	0	1.84			1.05	0.57	3.19	4.18	7.2	7.2	2.62	4.46
Del	18,308	8,215	1.54	3	0	1.03			2.06	2.00	0.94	4.38	5.2	7.2	2.89	1.95
FD	16,458	7,500	2.87	3	0	2.45			1.65	0.67	1.63	2.90	5.8	6.2	1.98	3.04
Del	23,190	7,627	3.15	0	0	4.08			1.85	0.45	0.58	3.15	4.3	6.3	2.06	2.77
HD	13,095	4,563	2.53	4	0	1.84			1.30	0.71	0.76	3.57	4.4	6.3	2.10	2.33
Del	17,912	6,653	3.61	1	4	4.91			2.09	0.42	0.51	1.90	5.0	5.2	1.50	3.14
HD	18,030	6,653	4.11	1	0	4.50			1.24	0.28	0.49	1.90	5.1	5.2	1.64	4.34
FD	17,345	12,569	2.03	1	0	1.90			1.12	0.59	0.67	1.85	4.8	5.8	2.43	1.92
FD	17,313	11,343	1.84	2	0	1.38			1.22	0.89	0.56	2.10	4.0	6.0	2.48	1.58
FD	16,215	12,815	2.19	5	0	1.64	2.20	3.61	2.61	0.74	1.46	3.43	5.7	7.0	2.04	1.74
FD	19,971	11,928	2.37	3	0	1.52	1.53	2.33	2.34	1.01	2.54	4.45	6.7	10.2	2.48	2.94
Wd	17,925	6,957	2.02	1	0	1.03			2.25	2.18	0.30	1.33	4.0	4.6	1.43	1.47
FD	14,620	12,327	2.21	1	0	1.60	0.52	0.84	0.77	0.92	5.25	10.66	8.5	10.1	3.84	3.54
FD	19,047	10,593	1.96	0	0	1.48			1.15	0.78	0.93	2.74	5.2	6.4	2.34	1.76
FD	18,000	13,715	1.35	0	0	0.65			0.64	0.98	0.87	2.18	5.1	6.1	2.29	1.45
FD	15,557	7,659	2.18	0	1	1.97			1.46	0.74	0.52	1.63	3.4	5.2	1.81	1.60
FD	17,300	6,108	2.33	30	1	0.97			0.60	0.62	1.19	2.43	5.4	6.0	1.97	2.24
FD	29,711	15,801	2.14	1	1	1.24			1.02	0.83	1.46	2.90	6.1	6.8	2.02	2.16
FD	38,011	10,855	2.84	1	0	2.74			1.65	0.60	0.75	3.91	5.2	7.1	2.36	2.44
PD	40,619	15,000	5.85	4	0	4.90			2.62	0.53	0.19	1.98	1.4	6.1	1.20	1.48
Del	59,631	41,500	2.56	5	0	1.59			1.20	0.76	0.46	0.67	5.1	5.2	1.09	1.60
FD	60,794	39,580	2.33	2	0	0.98			0.47	0.48	0.59	0.53	5.3	5.1	1.11	1.76

No.	Year & Date		Battle Designation	Force X Designation	Posture	Force Y Designation
4	Aug	16	Chartres	7 AD	A	First Army
5		23-25	Melun	7 AD	A	48 ID
601	Nov	10-11	Foret de Chateau-Salins	35, 26 ID & 4 AD	A-HD	11 PzD, XIII Corps
2		13-15	Morhange	4 AD & 35 ID	A	11 PzD, 361 ID
3		14-15	Bourgaltroff	4 AD & 26 ID	A	11 PzD, 361 ID
4		24-25	Baerendorf I	4 AD	A-HD	PzLr, 361 ID
5		26	Baerendorf II	4 AD	A	PzLrD
6		27-29	Burbach-Durstel	4 AD	A	PzLrD
7	Dec	1-2	Sarre-Union	4 AD	A	11 Pz, PzLr, 25 Pz
8		6-7	Singling-Bining	4 .\D	A	25 PzGr, 11 PzD
9	Nov	8-12	Seille-Nied	XII Corps	A	XIII & LXXXIX Cor
10		13-16	Morhange-Faulquemont	XII Corps	A	XIII & LXXXIX Cor
11		20-27	Serre-St. Avold	XII Corps	A	XIII & LXXXIX Cor
12		28-29	Durstel-Farebersvilles	XII Corps	A	XIII & LXXXIX Cor
13		5-7	Sarre-Singling	XII Corps	A	XII & XC Corps
701	1943, July	4-12	Oboyan-Kursk	S 6 Gd & 1 Tk A	FD	XLVIII Pz Corps
2	1944, Sept	13-17	Il Giogo Pass	U 85 ID	A	12 ParaRgt
3	Dec	16-17	Ardennes-Sauer	4 ID	HD	212 VGD
A- 1	1805, Dec		Austerlitz	F	HDA	Allies
2	1815, June	18	Waterloo	F	AHD	Allies
3	1862, Sept		Antietam	U Army Potomac	A	CSANV
4	1863, Jul	1-3	Gettysburg	Army Potomac	HD	CSANV
5	1918, March	21-26	Somme-Peronne	B	FD	G
6		27-Apr 4	Somme-Montdidier	B	FD	G
18601		Sept 19-20	Megiddo	XXI Corps	A	T 8 Army
40101	1940, March	13-14	Sedan	F elms 7 & 9 A	PD	G XIX Corps
41201	1941, June	21-25	Rovno (Ukraine 1941)	S elms SWAG	PD	1st PzGp
41601	Dec	12	Jitra (Malaya 1941)	B 11 IndD	HD	J 5 ID
43201	1943, Jan	12-18	Leningrad	S 2d AA	A	G elms 18 A
43203	Aug	3-5	Kharkov-Belgorod	53d A	A	167 ID
44190	1944, July	24-26	Cobra (St. Lo)	U VII C	A	LXXXIV Corps
45591	1945, Aug	9-16	Mutangiang (Manchuria)	S 5 A	A	J 5 A
50001	1950, June	25-27	Invasion of South Korea	ROKA elms	HPD	NKPA elms

*Abbreviations:

B = British	T = Turks	A = Armored
U = United States	D = Division	P = Para or Airborne
G = German	C = Corps	Gr = Grenadier
S = Soviet	Rgt = Regiment	Gd = Guard
F = French	Inf = Infantry	Pz = Panzer
J = Japanese	Gp = Group	Lt = Light

**For the 1st 81 examples these are based on reliable estimates of casualties inflicted by ground weapons only.

| | | | | Air % Firepower | | | Set Piece | | | $PR_x/$ PR_y | | % cas/day°° | | | | | |
Posture	N_x	N_y	S_x/S_y	W_{yx}	W_{vy}	P_x/P_y	Set Piece	Surp	P'_x/P'_y	PR_x/PR_y	CEV_x	x	y	I_x	I_y	SE_x	SE_y
HD	15,646	8,325	5.26	1	0	7.16				1.25	0.17	0.72	6.95	4.7	8.5	1.97	2.24
PD	17,232	6,000	7.53	0	0	7.75				2.21	0.29	0.19	5.98	1.4	5.3	1.03	2.13
FDA	43,587	11,185	4.19	1	0	2.27				1.09	0.48	0.82	1.99	5.4	5.9	1.14	3.21
Del	25,881	7,555	3.36	0	0	1.35				1.25	0.93	1.54	0.87	6.0	3.1	0.87	3.54
Del	21,860	6,519	2.28	0	0	1.16				0.74	0.64	0.89	1.08	4.2	3.4	1.27	1.98
HDA	7,935	5,366	2.24	0	0	2.05				1.25	0.61	0.37	2.09	1.3	5.2	1.41	1.26
PD	15,871	6,999	3.39	0	0	2.36				1.69	0.72	0.35	3.33	3.4	6.4	1.54	1.17
Del	16,232	6,713	2.14	0	0	0.80				0.88	1.10	0.16	1.07	1.2	3.6	1.01	0.76
PD	19,773	6,044	4.49	0	0	2.64				1.15	0.44	0.70	1.08	5.0	3.6	0.73	1.93
FD	15,224	5,044	3.35	0	0	1.23				0.65	0.53	0.51	1.21	3.2	3.4	0.92	1.52
FD	99,583	23,588	4.44	1	0	1.94				1.73	0.89	0.86	4.13	6.1	8.6	1.69	2.79
Del	92,393	28,382	3.07	0	0	1.38				1.00	0.73	0.87	3.23	5.9	7.8	1.74	2.54
Del	88,941	32,396	2.94	1	0	1.25				1.19	0.95	0.46	1.91	5.0	6.6	1.45	1.82
Del	90,078	30,712	2.85	0	0	1.13				0.85	0.76	0.27	1.32	3.2	5.9	1.13	1.29
Del	89,977	31,501	3.10	1	0	1.34				1.57	1.17	0.42	1.87	3.7	6.5	1.39	1.47
A	90,000	62,000	1.24	23	17	2.04				0.76	2.68	3.82	1.01	9.2	8.1	1.39	2.55
FD	15,721	3,700	6.03	19	0	4.08				2.34	0.57	0.71	2.72	3.9	2.3	1.46	3.14
A	8,634	10,000	0.94	0	0	3.25		0.33	1.07	0.77	0.72	0.78	1.34	2.5	4.7	1.93	1.71
AHD	75,000	89,000	0.86			0.94		1.73	1.63	3.69	2.27	9.33	30.33	6.0	9.7	13.88	6.54
HDA	72,000	139,000	0.51			0.54		0.35	0.19	0.29	1.53	15.83		7.7		12.74	10.93
HD	80,000	45,000	1.78			1.16				0.83	0.72	15.51	30.50	7.2	8.3	6.69	8.48
A	88,289	75,000	1.18			1.81				1.83	1.01	8.70	12.47	9.2	10.0	5.26	5.17
A	250,000	600,000	0.39			0.75		0.91	0.68	0.38	0.56	8.00	1.95	11.0	8.3	1.28	1.32
A	500,000	600,000	0.97			1.67				1.32	0.79	2.67	2.41	9.6	9.4	1.07	1.17
FD	51,170	18,250	2.66			1.43		1.92	2.75	5.20	1.88	0.98	12.33	5.9	11.0	2.54	1.57
A	45,000	48,000	0.37	69	9	0.69		0.71	0.49	0.37	0.76	5.00	0.83	10.1	5.5	1.53	3.07
A	150,000	132,000	0.79	4	22	1.22		0.75	0.92	0.30	0.32	11.67	0.50	11.0	3.8	1.30	6.42
A	12,000	7,000	0.50	0	0	0.87		0.87	0.76	0.40	0.52	10.00	8.57	10.0	8.6	6.33	9.30
FD	120,000	30,000	4.84	6	7	2.21	1.6		3.54	1.51	2.34	5.71	1.50	10.5	6.4	1.05	7.98
FD	70,000	15,000	5.12	25	28	2.38	1.6		3.81	1.57	2.43	5.56	0.90	10.3	4.6	0.60	6.05
FD	126,000	30,700	6.73	37	0	4.10				2.99	0.73	0.60	8.14	4.1	11.0	1.66	2.12
FD	147,000	75,000	3.97	3	2	2.70		1.09	2.94	3.16	1.07	0.85	6.00	5.6	10.6	2.68	2.53
A	38,000	60,000	0.68	2	3	0.88		0.83	0.73	0.31	0.37	15.79	3.06	11.0	8.7	3.78	7.15

No.	Year & Date	Battle Designation	Force X Designation	Posture	Force Y Designation	Posture
6701	1967, Jun 5	Rafah	Eg 7 ID(+)	FPD	Is Tal D	A
6702	5/6	Abu Ageila	2 ID	FD	Sharon D	A
6703	6-7	Gaza Strip	Pal 20 PLA D	FPD	Tal D(−)	A
6704	5/6	El Arish	Eg 7 ID(−)	FDD	Tal D(−)	A
6705	5/6	Bir Lahfan	3 ID	Del	Yoffe D	A
6706	6	Jebel Libni	3 ID	Del/PD	Yoffe D(+)	A
6707	7	Mitla Pass	3 ID, 4 AD	Del	Tal D	A
6708	7	Bir Hama	3 ID, 4 AD	HD	Yoffe D	A
6709	7/8	Bir Hassna	3 ID, 6 ID	A	Yoffe D(−)	HD
6710	8	Bir Gifgafa	4 AD(−)	A	Tal D(−)	HD
6711	8	Nakhl	6 MczdD	HD	Sharon D	A
6721	5-7	Jerusalem	Jord 27 IBde	FD	Central C	A
6722	5/6	Jenin	25 IBde	PD	Peled D(−)	A
6723	6/7	Kabatiya	40 ABde, 25 IBde	HD	Peled D	A
6724	6/7	Tilfit-Zababida	40 ABde, 25 IBde	HPD	Ram Bde	A
6725	7	Nablus	40 ABde, 25 IBde	HPD	Peled D(−)	A
6731	9	Tel Fahar-Banias*	Syr 11 IBde(+)	FD	Laner D	A
6732	9	Zaoura-Kola	11 IBde	FD	Mend Bde	A
6733	9	Tel Fahar	11 IBde	FD	Golani Bde	A
6734	9	Rawiyeh	8 IBde(−)	FD	Ram Bde	A
731	1973, Oct 6	Suez Canal Assault(N)	Eg 2 A	A	Mend D(−)	PFD
732	6	Suez Canal Assault(S)	3 A	A	Mend D(−)	PFD
733	7	Second Army Buildup	2 A	A	So. Comd(−)	HPD
734	7	Third Army Buildup	3 A	A	So. Comd(−)	HPD
735	8	Kantara-Firdan	2 A	HD	So. Comd(−)	A
736	14	Egypt Offensive(N)	2 A(−)	A	So. Comd(−)	HD
737	14	Egypt Offensive(S)	3 A(−)	A	So. Comd(−)	HD
738	15/16	Deversoir (ch FI)	16(−) & 21(−) D	HPD	Sharon D(+)	A
739	16-17	Chinese Farm (II)	16(−) & 21(−) D	HPD	Adan D(+)	A
7310	18	Deversoir West	2 A(−)	HPD	Adan D	A
7311	19-21	Jebel Geneifa	3 A(−)	Wd	Adan D	A
7312	19-22	Ismailia	2 A(−)	HPD	Sharon D	A
7313	21-22	Adabiya	3 A(−)	Wd	Magen D	A
7314	22	Shallufa I	3 A(−)	HD	Adan D	A
7315	23-24	Suez	3 A(−)	HPD	Adan D(−)	A
7316	23-24	Shallufa II	3 A(−)	HD	Adan D(−)	A
7321	6-7	Ahmadiyeh	Syr 7 ID(+)	A	7 ABde(−)	FPD
7322	6-7	Kuneitra	9 ID(+)	A	7 & 188 ABde(−)	PDW
7323	6-7	Rafid	5 ID(+)	A	188 Bde(−)	FPD
7324	7-8	Yehudia-El Al	5 ID(+)	A	Laner D(−)	HD
7325	7-8	Nafekh	1 AD(+)	AHD	Ori Bde(+)	HDA
7326	8-9	Mt. Hermonit	7 ID(+)	A	7 ABde (−)	FPD
7327	8	Mt. Hermon I	Para Bde(−)	PD	1 IBde(−)	A
7328	8-10	Hushiniyab	1 A & 9 ID(−)	HD	Laner D(−)	A
7329	8-10	Tel Faris	5 I & 1 AD(−)	HD	Peled D(+)	A
7330	11-13	Tel Shams	7 I & 3 AD(−)	FD	Eitan D	A
7331	11-12	Tel Shaar	1, 3 AD & 9 ID	PD	Laner D	A
7332	13	Tel el Hara	Iq 3 AD	A	Laner D	HD
7333	15	Kfar Shams-Tel Antar	3 AD	HD	Laner D(−)	A
7334	16	Naba	Jord 40 ABde(+)	A	Laner D(−)	HD
7335	19	Arab Counteroffensive	Syr 9 ID; Iq 3 AD;	A	Peled D	PD
7336	21	Mt. Hermon II	Syr ParaBde(−)	FD	1 IBde	A
7337	22	Mt. Hermon III	ParaBde	FD	1 I & 31 ParaBde	A

Abbreviations:

Is = Israeli
Eg = Egypt
Syr = Syrian
Jord = Jordanian
Iq = Iraqi
Pal = Palestinian

Bde = Brigade
D = Division
I = Infantry
A = Armored
P = Para or Airborne
Mczd = Mechanized

*Engagements 6732 and 6733 were part of 6731

Middle East Wars, 1967-1973

N_x	N_y	S_x/S_y	P_x/P_y	Set Piece	Surp	P'_x/P'_y	R-R	PR_x/PR_y	CEV	% cas/day x	y	SE_x	SE_y	Air % Firepower W_x	W_y
19,520	19,520	0.65	0.84		0.50	0.43	−15.13	0.25	0.58	13.85	3.59	2.03	3.78	12.14	31.42
18,450	19,280	1.01	1.81		0.32	0.58	−10.50	0.32	0.55	4.88	1.56	1.56	3.16	0	0
17,450	12,150	1.01	1.52		0.67	1.02	−12.36	0.28	0.27	1.79	0.45	0.61	1.77	2.82	29.23
12,750	6,912	0.63	0.77		0.67	0.52	− 9.77	0.34	0.65	1.76	1.95	1.34	1.66	0	34.32
10,050	10,450	0.59	0.66		0.67	0.44	−14.46	0.26	0.58	13.43	0.86	0.95	2.93	6.37	37.85
10,050	10,800	0.65	0.80		0.67	0.53	−11.29	0.31	0.58	4.48	0.65	0.82	1.87	0	31.31
13,500	10,200	0.78	0.80		0.83	0.67	−11.00	0.31	0.46	4.07	0.74	0.86	1.69	0	30.54
11,000	8,700	0.55	0.49		0.83	0.41	−12.77	0.28	0.68	5.00	0.69	0.90	2.19	0	27.16
22,000	7,250	1.81	1.81		0.83	0.67	− 8.69	0.37	0.55	2.50	1.24	0.87	2.41	0	20.94
3,500	3,600	1.02	0.58			0.58	− 8.25	0.38	0.66	12.86	1.67	1.48	3.52	0	0
18,450	18,780	1.51	0.55			0.55	−12.84	0.28	0.51	3.39	0.32	0.78	1.86	0	51.57
13,600	27,682	0.41	0.77		0.83	0.64	− 7.62	0.53	0.62	5.51	3.16	4.30	3.06	7.79	18.37
6,160	10,900	0.39	0.62		0.85	0.53	− 6.41	0.44	0.83	3.25	2.06	2.68	1.80	0	14.53
9,900	12,800	0.69	1.18		0.90	1.01	− 5.03	0.50	0.47	3.54	2.93	2.31	1.93	0	19.15
5,450	5,350	0.58	0.85		0.90	0.77	− 6.46	0.44	0.57	4.59	4.67	2.46	2.13	0	29.35
10,640	10,700	0.41	0.56		0.95	0.53	− 7.32	0.41	0.77	4.05	3.50	2.49	1.72	0	33.91
16,720	11,225	0.36	0.67			0.67	−11.59	0.30	0.45	8.10	4.76	2.28	2.47	0	86.45
8,560	5,850	0.36	0.58			0.58	−11.49	0.30	0.52	5.78	3.93	2.10	2.11	0	84.45
8,160	5,375	0.36	0.76			0.76	−11.68	0.30	0.39	10.42	5.58	2.46	2.82	0	88.44
4,350	5,350	0.74	1.76		0.54	0.95	−10.16	0.33	0.35	6.88	2.80	2.36	4.38	0	0
29,490	4,455	2.96	0.98	1.5C	3.19	4.06	5.67	2.13	0.52	1.36	6.17	0.70	1.19	16.27	66.60
22,850	3,020	2.98	1.06	1.5C	3.14	4.32	5.78	2.16	0.50	1.53	7.45	0.66	1.16	17.69	72.72
63,910	14,000	2.76	1.33	1.5C	2.55	4.41	4.95	1.99	0.45	1.25	3.21	0.78	1.06	10.65	41.86
45,160	10,980	2.93	1.51	1.5C	2.55	5.01	5.20	2.04	0.41	1.66	3.64	0.78	1.06	12.71	50.65
67,440	25,850	1.60	1.40	1.5C	1.94	3.53	4.19	1.84	1.52	1.04	2.71	0.83	1.21	11.26	23.09
81,160	43,400	1.42	0.82				− 9.05	0.36	0.43	2.0	0.88	0.60	1.41	6.93	31.18
57,910	28,600	1.93	1.34				− 8.94	0.36	0.27	2.33	0.91	0.59	1.61	9.90	30.10
30,970	22,790	1.43	2.07		0.35	0.72	− 5.17	0.49	0.68	1.61	1.76	0.90	1.51	0.33	0.08
36,840	28,700	1.08	1.55		0.57	0.88	− 5.61	0.47	0.53	3.26	1.66	0.64	1.23	11.89	40.91
18,180	16,200	0.70	1.00		0.79	0.79	− 6.61	0.43	0.54	4.40	1.39	0.67	1.35	21.16	51.21
35,633	16,200	1.21	1.31				− 9.16	0.35	0.27	1.54	0.62	0.44	1.13	10.51	35.41
23,860	17,000	0.91	1.28				0.32	1.06	0.83	1.89	0.88	0.65	1.26	16.16	44.54
14,629	10,900	0.95	1.22				−13.38	0.27	0.22	2.73	0.69	0.53	1.22	11.72	44.69
25,600	16,200	1.01	1.14				− 7.00	0.42	0.37	4.30	0.93	0.52	1.60	9.43	37.93
22,570	14,681	0.69	1.07		1.52	1.63	0.11	1.02	0.63	2.44	1.16	0.72	1.18	9.97	47.00
27,570	11,700	0.92	1.31				−10.53	0.32	0.25	2.44	0.64	0.48	1.27	9.97	61.30
22,750	5,745	1.03	0.34	1.7	2.37	1.61	− 5.54	0.47	0.29	1.54	2.18	0.84	1.34	30.16	74.19
17,750	3,630	1.66	0.60	1.7	2.77	2.75	1.77	1.35	0.49	0.99	2.75	0.90	1.00	39.02	69.73
19,525	4,958	0.91	0.38	1.7	3.14	2.03	3.77	1.75	0.86	1.79	5.04	1.04	0.97	30.76	74.98
21,984	6,300	0.84	0.35		2.43	0.85	− 5.94	0.46	0.54	2.27	2.38	0.93	2.56	20.89	73.35
12,500	6,946	0.80	0.84		2.30	1.93	− 5.12	0.49	0.25	4.00	3.60	1.15	1.02	20.79	72.33
31,350	5,234	1.25	0.41	1.7	1.52	1.06	− 4.82	0.51	0.48	1.91	3.82	1.05	2.36	19.91	86.01
1,583	2,692	0.36	0.85	1.7	1.46	2.11	3.25	1.65	0.78	6.32	1.86	1.21	1.24	68.89	91.27
14,683	12,733	0.63	0.92		1.65	1.52	− 7.20	0.41	0.27	2.55	1.18	0.83	1.18	42.40	79.00
23,750	17,833	0.84	0.32		1.72	2.27	− 6.65	0.43	0.19	2.10	0.84	0.69	1.14	32.33	76.03
9,400	16,100	0.76	1.62			1.62	− 6.33	0.44	0.27	1.68	1.09	0.65	1.09	34.89	80.63
21,500	14,700	0.83	1.46			1.46	− 6.15	0.45	0.31	2.09	0.95	0.55	1.11	23.44	69.47
2,500	11,000	1.36	0.77			0.77	−12.24	0.29	0.38	3.60	0.34	0.48	1.45	16.10	18.24
2,000	11,000	1.09	1.99			1.99	− 8.55	0.37	0.19	1.67	0.91	0.74	1.11	29.17	21.06
1,500	11,000	0.94	0.53			0.53	− 8.43	0.37	0.70	3.91	0.91	0.74	1.23	39.93	55.48
15,750	16,100	1.84	0.94			0.94	− 7.75	0.39	0.41	1.54	0.99	0.62	1.30	13.88	52.33
4,750	5,700	0.60	1.61			1.61	1.75	1.35	0.84	3.16	1.40	1.64	1.90	82.93	93.26
4,750	11,400	0.37	0.95			0.95	− 7.86	0.39	0.41	5.26	0.88	1.22	1.48	74.13	87.51

Index